Managing
the
Information
Ecology

Managing
the
Information
Ecology

---

*A Collaborative Approach
to Information Technology
Management*

Bruce W. Hasenyager

QUORUM BOOKS
Westport, Connecticut • London

Library of Congress Cataloging-in-Publication Data

Hasenyager, Bruce W.
    Managing the information ecology : a collaborative approach to
information technology management / Bruce W. Hasenyager.
        p.   cm.
    Includes bibliographical references and index.
    ISBN 0–89930–947–X (alk. paper)
    1. Management information systems.   2. Information resources
management.   3. Information technology—Management.   I. Title.
    HD30.213.H37   1996
    658.4′038—dc20   94–39344

British Library Cataloguing in Publication Data is available.

Library of Congress Catalog Card Number: 94–39344
ISBN: 0–89930–947–X

First published in 1996

Quorum Books, 88 Post Road West, Westport, CT 06881
An imprint of Greenwood Publishing Group, Inc.

Printed in the United States of America

The paper used in this book complies with the
Permanent Paper Standard issued by the National
Information Standards Organization (Z39.48–1984).

10 9 8 7 6 5 4 3 2 1

Dedicated to Patti, with love.

Acknowledgments

All books are personal but no book is done by one person alone. I gratefully acknowledge the contributions, large and small, made to this effort by the many people who have influenced it in its conception, in its creation, and in its production. My thanks to

- My mentors who helped me get it straight, especially Billy Himes, Chris Young, and Barbara Capsalis.
- My colleagues who helped me get it in focus, especially Gary Cathcart, Larry Gress, Rick Zahniser, Helga Minderjahn, Tim Tabor, Gordon Sollars, Len Silver, Gail McGee, and Dave Smith.
- The friends who helped me with the outline and who agreed to read the draft when it was it at its roughest — Lynda Applegate, Howard Benkov, Charlie Caputo, Lee Farmelo, Bobbie Harvey, Joan Hochman, Tom Lodahl, Charley Nobs, Susanna Opper, DuWayne Petersen, Kay Redditt, Chris Reid, Peter Rothstein, Howard Rubin, and H. Allen White III.
- My editors, Eric Valentine, Pat Steele, and Emily Okenquist, who so gently brought style to my language and substance to this book.
- My production manager, Dick Burr.
- Caroline Hasenyager, who spent hours with me making corrections, and Genny Hasenyager, who had the last pencil on the galleys.
- Tom Davenport for the phrase information ecology and the huge ideas behind the phrase.

Finally, I'd like to thank my many friends and co-workers at Booz, Allen & Hamilton, Citibank, Kidder Peabody, Merrill Lynch, and Chemical Bank who were patient with me while the ideas in this book were developed.

Contents

1

Information Ecology, Linkage, and Sustain and Transform

The hardest part of managing information technology is to get the business experts to work effectively with the technology experts—the business technology linkage.

Managing the business technology linkage requires that we understand the complex interrelationship between the *business* of our business and the *technology* of our business in a new, subtler way that is becoming known as the *information ecology*. It also requires that we understand and manage the significant tension between *sustain* and *transform* that underlies the transactions and decisions taking place in the information ecology.

Information ecology

The mechanical or architectural view of systems is appropriate when we think about a single computer program or even a small number of programs taken together as a single system, but as soon as the numbers get large, mental images of *biological* systems become more useful.

Very large systems are so complex that they become subtly unpredictable. Combinations of large systems (which is usually the case with large organizations) compound the complexity and multiply the unpredictability. Complexity grows out of the details of the programs themselves and it grows out of the interactions between programs and the computer hardware, between programs and computer operating systems, between programs and computers and networks, between the programs and the computers and the networks and users... and on and on. In our modern computing environments, everything depends on everything else directly or indirectly, intentionally or potentially. We have built, in each of our large organizations, an *information ecology*.

The machines and programs are not the only participants in the ecology. Humans dominate. They run the machines, write and maintain the programs, design the functions, operate the terminals, share or hoard information, allocate funds to one part of the ecology or another, and praise or complain about the way it all works.

A company's information ecology may be a modest one like a suburban garden or a huge complex one like Chesapeake Bay. It may be as rich and varied as a rain forest or it may be spare and fragile as high mountain tundra. No matter what the specifics of a particular information ecology, it is certainly much more complex, variable, subtle, and difficult to understand than its inhabitants acknowledge. It is capable of producing benefits far beyond what it so far has been asked for. It is also the source of risks that are very large and very poorly understood. The notion of the information ecology and its intricate involvement in every part of our business has been largely ignored by management experts and advisors.[1] In this book we will confront the complexity of the information ecology and focus on managing its relationships rather than its parts.

Management of the business technology linkage has become an important problem fairly recently. The complexity that has created the information ecology has been one cause for our increasing concern, the other is the pace of change and the penalty for not keeping up.

Sustain and transform

Sustain is a code word for the concepts, conventions, processes, and forces that tend to keep our businesses the way they are and *transform* is a similar code word for those things that make our businesses new, different, and more competitive. There is a crucial struggle between *sustain* and *transform*. The struggle is waged throughout our companies, but nowhere are the conduct and outcomes more important than in our use of computers and communications technology. Correctly balancing *sustain* and *transform* demands that we manage the confluence of business and technology much better than we have ever done—much better, indeed, than we have ever thought of doing.

Flaming arrows and little green men

Imagine yourself under attack.

- Imagine you're Custer at the Little Big Horn.
- Now imagine that a sympathetic extraterrestrial is passing by and just as you come under attack—bullets and arrows flying thick and fast—the extraterrestrial drops from his spaceship a super atomic disintegrater cannon kit, a user's manual, and a good luck message.
- All you have to do is read the manual, assemble the disintegrater, train the crew, revise your battle tactics, and zap Sitting Bull and the boys... victory is certain.
- Unfortunately, those angry Americans shooting arrows at you aren't about to take a break and let you figure out the new way of doing things.
- For all we know maybe General George *did* get a present from a friendly green person... but it wouldn't have made any difference. The outcome

wouldn't have changed because George and his troops had no skill, no experience, no process, and no plan for simultaneously sustaining their defense and transforming their weaponry and tactics. They just didn't know how.

That's our problem, too. In most large companies, we don't have skill, experience, process, or plan for simultaneously sustaining and transforming our information ecology. And the Indians are all around us.

The heart of the problem

The information ecology has grown in little more than a generation from a minor feature of a minor part of our businesses with negligible cost into a ubiquitous, irreplaceable, incomprehensible fundamental element which accounts for 2% to 20% of the company's expense base.[2] Important as the information ecology has become, the executive managers of most of our large companies have had no formal training and little experience in managing it and are inclined to ignore it as a strategic consideration. The most influential executives in our large companies consider the information ecology a service provided by people who are necessary but, in some sense, foreign to the *real* business that the company is in.

On the other hand, we read in *Business Week*, *Fortune*, *Forbes*, and the *Wall Street Journal* slick stories about how the CEO and the CIO of some obscure company converted their entire computer operation to a bunch of PCs, wrote all their programs in a new language, and now their expenses are a tenth what they were and everything they want to do works better, cheaper, and faster. Is there anything real behind these stories—anything relevant to us? Yes, there is.

- Small computers *are* 10 to 1000 times more cost efficient at computing than large ones.[3]
- Software developed with the best technology *can be* 10 to 1000 times cheaper to build than software developed with traditional technology and 10 to 100 times cheaper to maintain.[4]

It's not hard to conclude that a company like the ones they write about in the press can use the best technology and have a systems cost of 10% of traditional technology. If you're spending $200 million a year for your systems, the prospect of doing it for $20 million instead is highly attractive. Let's be conservative and assume that these kinds of savings don't scale up directly (nobody really knows). Let's say that the best technology for a big company will cost $100 million instead of $200 million. The best new technology can provide efficiencies that are strategically significant to most large companies

I imagine that a saving of that magnitude is large enough to attract considerable attention. Cutting cost to own and operate systems by half is an economic and technical reality. It's on its way and we can't stop it.[5] The benefits to be derived by changing the fundamental way we do business, however, are much greater even than the large efficiency benefits available from the best new technology.[6] Companies that master the new technology are going to come to market with a whole range of improvements including better marketing, billing and collection, order processing, customer service, more efficient administration, and lower cost of operations.

These and other benefits are to be expected from *business reengineering* efforts. And, of course, these are the benefits that really matter. Small companies, constrained by capital but not by unwieldy information ecologies dominated by legacy systems and established attitudes, will find the necessary changes easier to make than large companies. Big companies from other industries entering a market may be the most likely winners because they have the resources and can start with a clean slate.

- *The status quo can kill you.* A company in an information intensive business or in one where information systems have been an important barrier to entry will find the barriers disappearing and its old technology suddenly becoming an anchor that can drown its business.
- *It can happen very fast.* A significant feature of the best new technology is that new systems can be built two to ten times faster than the same systems with old technology. New competitors can appear with superior operations and systems even before a currently successful company knows they are there.

Now we get to the *sustain* and *transform* problem of technology in the large company: How can we transform our old technology information ecology into a new technology information environment while sustaining our ability to do our business every day? It's not easy.

- *It hasn't been done yet.* Nobody in the world has demonstrated, yet, that a very large company can make the transition from old technology to the best of the new technology.
- *We can't buy all the parts.* The products necessary to implement the best new technology aren't yet made or, if made, weren't designed to fit together or, if designed to fit, haven't been tried or, if tried, haven't been tried on a large scale.
- *Our guys don't know how to build it.* The programming staff in most companies doesn't have the conceptual basis, the design skills, or the implementation skills to build and maintain systems in the best new technology.
- *We couldn't run it if we had it.* The computer operations people in most companies don't have the conceptual understanding or skills to operate large-scale applications built in the best new technology and, if they had the understanding and skills, would still lack the process, procedures, and experience necessary to provide the high degree of reliability most businesses require.

- *Our business people don't appreciate the potential benefits of the best new technology.* The new technology and its possibilities are far outside the experience of most of us. Business training, experience, and expertise give no appreciation for the vast potential made available by the new technology.
- *Our technology people don't appreciate the subtle business pitfalls in reengineering.* Appreciation of the concepts and details of the best new technology is insufficient in itself to design and build the new systems necessary to compete effectively.
- *Our technology and business people don't know how to work together to combine their strengths and get the benefits.* At best, business and technology people coexist peacefully; at worst, they undermine each other's effectiveness. They don't have the inclination or skills to improve this situation.

Let's review:

- *We have a huge investment in our present systems.* They are expensive to own and operate.
- *Our present systems are critical to our business.* We can't function without them.
- *But it really can be a lot better.* We know that there is a better kind of technology that would give us significant cost advantages if we could convert to it.
- *Technology change without business change is a loser.* Much of the opportunity is lost if we don't reengineer the business at the same time we change the technology.
- *Skills are short.* Even if we were willing to make the investment, our people don't yet have the necessary skills either to make the change or to operate the environment that would result.
- *New competitors won't have our problem.* Most of the barriers that make this transformation difficult for us don't affect smaller companies in our industry as much and don't effect possible new entrants in our industry at all.
- *Our business and technology people are fundamentally unready to do the necessary cooperative work.* Neither business nor technology people alone can achieve the transition to the best new technology, but they are ill prepared to work together.

I've asserted that a central problem of technology management in large companies is to *sustain* the business with old technology and simultaneously *transform* it with the best new technology. Solving this central problem is not a project... it is a process. Specifically, it is the process of managing effectively the business technology linkage. Keep in mind that the dramatic superiority of today's best new technology over yesterday's may shrink to insignificance when we encounter tomorrow's best new technology. It is a cycle that repeats and we need to master the cycle, not just this particular change. We are riding a river of change. Until recently the currents have been gentle; now here come the rapids. The rush of change is accelerating and the skills needed to manage change become more important every day and require the full commitment and cooperation of both business and technology experts.

It is broadly agreed among management theorists that continuous innovation and improvement are essential to continuing competitiveness. This is a feature of business in general, not just the information ecology. The transformation we are talking about in this book is from a business based on old information technology to one based on continually adopting the best new technology, but much of the conceptual framework would be the same no matter what transformation we were talking about. We'll examine the ideas of linkage, ecology, and *sustain* and *transform* in the context of information technology but it may be useful to keep in mind that the tensions and biases built into our culture which tend to favor *sustain* over *transform* are common to many aspects of business and that the solutions may well be common too.

The book addresses and answers questions like these.

- *What's in the information ecology?* What are the major parts of the technology? Who are the people who work in the information ecology? What do they do? What attitudes do they have about each other?
- *What is the cost structure of the information ecology?* What does it cost to own and operate? What is the money spent on? Are we spending enough already?
- *How do we know if we are spending enough or too much on the information ecology?* How do we decide what to spend it on? How do we decide which processes to *sustain* and which to *transform*?
- *Why do our business and technology people work together so poorly?* Why do they think such rotten things about each other? How did it get that way? Is it their fault?
- *How can we improve the way strategy makers meld business and technology strategy?* When is it necessary for the CIO to be part of the CEO's inner circle and when does it not matter? How can we improve the way tactical decisions meld business and technology? How can we connect the strategy and the tactics?
- *How can we use teams to both sustain and transform the information ecology?* Who's in charge? Who's accountable? Does organization matter? How do we measure their performance? How do they interact with the hierarchy? How can we use technology itself to improve teamwork?

This book embodies 30 years of observations and experiences, many successes and enough failures. Much of the content draws on and reshapes familiar management ideas into the specific context of the information ecology. Some of the material presents ideas from industry and academic sources that, I believe, should be much better known than they appear to be. And, some of the ideas are completely new, at least to me. In aggregate, the ideas of this book describe a new way of thinking about and doing business technology linkage—a new way that recognizes the complexity and ambiguity of the information ecology and that breaks the grip that *sustain* has clamped on our businesses and allows us to reap the continuing benefits of *transform*.

Notes

1. Tom Davenport of University of Texas is the leading proponent of the ecological view of information systems. His view of the ecology is slightly different from but not incompatible with the sense in which we use that notion in this book. Davenport emphasizes more the multiplicity of information types and focuses more strongly on information processes. See Selected References for specific citations.
2. Booz, Allen & Hamilton estimates the Information Technology (IT) expense of the average large American manufacturing company as about 2.4% of total expense. A.T. Kearney has reported that the most information intensive Industry is investment banking and the most information intensive single company they have encountered in that industry has IT expense of 22% of total noninterest expense.
3. In 1994, a typical mainframe computer cost more than $200,000 per MIPS (million instructions per second) and a typical microcomputer cost about $2,000 per MIPS. The efficiency advantage of small computers grows when compared to larger and larger computers until a point is reached when larger computers can no longer be built practically. At that point additional computing power is only possible by adding more computers and the efficiency advantage of microcomputers is multiplied.
4. Direct measurement has shown productivity advantages of 10 to 100 for best practices in development and maintenance compared to average practices (see Jones 1986 and Rubin April 1992). Another factor of ten is easily available through the use of reusable components.
5. Appendix A introduces the significant features of the best new technology. It discusses traditional computing and contrasts it with network computing. It explains the client-server concept and describes how computers communicate. It examines the dramatic changes underway in how computer software is developed and maintained, describing the growth of software standards, "snap-together" systems, and objects.
6. See Hammer 1990 and Hammer and Champy 1993.

2
Cost Structures…
What Does the Money Really Buy?

The purpose of this chapter is to examine the way big companies spend their information technology money and what they get for it. Along the way I will develop a case to support these assertions:

- The way we use information technology is fundamentally inefficient.
- The key to more productivity in our information ecology is better use of our human resource in both the business and technology.
- As much as two thirds of our system designers' and programmers' effort is spent doing work that may have no strategic significance to the company because we have inefficient and inappropriate business technology linkage.

To illustrate the cost structure of a large company's information ecology, I have constructed an example of a fictitious large company intended to be representative of the companies I am describing.

Let's call this representative company *National Necessary Services Corporation*. The people who work for National Necessary Services Corporation call it *NatNec*.

NatNec is a large services company with 10,000 people in a four-building home office campus, 5,000 people in four regional operations centers, and 5,000 more people in 100 branches scattered around the United States. The information ecology at NatNec is pretty typical: two large mainframe data centers, a massive star network to connect the branches and regional offices to the data centers, local area networks (LANs) in each branch and scattered in the headquarters and regional offices, 100 application systems, which are grouped into the usual stovepipes, and a total information technology (IT) staff of about 800 people—500 in the central IT organization and 300 in support roles in end user organizations.

NatNec spends $178 million a year on its information ecology. The typical[1] service industry company spends 6% to 8% of gross revenue in their information ecologies. NatNec spends 10%. Technology intensive companies can spend up to 20% of their total non-interest expense on technology. NatNec spends 12.8%. The table in Exhibit 2.1 shows NatNec's overall expense structure.

$ Millions	Information Ecology	Engineering	Marketing & Sales	Distribution	Manufacturing	Management & Staff	Totals
People	$ 50.6	$135.7	$266.0	$133.2	$365.2	$127.3	$1,078.0
Space	5.4	12.8	25.4	12.8	35.9	12.2	104.5
Equipment	106.5	2.7	2.7	1.3	7.3	2.5	123.0
Services	11.8	1.4	16.0	5.3	11.0	5.1	50.6
Other	3.8	2.7	13.3	2.7	7.3	6.4	36.2
Totals	$178.1	$155.3	$323.4	$155.3	$426.7	$153.5	$1,392.3

Exhibit 2.1   Overall Expense Structure by Major Business Process of Representative Company

We are going to examine several questions about how NatNec spends their $178.1 million, including:

- **Cost to own and operate.** How much of the total is directed to acquiring the parts of the information ecology and how much is directed to maintain the parts they already have?
- **Component costs.** What is it that they buy?
- **Functional costs.** How much do the various functions of the information ecology cost?
- **Strategic allocation.** How much of the money is directed toward *sustain* and how much toward *transform*?

When we have completed the examination, we will conclude that costs are not what constrain us from moving toward the best new technology.

Cost to own and cost to operate

If we were talking about a fleet of company cars and trucks instead of an information ecology, we would talk about "the cost of ownership" and "the cost of operation" of the fleet. Exhibit 2.2 shows NatNec's "cost of ownership" and "cost of operation" for the information ecology.

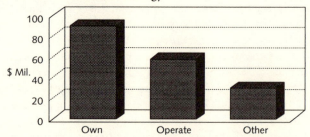

Exhibit 2.2   Cost to Own and Operate a Representative Information Ecology

In "cost to own," we include all the expenses associated with establishing the information ecology: cost of computers and other equipment, cost of facilities, costs of purchased software, and so forth. In "cost to operate" we have costs of operations personnel directly associated with the IT function, costs of maintenance, costs of training, and so forth.[2]

The first thing we notice is that NatNec's information "fleet" is expensive to own and relatively expensive to operate.[3] Is there anything we can say about the ratio? For comparison purposes, think about a car that costs $9000 a year to own and $6000 a year to operate, the same proportions as NatNec's IT. The $9000 might be a three-year lease on a pretty good car. The $6000 might represent 40,000 miles at $.15 per mile. That seems reasonable—the cost to operate covers consumables (gas, oil, tires) and maintenance. Does the same ratio for cost to own/cost to operate (3:2) seem reasonable for an information ecology?

This ratio could come from a low cost to own... but it doesn't. As with most companies, there's nothing cheap about the $90 million a year NatNec spends to own its IT. Since an information ecology doesn't have much in the way of consumables (only electric power and paper come quickly to mind), we've got to wonder why the cost to operate is so high.

In my opinion, the high cost to operate an information ecology is a reflection of the immaturity of the technology and of our limited mastery of it. Our use of information technology is essentially inefficient. In most large companies, today's IT is mind-bogglingly complex and it takes a lot of smart, hard-working people to hold it together—operating and analyzing the functioning of the data centers and networks, maintaining the hardware and software as the business evolves, and helping end users master the complexities of the rapidly changing technology. A rule of thumb might be: *if we make the information ecology simpler and easier to maintain and operate, its costs will drop.* We might imagine a management principle[4] like the following:

Potential Principle: We will invest to simplify our information technology infrastructure, applications, and management processes.

The Structure of IT expense

Let's look inside the NatNec IT expense and see what they are buying with $178 million every year. As illustrated in Exhibit 2.3 on the next page, one breakdown might be:

- **Machines:** the computers, PCs , communication boxes
- **People:** employees and consultants
- **Places:** buildings and other facilities
- **Services:** telecom services, information services, maintenance services and training
- **Software:** purchased programs

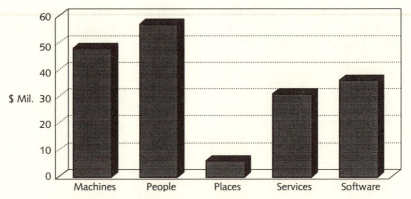

Exhibit 2.3   Representative Company IT Expense Breakdown

The typical company will show lower proportions for machines and software and higher proportions for personnel than NatNec because NatNec has made a significant investment in PC and LAN infrastructure. All the people in the branches and a big percentage of the headquarters and regional office folks have PCs . This drives up the hardware and software proportion of the IT expense. NatNec has realized some savings in mainframe computer equipment, network expense, and network management people expenses to offset the increases in hardware and software costs. The services and people proportion of the expense is accordingly lower.

Two observations to draw from the overall chart is that people expense is large compared to the other categories and the workspace costs (even including the data centers) are relatively small. The typical company spends about the same percentage on workspace but up to 40% of total information ecology costs on personnel. Also we should note that purchased software expense is beginning to approach the overall hardware expense. This is partially a result of the investment NatNec has made in its PC/LAN infrastructure, but it is true to some extent in the mainframe portion of the IT infrastructure as well. The typical company spends a much smaller proportion of its budget on software.

Exhibit 2.4 compares NatNec's IT expense distribution percentages (the right of each pair) with the average percentage distribution for all IT budgets in 1989 (a year selected to represent IT cost structure before most companies made investments in network computing infrastructures)[5] A company that has not made a big push yet into giving a large proportion of its people PCs on a network, is more like the left-hand side of each pair.

No matter which of these profiles fits your company, the key point of the breakdown is that *people expense is somewhere between very important and most important.*

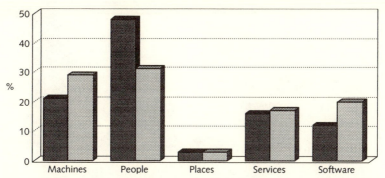

Exhibit 2.4   Representative Company's IT Expense Structure Contrasted with Typical Expense Structure of Companies Before Infrastructure Investment in LANs and PCs

Somehow the importance of people keeps getting overlooked in the management of this resource. We get involved with hardware and software and lose track of personware.

> *At the beginning of the computer era machines were scarce, dear, and poorly understood compared to the role people played in their use. Today they are plentiful, cheap, and well understood compared to the role people play in their use.*

This observation might lead us to another management principle.

Potential Principle: **We recognize that skilled personnel is the scarce resource in the information ecology and we will manage our investments in hardware and software to make maximum use of the scarce resource.**

Traditional functional breakdown of IT

The following is a fairly traditional breakdown of the information ecology into component parts and Exhibit 2.5 on the next page shows how NatNec's IT expense breaks down by function:

- **Data Center:** rooms, mainframes and their necessary software and peripherals, operators, and systems programmers.
- **Telecom:** data communication lines, network equipment, network operations center, network operators, network administration people, and network planners.[6]
- **Development:** programmers and all their gear.
- **Shared services:** overall IT management and planning, standards, technology scan, research and development (R&D).
- **End user:** terminals, PCs and LANs used by the business outside of IT, people necessary to administer and operate this gear.

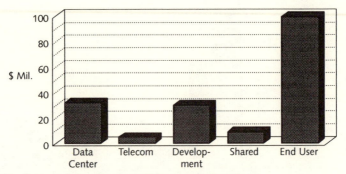

Exhibit 2.5   Representative Company IT Expense by Function

Obviously, the most prominent feature of this breakdown is that the "end user" function accounts for 57% of the total.[7] Here is a dramatic illustration that the information ecology has escaped the data center. It's even escaped the IT function all together! End users represent the portions of the information ecology that are controlled by the business units themselves without help or reference to the technology organization per se. In some companies, this means PCs and LANs that are essentially unknown to the central IT organization. In others, like NatNec, connections between the IT organization and the end users are closer and the PCs and LANs are counted as part of the overall IT function. The quality of these connections is critical to the overall effectiveness of the technology.

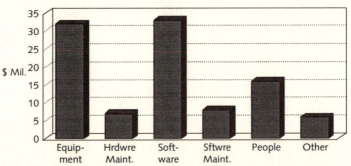

Exhibit 2.6   End User IT Expense in a Representative Company that Has Made a Significant Investment in PC/LAN Infrastructure

NatNec's investment in PC/LAN infrastructure for the branches and elsewhere is combined with pretty lean data center and telecom functions. This dramatic shift to end user expense is the concrete evidence of the PC revolution. Fifteen years ago there wasn't *any* expense in the end user category. Here's dramatic evidence of the power (or, at least, the lure) of the best new technology. We can't tell from this analysis if NatNec is getting benefit from this change, but Exhibit 2.6 shows more about how exactly NatNec is spending the end user dollars.

NatNec user areas have nearly 11,600 PCs and 6500 terminals. Of the PCs, nearly 9200 are attached to one of 169 LANs. NatNec is very aggressive in rolling out this PC LAN infrastructure and expects to replace the hardware every three years and to increase the software in use by $1000/PC/year. Depending on the size of the LAN, there are one to eight full time equivalent people doing network administration and security for each LAN. The terminal support comes from the Telecom function. In total there are 272 people supporting the end user portion of the information ecology.

A shareholder or director of NatNec might look at these numbers and tell the management,

> *This is a very large investment in infrastructure. I'm aware that there were partial offsetting savings in terminals and associated network expense, but now that you have installed the foundation for the best new technology, I sure hope you can complete the transition without dropping the ball! There is now at least 200 times as much computing power outside the data center as inside. We are going to have to get something pretty wonderful out of all that power!*

In my opinion, NatNec's end user investment in infrastructure was a necessary, but not sufficient, condition "to get something pretty wonderful." Success comes from a very complex combination of business end user and system developers working together. Conversion to the best new technology cannot be done with a checkbook alone.

Stuff in the cracks

In Exhibit 2.5, the functions included in "shared" are: strategic planning, architecture and standards, technology scan, and what is called "R&D" or sometimes "Advanced Systems." These functions are less than 4% of NatNec's information ecology but, because these functions are intensely involved in choosing the direction of technology, they have a disproportionate effect. The entire "shared IT expense" represents the steering gear on the information ecology. This stuff in the cracks, especially the monitoring and selection of standards, is of vital importance and is probably underfunded. The size of the numbers, however, will always be small when compared to the traditional IT functions.

The system development organization

There are 327 people in NatNec who comprise the system development organization. Their job is to maintain the existing application programs and to build new ones as required. Of the total, 27 are managers and administrative types, 12 are database administrators, and 288 are programmers and analysts at various experience and skill levels. This is a very small system development organization compared to the typical large company. NatNec supplements their system development staff with an above average use of contract professionals.

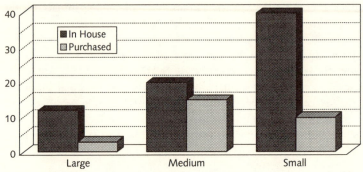

Exhibit 2.7   **Representative Company In-House and Purchased Application Systems by Size**

The developers are expected to *sustain* the existing set of application systems. NatNec has 100 application systems (see Exhibit 2.7). The big ones (over a million lines of code) are the absolute heart of NatNec's business. The medium and smaller application systems range from vital to nice to have. Most of these applications fall in NatNec's familiar stovepipes, that is, along established department lines.

Painfully few companies actually measure developers activity in a meaningful way, so one of the mysteries of the information ecology is "what exactly do the developers do?" In a recent survey, senior IT executives *estimated* that their developers divided their time as shown in Exhibit 2.8.[8]

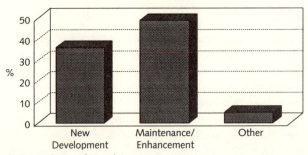

Exhibit 2.8   **Estimated Use of Development Resource**

On the surface this seems simple enough. About 40% of the time developers are building new systems and more than half the time (say 55%) developers are maintaining and enhancing existing systems. The development of new systems is easy enough to understand, but what is actually going on in the 55% called Maintenance/Enhancement?

Developers are constantly making changes to application systems that are already in production. It is often unclear why these changes are made and how they are selected. Through a set of unusual circumstances, I had an opportunity once to get an important insight into this question.

Because of severe pressure for cost reduction, one group of developers with whom I worked had been intentionally cut back from a normal level to the absolute minimum set of people necessary to fix defects and respond to regulatory changes. This cutback, painful as it was for the organization, created an interesting example of an almost pure maintenance organization. They weren't expected to do any new development; users had been told to expect absolutely no new functionality. Enhancements were to be done only after all maintenance tasks were completed. Consequently, it was expected that few if any enhancements were likely to be done.

In this unusual example, there were 186 people maintaining 53 application systems.[9] They made 11,000 changes in the year I studied them! At the end of the year, the application systems did essentially the same things that they did at the beginning of the year. Why did these bright people make all these changes and what did the company get for the nearly $20 million they cost? The people who made all those changes kept records of what they did. They classified each change as:

- **Corrective**: a change necessary to fix a problem that resulted from defective coding, design, or specification of the systems, "a bug."
- **Adaptive**: a change necessary in order for the system to continue to operate in response to a change in the business environment, the data center operations environment, or the regulatory environment.
- **Perfective**: a change in the way the system works that makes it perform better or provide improved functionality, "enhancements."

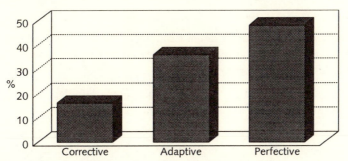

Exhibit 2.9   Changes by Type in a "Pure Maintenance" Environment

Exhibit 2.9 shows the percentage breakdown for the 11,000 changes. The amazing thing about these numbers is that only a sixth of the changes were made to fix problems. *Even in a pure maintenance organization, half the changes were enhancements!*

Let's put these observations together with the senior techies' estimates of how developers spend their time and take a closer look. Putting the numbers together with a little "Kentucky windage" (Exhibit 2.10), we estimate that the typical development resource is used about 30% for really maintaining systems—sustaining our information ecology. But accepted wisdom says our developers are so mired in maintaining legacy systems that we can't marshal the resources to change things without massive additional costs. This analysis says that *real maintenance requires less than a third of the resource*, but our developers are mired down in making small, inconsequential changes to legacy systems, wasting their potential to make significant changes. The forces of *sustain* have absorbed the system development resource totally, leaving nothing to *transform*.

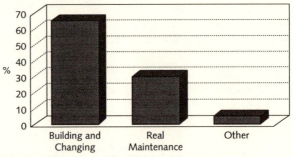

Exhibit 2.10   Estimated Allocation of Development Resource

Cost to sustain and cost to transform

So far, we've examined the overall cost of the information ecology from several perspectives—costs to own and operate, costs by expense category, and costs by IT function. Now we take another view, which reveals a novel aspect of the information ecology.

We've posed the problem:

> *How can we transform our old technology information environment into a new technology information environment while sustaining our ability to do our business every day?*

You've probably heard or participated in a conversation about this question in which somebody took a position something like this:

> *Well, maybe the techies know how to get all those great benefits and maybe they don't, but it's all academic anyway because, with all the money we're already spending on this systems stuff, we sure aren't going to spend a bunch more to find out.*

The chances are quite good that we are already spending enough to transform the information ecology, but we're spending it on relatively meaningless changes and enhancements to legacy systems.

To demonstrate that, Exhibit 2.11 is another cut of NatNec's IT numbers. The point of this breakdown is that while there are some elements of the information economy that are dedicated to keeping things the way they are (operations people, maintenance, and so forth) and there are elements dedicated to changing things (strategic planning, training, and so forth), *the bulk of resources in the information ecology are not intrinsically dedicated to either.* They are in some sense discretionary. If we chose to use them to *sustain* the present version of the information ecology, that's what will happen. If we choose to use them to *transform*, then that's what will happen.

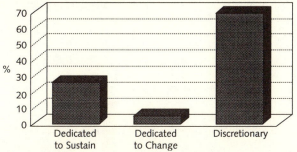

Exhibit 2.11 Most of the Representative Company's Resources are Discretionary with Respect to Their Use to Sustain or Transform the Information Ecology

Some of this chapter's observations include:

- The cost to operate our information ecology is quite high relative to the cost to own it. I suggested that this is a feature of the immaturity of the technology and our relatively limited mastery of it.
- I argued that productivity of the information ecology was mostly concerned with people issues rather than equipment issues.
- We observed that the development organization is a key area of flexibility and embodies more potential for creating change at its present expense level than most people think.
- The entire information ecology has a great deal of discretionary resource—not whether or not to spend the money, but how. We can take a strong orientation toward sustaining our existing situation or a similarly strong orientation toward transforming it. It is a matter of will and skill, not a matter of resources.

Chapter 3 introduces some of the things we can do at a strategic level to verify that we are spending the right amount on technology and that it is being spent on the right things.

Notes

1. Remarks about the "typical" company's expenses are based on figures produced by the Gartner Group in their 1991/1992 Information Technology Budgets and Practices Survey (See Flynn 1992).
2. Note that "cost to operate" doesn't include the costs of all the end users of the systems. I suppose an argument could be made that many of the people we employ as

users of information technology are "operators" of the information ecology. If a salesman uses his car to call on customers, we probably wouldn't think of the salesman as part of the fleet cost. If, on the other hand, we think about a fleet of bulldozers, the operator is certainly part of the cost to operate of our earth moving fleet.

3. We also notice there is an awful big "other" that we don't understand. We will spend some time later in this chapter understanding the "other." For the moment, let me just say that "other" is the $30 million for the development function and until we understand better what happens in that function, it isn't clear if the work represents creating new parts of the information ecology (cost to own) or if it represents maintaining the information ecology (cost to operate).

4. Throughout the book, I suggest management principles for the information ecology. These principles are summarized in Appendix B.

5. Average 1989 information service (I/S) budget data from "Human Resource and Productivity Challenges in Information Services" Touche Ross Information Technology Consulting Services, Second Annual North American Survey, 1989. They also say in the paper that the 1989 distribution was practically identical to that in 1988.

6. Voice telecommunications is very often included in the telecom function. The technology is changing in such a way that voice and data increasingly use the same equipment and lines. In the long run, voice and data will be indistinguishable. Voice telecom expense almost always is much larger that data telecom expense. Fifteen years ago the ratio of voice expense to data expense was 20:1. Now it may be 5:1. Because voice is a big issue and a big number and because it doesn't really have much impact on what I'm talking about, I've left it out of this discussion.

7. The typical company doesn't know very much about how much end user expense they have. Estimates of unrecognized expense range from 4% to 90% on top of the formal IT budget. Twenty-four percent of the Gartner Group survey respondents estimated more than 31% was off budget.

8. See Booz, Allen, & Hamilton 1992. The numbers are the arithmetic means of the responses from the 352 respondents. That's why they don't add up to 100%.

9. The number of people required for the minimum set depends on the specific skills of the people and the specific details of the application systems. I believe that the fairly large number of people required in this example is typical of our complex, heterogeneous legacy information ecologies.

3
Spending Smarter

The most complex and politically charged questions in business have to do with allocating the organization's resources. In Chapter 2, we looked at how money *is* spent in a representative large company. At the highest level of the business technology linkage are the questions about how much *should be* spent on the information ecology and *how* it should be spent. More specifically,

- *How much is enough?* How do we know how much of the aggregate corporate resource to devote to the information ecology?
- *How should we spend it?* Given that we know how much to spend, how do we decide at both the strategic and tactical levels how to spend it?

This is a judgment process for which there is no algorithm, so the purpose of this chapter is to discuss the questions and arrive at a practical, if not entirely satisfactory, method for getting to a useful result. Our focus will be on process and method, but underlying these should be a continuing awareness that the company is best served when business and technology expertise is combined. Most significantly, we will conclude that a company with a clear shared vision including pursuits and measures will make these decisions with much more confidence than a company that is less well equipped.

How much do we spend?

Does our company spend the right amount of money on the information ecology? Do we spend it on the right things? Typically, the finance staff, or corporate planning staff, or a knowledgeable consulting team, will probably start to answer this question by rounding up all the numbers on what the company spends now. This step, by itself, is not obvious. There are very large companies who've never asked this question and could not answer it. There are good reasons why it's not easy to find out how much the information ecology costs.

- *Concept:* It isn't common for any accounting group to keep records of the costs associated with the information ecology. Generally the idea just doesn't occur.
- *Classifications:* The books and records of the company don't have a caption "information ecology." The captions for expense classes may have been modified at some recent time to reflect the categories of expense incurred by the various parts of the information ecology, or they may not have been. The chances are pretty good that there is confusion about how to record these expenses and different control people may have resolved this confusion in different ways.
- *Transfer pricing and expense allocation:* Major expenses incurred in one part of the company may be transferred to another either in a transfer pricing arrangement or an allocation. Only rarely are these transferred and allocated expenses separated from real expenses. Sorting them out can be a major complication.
- *Capital items:* There are different accounting treatments for alternative approaches to procuring pieces of the information infrastructure.[1] These differences result in significant interpretation issues when we try to analyze expenses.

The bottom line here is that it can be quite difficult to find out how much we are spending on the information ecology. Even so, it's work worth doing. We may discover that our intuition is an imperfect guide to investment decisions, but it's hard to imagine a circumstance in which not knowing where we are is better than knowing. The information ecology is too important to be ignored, its costs are too large to be hidden, and its value too great to be shrugged off. This analysis should be the minimum duty for a CIO. Good practice includes the following.

- *Work with direct costs only.* Ignore allocated cost. Ignore transfer prices.[2]
- *Fit in with the literature.* Several consulting companies, publishing companies, and universities do continuing data collection on the costs of various parts of the information ecology. Look at as many of these as possible before going to work. It may prove useful in the long run if the numbers can be sliced and diced to be compared with other studies.
- *Put it in a context.* The context will depend on how each company works, but something is required to keep the numbers from "flapping in the air." When expenses are being classified in a novel way, it is insufficient to say that an item is "information ecology" or "not information ecology." If it's not, it must fall into some other category and all the categories must add up to the company's total expense. The table in Exhibit 3.1 is a sample of a context for NatNec.

$ Millions	Information Ecology	Engineering	Marketing & Sales	Distribution	Manufacturing	Management & Staff	Totals
People	$ 50.6	$135.7	$266.0	$133.2	$365.2	$127.3	$1,078.0
Space	5.4	12.8	25.4	12.8	35.9	12.2	104.5
Equipment	106.5	2.7	2.7	1.3	7.3	2.5	123.0
Services	11.8	1.4	16.0	5.3	11.0	5.1	50.6
Other	3.8	2.7	13.3	2.7	7.3	6.4	36.2
Totals	$178.1	$155.3	$323.4	$155.3	$426.7	$153.5	$1,392.3

Exhibit 3.1   NatNec's Overall Expense Structure

The shaded box in the lower right corner is the keystone. It's the number that must match the total expense of the company. It's useful to select the major processes of the company as the other categories in the context chart. The process view of a business is likely to be more robust than a line of business view—the process structure of a business doesn't change anywhere near as quickly as the organization chart. Given a process view, it's possible also to make the chart in Exhibit 3.2, which shows how the information ecology is put to work supporting the company's basic processes.

$ Millions	Engineering	Marketing & Sales	Distribution	Manufacturing	Management & Staff	Totals
People	$135.7	$266.0	$133.2	$365.2	$127.3	$1,027.4
Space	12.8	25.4	12.8	35.9	12.2	99.1
Equipment	2.7	2.7	1.3	7.3	2.5	16.5
Services	1.4	16.0	5.3	11.0	5.1	38.8
Other	2.7	13.3	2.7	7.3	6.4	32.4
Information Ecology	10.8	43.3	37.5	71.8	14.7	178.1
Totals	$166.1	$366.7	$192.8	$498.5	$168.2	$1,392.3

Exhibit 3.2   Overall Expense Structure by Major Business Process of Representative Company with Information Ecology Allocated to Major Processes

- *Do a separate analysis for capital.* Investigate how much capital is in use to support the information ecology and put it in a similar context. Also, it might not be a bad idea to run the analysis back a few years if possible.

Let's go back to what we've learned about NatNec. We know it costs $178 million to run NatNec's information ecology and that cost has been roughly flat for a few years at about 13% of total cost. We also know that NatNec employs about $500 million in capital and that number has grown steeply. So what? Are these the right numbers? Are these the right patterns?

What's the right number look like?

As a thought experiment, imagine that we are spending exactly the right amount of money in the information ecology and we are spending it on exactly the right things. In theory, we might observe the following:

> *If we spent any less or any more or if we spent it any differently, the present value of our future earnings would decrease.*

Just thinking about that observation is sufficient to convince me that we'll never know if we have exactly the right number. After all, to know if any particular number met those criteria we would need perfect knowledge of how our investments and other actions affect future earnings—a more complete model than we are likely to have of our business. Furthermore, we would have to have perfect knowledge of the how our competitors, the markets, and all other environmental factors will behave—not likely either. No, we're never going to know if we have the right number, so let's ask if we can come up with a good number.

What's a good number look like?

We know that tolerating ambiguity and making decisions under uncertainty are at the very heart of the executive's job. The process we are investigating in this chapter is full of ambiguity and uncertainty. There is no fail-safe answer; no foolproof algorithm. When we set out to allocate our resources, we never have the comfort of knowing exactly what to do. Our talents, skills, and experience are brought to bear to produce a judgment. The quality of the judgment is difficult to know, but it is not unreasonable to think that an informed judgment is better than an uninformed one. This section investigates some approaches to making our judgments about total resource allocation more informed.

Let's try another thought experiment. Imagine the amount we are spending on the information ecology is about right and, by and large, we are spending it on the right things. If we are investing appropriately, we might observe the following:

- We are getting as much or more value for our money as other smart companies in similar situations are getting.
- We are getting as much as we had expected to get for our investments or more.
- We have realistic expectations about change and our investment in *transform* is consistent with those expectations.

If we find these things to be true, we might be comfortable that our investments in the information ecology are about right. These are, however, fairly complex criteria and how to test them isn't obvious.

Relative value and resulting value

The first thing we'd like to know is how we're doing compared to other companies. If we are going to determine whether or not we are getting good value relative to other smart companies in similar situations, we need to know what the measures of value are and who we should compare ourselves to.

Ideally, we would know as much about the cost dynamics of other smart companies as we know about our own. We would like to be able to compare their unit costs to ours for practically every thing we do. This kind of information isn't easy to come by. Furthermore, the companies to which we would like to compare ourselves probably aren't the same ones for every function and may not to be the ones that first come to mind. Most useful of all is a comprehensive comparison of how our company's basic *processes* compare with the best practices in these basic processes, regardless of industry. The standard we wish to use for our measurement is the best one, not the nearest or most convenient one.

Once we know how we're doing compared to other companies, we need to understand how well we do compared to our own plans, projections, and forecasts. One of the most useful and comforting skills we can have is the ability to forecast accurately. If we allocate resources with an expectation that they will return a certain value and they do, we build confidence in our forecasting and have more trust in the next forecast. Good forecasting is prima facie evidence that the mental models we applied were relevant and useful. Relevant and useful mental models are a good foundation for successful allocation. So, if it turns out that we are pretty good at forecasting value received for resources invested, we will trust more in our estimates of what is needed.

Some research into our investment history will reveal how well we anticipate the results of our investments. Accuracy is important. Consistently *underestimating* the value of information ecology investments is as likely to indicate a failure of understanding as consistently *overestimating* their value. If we discover that we have done a good job allocating resources to information ecology investments and we got the results we expected, we can feel confidence in our mental models of how the business works. If we learn otherwise, we are obliged to reexamine what we believe to be true about how the business works.

Expectations of change

Another way to shed light on whether or not we are spending the right amount in the information ecology is to compare the amount of resources we are allocating to the areas in which we anticipate change.

Imagine that we had a breakdown of the corporate expense base by process like the one we looked at above. Imagine further that we divide the information ecology into costs incurred to support *sustain*, costs incurred to support *transform*, and costs that could go either way depending on our actions. The table[3] would look like Exhibit 3.3. Appended at the bottom of the table are the expectations we hold about the business and how technology change may influence it.

$ Millions	Engineering	Marketing & Sales	Distribution	Manufacturing	Management & Staff	Totals
People	$135.7	$266.0	$133.2	$365.2	$127.3	$1,027.4
Space	12.8	25.4	12.8	35.9	12.2	99.1
Equipment	2.7	2.7	1.3	7.3	2.5	16.5
Services	1.4	16.0	5.3	11.0	5.1	38.8
Other	2.7	13.3	2.7	7.3	6.4	32.4
Information Ecology						
Sustain	2.6	13.3	10.5	10.8	9.1	46.3
Transform	8.2				0.7	8.9
Discretionary		30.0	27.0	61.0	4.9	122.9
Totals	$166.1	$366.7	$192.8	$498.5	$168.2	**$1,392.3**
Expected technical transformation potential	moderate	moderate	very high	high	high	
Expected benefit from transformation	moderate	high	high	moderate	moderate	
Expected likelihood of competitive pressure	low	high	high	high	low	

Exhibit 3.3   Cost by Process Augmented with Estimates of Transformation Impact

- *Expected technical transformation potential:* our opinion about how much the technology might impact the process if we chose to transform it. Our intuition about this topic would be enriched by brainstorming or similar exercises.
- *Expected benefit from transformation:* our opinion about how much the process would benefit if we applied a major technology transformation to it. Our opinions would be better informed after appropriate business process reengineering (BPR) feasibility work.
- *Expected likelihood of competitive pressure:* our opinion about the likelihood that a competitor will exert significant pressure on our business by making a technical transformation or other change. Intense competitive analysis would help here.

We now have a framework for matching our expectations about change with the realities of our information ecology. This type of analysis might be described as "quantifying smoke," but a disciplined effort to make and understand the various judgments gives us a much more informed framework for decision making than we have without doing the work. Of course, this frame cannot be applied mindlessly, but it can serve as a foundation for discussing the allocation of resources. We shouldn't expect that preparing an exhibit like Exhibit 3.3 will make a strategy "jump out at us," but the work necessary to prepare such an exhibit will be excellent preparation for the discussion in which a strategy will be forged.

Working out the number

Let's assume that NatNec has brought together all the information I have been describing. In addition to the analysis that has led to the exhibit, NatNec has learned that:

- NatNec has lower unit costs for delivering their products than most, but not all, of their competitors.
- NatNec's cost ratios in basic activities and corporate functions are significantly worse than the best practices but stack up reasonably well against other companies in their industry.
- Significant projects routinely perform better than they expect and they usually get more benefit from changes than they anticipated. Differences are dramatic.

Given this set of information, what can NatNec say about whether or not $178 million a year is the right number to spend on the information ecology? Here's the summary I might make of the situation.

- NatNec is in an information intensive business. Thirteen percent of their total expense base is in the information ecology. They seem to be using their systems about as efficiently as their competitors, although other smart people in other industries have figured out how to be more efficient in important ways.
- NatNec consistently underestimates the value of innovation and change to their business. They may have created a climate where people have an exaggerated fear of failing. This possibility is reinforced by the very small amount of resource being allocated to *transform*. Most of the company isn't trying to innovate, even though there is a sizable resource available.
- Their marketing, sales, distribution, and manufacturing processes dominate their cost base and they have a high potential for technical innovation. Furthermore, they anticipate competitive pressure developing in these areas.
- Putting resources into *transform* for engineering and management is pretty silly when distribution and manufacturing are the areas where there is high potential and high likelihood of competitive pressure. It seems that there is much discretionary resource that could be turned to *transform* if they choose.
- NatNec should assume that the $178 million is a big enough number. They should make a strong push to examine their climate for change and to focus a lot more discretionary resource on *transform* for the next year or so. *Transform* ramps up slowly so they will have time to improve their climate for change and to read the competition better before they have to commit irrevocably to any changes in the underlying processes.

The thought process around this question can be complex and can include a wide variety of considerations. In addition to the evaluations I have already described, there are others that have been recommended or used from time to time to support these strategic judgments, including,

- *Capacity analysis:* An analysis of how much of the present available capacity we are using. This can apply to computers, networks, applications, training facilities, development staff, and so forth.
- *User satisfaction survey:* analysis of how well the users believe their needs are being met by the techies. I have never seen an analysis of how well the techies think their needs are being met by the users.
- *Hardware and software inventory:* An analysis of the present complement of computers, communications capabilities, and software in the information ecology. This inventory is usually the first step agreed to by anyone working on the "problem." Often, it is the only step. These inventories are difficult and time consuming to do in detail and can serve as a bureaucratic alternative to thinking.
- *Software quality assessment:* An analysis of how well the existing complement of application software meets some set of quality criteria. The choice of criteria is critical, of course, to the value of the assessment. These analyses are not done often enough in most companies.
- *Skills inventory:* A survey of the available breadth and depth of skills in the *technology* organization. I've never seen anything like this applied to the *business* side of the relationship. Like hardware and software inventories, these are hard to do and difficult to interpret and can serve as an alternative to thinking.
- *Information technology assessment:* One of several names for a study or survey that combines some or all of these surveys and assessments to produce a multidimensional view of the quality of the information ecology. It is often revealing.

Better top level resource allocation decisions are made when more of this kind of information is available. None of this data gathering and assessment, however, can serve as an alternative for the involvement of the key decision makers. Given that key decision makers will be actively involved in managing the information technology, we can suggest another management principle.

Potential Principle: We will analyze and manage information technology expense and capital investment in the aggregate.

Strategic resource allocation

Let's say that we have a pretty good number for the total to be allocated to the information ecology. As we've seen, a lot of the resources are discretionary in the short or intermediate term. That is, there's money we definitely will spend, but we have a variety of options about how to spend it. The metaphor I like for this situation is that we have a river of money flowing through our information ecology and it's up to us to see that the right things get watered.

Strategic resource allocation for the entire company is conceptually a matter of examining how we are presently allocating a resource and then adjusting the allocation to correspond best with our business judgment. The stuff that's new when allocating resources to the information ecology includes:

- *We are going to look at the information ecology as a whole:* Taking the information ecology as a whole and allocating it across our strategic dimensions is not unheard of, but it's rare. More commonly, we allocate expense and capital dollars separately from each other but aggregate each across business units—the typical business plan and budget process.
- *We are going to examine unusual dimensions:* Many companies are accustomed to allocating resources along dimensions like business unit, market segment, geography, distribution channel, or product. We are going to discuss allocating the information ecology resource according to a couple of novel dimensions.

Conceptually, as I said, strategic resource allocation is a multidimensional process. Practically, it seems, allocation is pretty one dimensional. I don't know how allocation decisions get made in every company, but in several I've worked in it goes this way.

- *Everybody makes a budget request for the next year.* Revenue and expense forecasts are built-up by some (usually complex) process for every small unit of the company. Time and information are usually sufficient only to make very approximate plans. The requests are usually very conservative, that is protective of the interests of the people making the detailed forecasts. The detailed budgets are added up and mapped into the usual set of P&L statements. P&L managers (sometimes important cost center managers too) make presentations to upper management. The finance types consolidate all the P&Ls into the usual top level presentation format and present it to executive management.
- *Executive management rejects the aggregate plan.* The pro forma aggregate financials are examined by the executive managers and are judged to be undesirable, by which they mean they would not be pleased with a real result that looked liked the pro forma.[4] Occasionally, they will question what appear to be unrealistic revenue forecasts. More frequently they will object to aggregate costs. They may set overall profit goals at this point and give some indication of where profit forecast adjustments are expected. If so, these are the topmost allocation decisions.
- *Changes are mandated.* Revenue adjustments and cost reductions are mandated level by level down the organization. These mandated changes in the business plans are based on the judgment of the appropriate mem-

ber of the hierarchy. These are real allocation decisions. Usually made in haste. Usually made with little analytical framework.

- *Revisions are made.* Based on the allocation decisions of those above in the hierarchy, adjustments are made. Usually time has run out for any detailed planning by the time these revisions are required. If the original submission was done by an experienced player of this game, the adjustments can be made without seriously reducing the options available at this level of the hierarchy. Allocation decisions not already built in (i.e., most of *sustain*) can be made at this level and below at any later time.

It's easy to see from this description that allocation done this way is primarily a divvying up of resources along the organizational hierarchy, a one-dimensional allocation process. It's also easy to see that a strategic focus is likely to be diluted and eventually lost without extraordinary additional effort being applied to preserve it. The only mechanism in this process to achieve cross-linkage between business and technology is at the very beginning when low-level units make their initial plans. Coordination of business and technology happens at this level or it doesn't happen at all, and all of the tops-down allocation decisions are made in complete ignorance of any of this low-level planning.

Resources identified as *transform* are the only ones that are identified in this process as discretionary, thus the only ones ever cut. Discretionary resources survive at a level low enough to hide them and are allocated there. This kind of resource allocation process is an important force that biases our companies toward *sustain*.

The dynamic dimensions

The *dynamic* dimensions are *sustain* and *transform* and *risk*. We've already seen a breakdown of NatNec's information ecology resource allocation[5] by *sustain* and *transform* versus business process (see Exhibit 3.4).

$ Millions	Engineering	Marketing & Sales	Distribution	Manufacturing	Management & Staff	Totals
Information Ecology						
Sustain	$ 2.6	$13.3	$10.5	$10.8	$ 9.1	$ 46.3
Transform	8.2				0.7	8.9
Discretionary		30.0	27.0	61.0	4.9	122.9
Totals	$10.8	$43.3	$37.5	$71.8	$14.7	**$178.1**

Exhibit 3.4   Allocation of Information Ecology Resources in a Representative Company by Major Business Process Versus Sustain and Transform

Remember, in most large companies, *discretionary* turns into *sustain* unless we specifically focus it on *transform*. Insights from this table are scarce. We've already noted that very little of the information ecology is focused on *transform*, but there's a lot of potential. We also observed that we may not be putting the *transform* resources against the highest payoff business processes. Beyond that, there's little to say.

Resources devoted to *transform* have an importance to the company that is disproportionately large. If we choose to shift the resource balance toward *transform* in the company, the details of the new transform-oriented work will probably be well known even at the strategic level. One view of the transform-oriented resources, however, may not be obvious. I speak of an understanding of how *risky* the transform activities are.

Transform activities have various associated risks.

- *Feasibility can fail.* Exploratory activities can fail to have any useful result. If we set out to discover a better way to build widgets, we might not find one.
- *Development can fail.* If we set out to apply a technology to a problem, we can fail to solve the problem. Risk is raised by unfamiliar business process, unfamiliar technology, large size, and more complexity.
- *Development can succeed poorly.* This is not a complete failure, but the budget or schedule is missed. Same risk factors.
- *Implementation can fail.* We can set out to apply a system and fail. Risk factors are an unfamiliar business process, an unfamiliar target group, an unfamiliar system, or a challenging schedule or budget.
- *Implementation can succeed poorly.* This is not a failure, but budget or schedule is blown. Same risk factors.
- *Unexpected poor business result.* We tried it and it didn't work. It didn't sell or it drove customers away. Risk factors include an unfamiliar market, and unfamiliar business, and unfamiliar process, and a little bit of everything else we can fail to understand.

We can summarize and think about three kinds of transform risk: feasibility risk, development risk, and implementation risk. Ultimately, of course, it's all business risk, but we would like to eliminate some of the risk associated with change by doing good feasibility analysis, good development, and good implementation. Imagine a table like the one in Exhibit 3.5. The entries in the table are the percentages of the total resources allocated to *transform* that fall in each category. The numbers in the example show a reasonable allocation of *transform* resources.

	Low Risk	Moderate Risk	High Risk	Total
Feasibility	2 %	3 %	10 %	15 %
Development	20	10	5	35
Implementation	40	10	–	50
Total	62 %	23 %	15 %	100 %

Exhibit 3.5   Representative Distribution of Transform Risk

By *reasonable,* I mean:

- *A healthy portion of the total transform resource (15% of total) is devoted to feasibility.* Feasibility work is relatively cheap, so a lot of things can be examined for fairly little investment.
- *Much of the feasibility work is relatively high risk (10% of total, 66% of feasibility).* We want to push the edge of what's possible here. Failure in a feasibility study is just another name for education.
- *We shift resources toward less risky activities as we move toward development (only 14% high risk).* There are probably many fewer development project teams than feasibility teams. Although there is a shift toward safer choices, significant risk remains.
- *Implementation uses the bulk of the transform resource (50%) and is risk controlled (no high risk implementation).* We want to get things done and we want them to work right away. We believe that our willingness to accept more risk in feasibility stages justifies our focus on low-risk implementations.

This table shows a reasonable risk balance across the *transform* portfolio, but it doesn't say anything about the absolute amount of *transform* we are introducing into the environment. Like the blind men and the elephant, we need a variety of views of the allocation of resources before the real strategic shape emerges.

Multidimensional allocation

Exhibit 3.6 is a copy of one of the tables we used earlier in the chapter. It is a high-level aggregation of the resource allocation (expense base) broken down in two dimensions—resource category (summary expense class) and business process. If we juggle these numbers around, we will eventually arrive at what feels to be a proper balance. That is, we will feel that we are spending the money on the right categories in the right processes.

$ Millions	Engineering	Marketing & Sales	Distribution	Manufacturing	Management & Staff	Totals
People	$135.7	$266.0	$133.2	$365.2	$127.3	$1,027.4
Space	12.8	25.4	12.8	35.9	12.2	99.1
Equipment	2.7	2.7	1.3	7.3	2.5	16.5
Services	1.4	16.0	5.3	11.0	5.1	38.8
Other	2.7	13.3	2.7	7.3	6.4	32.4
Information Ecology	10.8	43.3	37.5	71.8	14.7	178.1
Totals	$166.1	$366.7	$192.8	$498.5	$168.2	$1,392.3

Exhibit 3.6   Representative Company Expense Base by Major Business Process and Summary Expense Class with Allocated Information Ecology

That's a good thing to do, but it's not enough. We are still ignorant, for instance, of how resources are balanced across geography, or across business units, or across market segments. Each dimension of the business gives us another set of ways we may wish to balance. Almost everybody uses *resource categories* and *business units* as basic allocation dimensions. A couple more that are common, especially in large companies, are *geography* and *market segments*. I have already urged you to add the *fundamental processes* of your business and the *dynamic dimensions* to the list. The aggregate list becomes: resource categories; business units; geography; market segments; business processes; *sustain* and *transform*; and activity risks.

These may not all make sense for every company, but if we used all seven of these dimensions, we could generate 21 distinct two-way tables like the preceding one. Each table would show us the balance of one of these dimension against another. If we add dimensions, the number of two-way comparisons grows rapidly. Seven dimensions seems about right.

I said earlier in the chapter that there aren't any foolproof algorithms for strategic allocation, but an informed judgment is likely to be better than an uninformed one. Creating and pondering these two-way tables is a worthwhile activity for executive management.

Allocation and the vision

The last few sections have discussed how to determine if we are spending roughly the right amount of money and on the right kinds of things in the information ecology. In most of our companies, these choices tend to bubble up from the organization's lower level and are coerced into an acceptable size by a top-down, hierarchy-oriented allocation process. I have advocated a multidimensional balancing act instead. Let's suppose that we adopt some form of the allocation analysis I have proposed for our executive management and we have arrived at a balance of resources that we feel meets the needs of the company. In short, we know what we're going to spend and how the money is allocated across key dimensions.

How do we decide what to spend it on and what, specifically, we are going to do? That is also an executive management prerogative. As a practical matter, however, executive management probably doesn't think up projects as often as it reacts to projects presented to it. However it works, I have never seen a situation in which insufficient ideas were available to make use of the resources available and then some. It's always a matter of choosing among projects and sometimes adjusting the scale or pace of the ones chosen.

Where do the ideas come from? How do we know which ideas contribute to the business in really important ways and which contribute only incidentally or tangentially? If we have to choose between important ideas, what criteria would we apply? The answers are found in our understanding of *shared vision*.

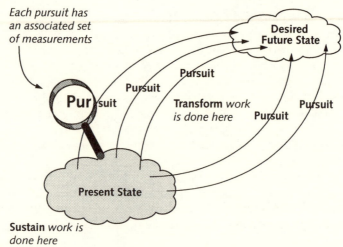

Exhibit 3.7   Shared Vision Conceptual Design

Shared vision is not a mystical concept and it is not in the least "blue sky, fuzzy wuzzy." A shared vision is a very powerful planning and coordination tool. It consists of three parts, which are depicted in Exhibit 3.7.

- *Desired future state:* a description of "how it would be if it were right" at whatever level of detail suits the purpose of the group developing the vision. This is the goal of all the work. It must include, as a minimum, some concrete way to measure how close we have come to the desired future state. A desired future state can be summed up as an appropriate mission statement, but is more powerful if it is more detailed.
- *Pursuits:* programs of action intended to bring about the desired future state. At the most general level, pursuits are quite broad. A company might, for instance, establish high level pursuits such as *acquire the industry's best qualified staff* or *become the dominant player in the widget market.* Pursuits should be broad enough so that there are relatively few, say five to ten.
- *Measures:* program metrics. The desired future state as a whole and each pursuit individually must have a set of measures associated with it so that we can unambiguously determine whether or not the work we do advances the pursuit and if progress on the pursuits creates progress toward the desired future state.

Ideally everyone in the entire organization would have exactly the same understanding of an extremely detailed version of the desired future state. Such an ideal is not likely to be achieved in an organization of any considerable size. More likely, we will have a situation like the one pictured in Exhibit 3.8.

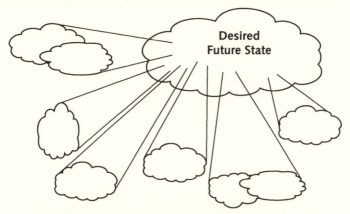

Exhibit 3.8 Desired Future State Must Be Seen Consistently but Not Necessarily Identically by All Participants in the Shared Vision

Each person who participates in a shared vision understands the overall desired future state in pretty much the same way, but each person also understands some particular portion of the desired future state in more depth of detail than others. Pursuits and associated measures will be developed for each subset of the vision. This phenomenon should be made part of the process. Each new group of people enrolled in the shared vision should be encouraged to elaborate their view with details that are particularly interesting to them and to coordinate their subpursuits and measures with the higher level pursuits of the overall vision. If the executive managers have a high-level understanding of the desired future state, then it will be expanded and enriched when the marketing team or the widget business or the management of the newly acquired subsidiary are enrolled in the vision, add their details to the desired future state, and articulate their additional supporting pursuits and measures.

Expanding the vision in a way that ensures all the enriched views are consistent is a problem in group dynamics that is reasonably well understood, but it does require work. Resources must be focused on vision creation, coordination, and maintenance. Although the cost of the vision is not insignificant, it is dwarfed by the benefits. Let's see how allocation works in a company where there is a broadly shared vision.

Project ideas come from everywhere

Ideas come top down and bottom up. They come from the business and from the technology people. Ideas affecting both infrastructure and applications can come from system developers or infrastructure operations. Ideas can come from customers or even competitors. Given an idea, how might we discover in which quadrant of Exhibit 3.9's picture it belongs?

	Bad Ideas	Good Ideas
Important to our business	Salvage?	Winners
Irrelevent to our business	Washouts	Honey traps

Exhibit 3.9   Ideas Can Be Classified for Business Planning Purposes

Usually sorting out bad ideas is fairly easy as long as they are examined honestly. If there is an honest disagreement over the quality of an idea, it probably reflects either a lack of factual information or a conflict of mental models, principles, or values. In a company with a broadly shared vision, people's values, principles, and mental models are synchronized to a large extent in the process of building the vision. In fact, verifying common values, principles, and mental models is the best way to start building a shared vision. Given a shared vision, bad ideas can quickly be sifted out by a judicious application of fact. Sometimes a bad idea can be salvaged by being revised or reworked, moving it from the left to the right side of the chart. We might want to try that, if the idea is relevant to our business.

In many companies, the toughest part of this winnowing out of ideas is to separate the winners from the honey traps. In the company with a broad shared vision, it's a snap.

> If the idea supports a pursuit, it's relevant. If it doesn't support a pursuit—no matter how wonderful it may be—it is irrelevant to our business.

It's just that easy. Anybody who shares the vision can do it—including the person who came up with the idea in the first place. Honey traps just don't come up. The decision whether to try to salvage a bad idea is just as easy—does the idea support a pursuit?

It's possible, of course, that an idea could be outside the mental models of the people who share the vision and a very good idea could be passed over because it doesn't fit with an inadequate understanding of the business. To provide some protection from this failing, we need to:

- *Establish valid linkage.* If we freely test each other's assumptions and mental models, they will be robust. The organization and processes of the organization need to be arranged so that it is possible for the various experts in different part of the business to understand and challenge each other's ideas.
- *Maintain the vision.* Shared visions must be continually renewed and tested. Maintaining a shared vision is a group process that requires a great deal of meeting and re-meeting. If a new winner idea arises outside

of the paradigm, it should begin to have a following in these vision maintenance sessions.

These techniques will lessen but not eliminate the risk of turning our backs on the winner that is outside our mental models.

The shared vision gives us an enormously powerful tool for focusing on winners. It also gives us the machinery for choosing among competing winners when we allocate resources. Competing proposals for projects will be framed in the language of our pursuits including the associated measures of progress along the pursuit. It's this progress that constitutes the *return* from the proposed allocation of resources. Some of the connections among the hierarchy of pursuits may be judgmental, but it should be possible to make at least qualitative comparisons of return on investment among the competing proposals. Balancing resources across various dimensions comes as the last step in the allocation process in a company that does planning and resource allocation through a shared vision. The importance of shared vision to resource allocation leads to another suggested management principle.

Potential Principle: **We will invest in the creation and maintenance of a shared vision to support resource allocation and other key decision-making activities.**

This chapter has addressed the questions *how much should we spend on the information ecology?* and *how should we spend it?* Our objective was to get to a useful approach rather than an exact answer.

We started out by talking about gathering information about how much we spend now. I gave some advice on this data gathering activity:

- Work with direct costs only.
- Fit in with the literature.
- Put it in context.
- Do a separate analysis for capital.

I argued that it was impossible to know for sure what the right amount was to spend on the information ecology. I went on to say that we might have confidence that we were close if

- We get as much value as other smart companies are getting.
- We get as much value as we expect from our investments.
- Our investments are consistent with realistic expectations about change.

We finished up the chapter with a discussion of how shared vision can be used to substantially improve the planning and allocation process. We will expand on the notion of shared vision in Chapter 4 when we get down to the details of business technology linkage.

Notes

1. Purchases, operating leases, and capital leases get very different accounting treatments even when they represent the same transaction from a practical point of view.
2. This requires that the scope of your analysis be corporate-wide or at least wide enough so that transfer pricing arrangements are included.
3. The numbers in this exhibit represent all of NatNec's costs except for approximately $200 million to finance their balance sheet.
4. What message do you imagine the organization gets from this step?
5. We are ignoring for this illustration the important fact that all resources, whether or not they are within the information ecology, are focused either on *sustain* or *transform*. If we reconstruct the original table to show all the resources classified as *sustain* or *transform* we have another one of the 21 allocation balancing tables.

4
What Is Linkage All About?

Business technology linkage has become a focus of attention because imperfections in our processes and organizations hinder our ability to perform. Poor linkage; big imperfections. Good linkage; fewer imperfections.

- *Linkage is good* when business need and technical solution feel like they fit together smoothly.
- *Linkage is good* when things seem to work out even better than we thought they would.
- *Linkage is good* when the customer feels that our company works better than the competition.
- *Linkage is good* when we feel that "users" and "techies" are names of roles instead of terms of class distinction.

We've done a lot of talking about linkage without ever saying exactly what the term means. Here's a try for a real definition: *linkage* is the condition wherein different people make choices while constrained by a common set of values, principles, and a common vision.

The definition says that you and I are linked if, as we go about our business—picking courses of action, settling priority conflicts, doing something one way rather than another—we choose those actions, not from every possible choice, but from a constrained set of choices.

- Our choices are constrained by a set of *values*: statements about what is important.
- Our choices are constrained by a set of *principles*: statements about how we are going to do things.
- And our choices are constrained by a *shared vision* of the way we would like things to be and the way we plan to get there.

When we examine all the possible things we could do, we reject those that aren't proper or desirable. We reject those that are incompatible with the way we do things. We reject those that don't move us along the path to our common vision. If you and I make our choices only from options that are left, we are *linked*… and what we choose to do will fit together. A lot of us are uncomfortable with the idea of being constrained. It doesn't feel quite right. Freedom is an important value to most of us. I'd like to point out that the constraints that are imposed by agreeing on values, principles, and vision only constrain us from making choices which would be wrong. There are still an infinite number of choices that are not constrained, allowing plenty of latitude for personal ingenuity, invention, and creativity. Let's look at the constraints more carefully to see how this works.

Values are easy enough to list: honesty, integrity, loyalty, customer satisfaction, empowerment, competence, flexibility, consistency, profitability, thrift, quality, robustness, harmony, and on and on. We have a lot of words naming values. When we are trying to build linkage, we select a set of values to which we wish to adhere. This is a tricky process. It's easy enough to pick a set of words, but when we intend to put them to practical use, things become more difficult. For instance,

- *We need to be very clear about what the words mean.* It has to be clear to everyone when an action is consistent with a value and when it's not.
- *We need to pick a limited set.* The set of values we select should be the ones we wish to make most important in our actions. If we have too many, they don't help much in constraining our choices.
- *We need to try for consistency in the value set.* If, for instance, we have both harmony and honesty in our value set, we may be setting the stage for a lot of conflicts.
- *We need to be willing to pay for these values.* The cost may be incurred in comfort, convenience, or current expense.
- *We need to be willing to "walk the talk."* If the values are not adhered to, especially in very public ways like company policy or executive behavior, they will immediately cease to be useful.

If you don't think that a public affirmation of values constrains decision making, ponder these examples for a moment.

- Imagine we have espoused *competence* as an important value of our company. What does this say about hiring policy? Training and compensation? Promotions? Layoffs?
- Imagine we have espoused *empowerment* as a value. What does that say about organization structure? Decision making? Dealing with mistakes? Dress codes?
- Imagine we adopt *loyalty* as an important value. What does that say about promotion policy? Internal mobility? When new skills are needed? When new opportunities arise?

Most likely, values have broad applicability in our company. It would seem reasonable for a single set of values to inform the company's decision making at all levels.

Principles are a little more specific, and they tend to support the values we select.[1] Instead of being simply words, principles are full statements of how we will do things. Furthermore, they have to be more than "motherhood and apple pie."

We will treat our customers well is not a principle. No one would argue that we should treat customers badly. *We will ensure customer satisfaction* even *if that results in short-term cost to the company* is a principle. It is possible to argue in support of a contrary position that we should ensure customer satisfaction *unless* it results in a cost to the company.

We will empower our employees is not a principle. No one would argue to repress our employees. *We will delegate decision making to the lowest possible level* is a principle that has enormous consequences.

Principles are associated with some specific domain of application that can be either broad or narrow. The two principles in the preceding examples are very broad, probably applicable across the company, but still limited. For example, *We will ensure customer satisfaction even if that results in short term cost to the company* is broadly applicable to all customer interactions, but it isn't relevant to most financial, human resource, or marketing decision making. Take for another example, the information technology principle *We will prefer open standards to proprietary standards and proprietary standards to internal standards*, which is strongly espoused by many good information technology managers, but is useful in only a fairly narrow range of decision making.

Exhibit 4.1 is a set of principles adopted in the very narrow realm of financial systems design. Even though these principles were applicable only in their narrow domain, these few simple principles served as a powerful coordinating mechanism for several teams of system developers who were simultaneously overhauling the financial systems of a very large corporation.

- Paper should not move.
- Numbers should be entered only once.
- Every change should be traceable to the source of the change.
- Every composite number should be analyzable.
- Users should maintain their own systems.

Exhibit 4.1   Principles from the Realm of Financial Systems Design

Whenever a group works together for a while, it develops principles. We hear,

- Stick around and you'll pick up the way we do things here.
- Well, stranger, I don't know about where you come from, but around here we...
- Maybe we're a little odd, but it's our way, you know.

These principles are rarely written down, but they are usually well understood by all the group's members. Newcomers are expected to conform. These principles reflect a set of values, also not documented. Unwritten and often unspoken values and principles strongly influence the group's behavior. Choices are constrained. The members of the group are linked. These informal principles may work well enough, but ugly things happen if people think they are adhering to the same principles but aren't. It's a *very* good idea to write these down.

As we discussed in Chapter 3, *vision* has three parts. The first is an understanding of what things will be like when they're right, the *desired future state*. This is more than a goal statement or a mission statement, although these may be included. The description of the desired future state can be in any form that works for a particular group. It can be a statement of where we want to go. It can be in the form of a formal future scenario or a possible future interview of participants after they have been successful. It could be a science fiction story. I saw one that included a music video! The form doesn't matter. What matters is sufficient clarity so that people in the group are comfortable that they understand the desired future state the same way.

The second part of the vision is a set of *pursuits*. There should be a reasonably small number of pursuits that constitute the most important things that have to happen to take us from our current state to the desired future state. As work progresses, projects and tasks are developed within each pursuit to move it forward.

The third part of the vision is a set of *measures*. Some measures will determine whether or not we are making progress on the pursuits and some measures will determine whether or not we are making progress toward the desired future state.

In the absence of real pursuits and measures, a desired future state could be a fairly airy fairy item. The pursuits represent real work to be done. The measures tell us if we are getting the work done and if we are moving in the direction we have set. Let's say, for example, that an important part of our desired future state is a *highly skilled workforce*.

We might establish a pursuit aimed at this part of the vision, for instance,

> Pursuit: *Upgrade the quality of the workforce through training, improved hiring, and elimination of substandard performers.*

This begins to put some meat on the bones. We can imagine projects such as:

- Identify needed skills
- Set performance standards
- Analyze the existing workforce
- Establish training programs
- Improve recruiting processes.

Measures might include:

- Percentage of staff who have completed designated training
- Percentage of new hires who meet performance guidelines
- Percentage of staff measured as substandard one year after being identified as substandard.

There might be an overall measure of

- Percentage of staff meeting required skill levels.

This example begins to show the power of the vision in supporting linkage. *Values* constrain choices in a very general way. *Principles* constrain choices more concretely, but still leave things quite general. The *desired future state* says, Only do things that take us there! The more detailed the *desired future state*, the more it constrains our choices and the faster and easier our decision making becomes. If we mutually agree to the *desired future state* as a constraint, we will choose to carry out our work in ways that will probably fit together, even if we do nothing else to coordinate them!

Add to that an agreed-to set of pursuits, and we have an extremely powerful mechanism for coordinating our activities. We are

- Constrained by agreed-to values and principles to work in certain ways.
- Constrained by an agreed-to desired future state to work toward certain goals.
- Constrained by agreed-to pursuits to work on certain specific activities.

And we have an *agreed-to set of measures to see how well we're doing*. One of the most important results of this kind of linkage is that it firmly shifts our decision-making focus away from the way things are and toward the *desired future state*. We spend a great deal less time and energy solving today's problems, devoting the energy instead toward creating the future we want. Values, principles, and shared vision make an extremely powerful formula for effective business technology linkage.

Why we care

It would be fairly easy to argue that good business technology linkage is important because information technology is so important in our businesses today. You know how that goes: information technology is everywhere… it's a rapidly growing part of our expense base… imaginative use of it makes winners… blunders make losers… and so forth.

All that is true, but it doesn't explain why a senior executive needs to be concerned with linkage any more than with, say, cash flow or employee benefits or investor relations. Why single out business technology linkage? Our experience, our preconceptions, and our mindsets work to help us see the flaws in the many parts of our organization—we know when advertising isn't working, or there's too much overhead in sales, or when manufacturing can't adapt fast enough. This body of experience, however, doesn't help us much with the role of information technology in our organizations. Being insensitive to problems in business technology linkage is a low grade problem as long as we are focused on *sustain*. It becomes a vital concern when we shift to *transform*.

When we started using computers we substituted capital for labor. The technology wasn't expected to add anything to our business. It was expected to do some part of our business cheaper, faster, and better. Since we already knew the business, there was nothing particularly important for us to learn about this substitution. Specialists did it and other specialists operated the results. Business went on the same as before (except, of course, cheaper, faster, and better). Someplace along the line, however, whether we noticed it or not, the *business* of our business was changed by the technology we used.

- *We did more business transactions with the new technology than would ever have been possible with the old technology and the quantitative changes became qualitative.* For example, no matter how many reservation clerks we hired, we never could have supported a modern airline's reservation process without computer technology.
- *The way we did the transactions began to change.* For example, inventory and pricing information was constantly available in branches so orders and commitments could happen closer to the customer.
- *New kinds of transactions were introduced.* For example, a check could be guaranteed at a point of sale or a bill could be paid on the telephone.

These changes were easiest to see in our manufacturing and process industries, but service industries have gone through the same kinds of changes. Because of the introduction of information technology, we are now doing different things in different ways at different rates and volumes. If this doesn't amount to being in a different business, it's hard to say what would! The *business* of our business is different.

Now ask yourself, *Who understands the new parts of the business?* Who can fix it if it breaks? Who can change it if it needs to change? Who can make it better, if it isn't perfect? Who will know if it's broken, or needs to change, or could be better? Who *sustains* the business; who *transforms* it?

I suggest that no matter how you answer these questions, your response will involve "business people" and "technology people." How could it be otherwise? That's linkage the way techies think about it. *Sustain* and *transform* is a *permanent* challenge to every company, a challenge that requires a *melding* of expertise between the *traditional* business of business and the *new* business of business. Here's another suggested management principle.

Potential Principle: We will invest in describing, designing, measuring, and improving our business technology linkage.

Mindsets, specialties, and leadership

Mindsets, habits of thought, both serve us and constrain us. Having mindsets is desirable and unavoidable. Not having mindsets is like not having a mind. Unexamined mindsets, however, lead to all sorts of mischief. We will dig further into mindsets soon, but for now I want to *examine* the mindsets that many of us have around the topics of how business and technology relate. Itemized in Exhibit 4.2 are real mindsets. Not everyone's, of course, but typical of enough people to shed some light on the linkage problem.

Business Person Mindset	Technology Person Mindset
• I have ultimate responsibility for this part of the business.	• I have ultimate responsibility for making this part of the business work.
• The techie doesn't understand the business.	• The user doesn't understand the way things work.
• I work for the company; the techie works for me.	• The user and I work for the company.
• The techie cannot be relied on to deliver systems or changes on time.	• The user cannot be relied on to do his part of the work.
• The techie is in love with technology.	• The user is ignorant about technology.
• The techie doesn't understand what' s really happening in the business.	• The users never include me in anything until it's too late.
• The techie doesn't care enough about cost.	• The user doesn't care enough about quality, reliability, and flexibility.
• I could replace the techie by outsourcing the whole function.	• I could replace most of the users with good technology.
• The techies just don't understand their place in the company.	• The users just don't understand the place of technology in the company.

Exhibit 4.2   Mindsets on How Business and Technology Relate

And, of course, there is the food chain. Every company embodies in its culture a sure and certain knowledge of which jobs are the fish and which are the fish food. In most companies, technology people are fairly low in this hierarchy. It started out that way when we were doing capital substitution projects, "computerizing" our functions. The people who did the "computerizing" didn't have much to do, really, with the company. They took the function they were pointed to, analyzed it, and "computerized" it. *Technology people and their systems inherited the class standing of the clerks they displaced.*

I am going to argue at length later that class distinctions and the associated behaviors are a major problem in linkage. Before we get to that, however, I'd like to point out that linkage in the context of *sustain* is less of a problem than linkage in the context of *transform*.

- **Sustain** is involved with maintaining the quality of the status quo. Once we have reached a reasonably satisfactory state, sustaining the state requires relatively little communication, agreement, or coordination. Everyone just keeps on doing what he is doing. Improvements, if any, are gradual and not threatening. *Sustain* requires good process management—stability, predictability, measurement, recoverability, and cost and quality control.

- **Transform** is involved with successful change. Transformation requires invention, creation, and innovation. Once we have agreed to change, accomplishing the change requires intense communication and coordination. Everybody has to do things differently and all of the changes must happen in the right order at the right time. Improvements are dramatic, sudden, and often frightening. *Transform* requires good project management—planning, consensus, mobilization of resources, communication, training, feedback, and change control.

The various specialists in a company typically deal with different mixes of *sustain* and *transform* and they develop different degrees of skill and experience with the associated management techniques. The chart in Exhibit 4.3 illustrates the point.

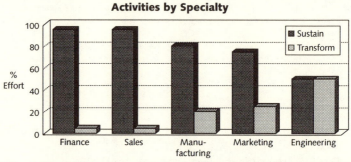

Exhibit 4.3   Estimated Proportions of *Sustain* and *Transform* Work in Various Business Functions

The numbers I used to draw the chart are my estimates based on experience and observation.[2] Whatever the numbers in your company, there is likely to be a range of *sustain* and *transform* across the specialties.

If you work in a *sustain*-dominated specialty, you'll develop *sustain*-oriented skills and a *sustain* mindset. You become a *sustainer*. Likewise, if you work in a *transform*-dominated specialty, you'll develop *transform*-oriented skills and a *transform* mindset and become a *transformer*. As a rule of thumb, it is easier for sustainers to build linkage with other sustainers and transformers to build linkage with other transformers than it is for linkage to develop between sustainers and transformers.

General managers have a vested interest in making all kinds of linkage work within their organizations. It appears likely that a sustainer general manager would be better at encouraging linkage between *sustain*-oriented specialties and better at managing *sustain* activity. A transformer general manager would be good at encouraging linkage between *transform*-oriented specialties and better at *transform* activity. Of course, they both need special techniques to link *sustain*-oriented specialties with *transform*-oriented specialties. Exhibit 4.4 lays out the possibilities for combining manager skills with business need.

	The Manager is a **Transformer**	The Manager is a **Sustainer**
Business needs **Sustain** activity	• Linkage between transform oriented specialties is strengthened. • Transform skills are reinforced. • Transform oriented specialities gain authority. • Sustain oriented specialities are encouraged to acquire transform skills. • *Business likely to be disrupted and become unstable.*	• Linkage between sustain oriented specialties is strengthened. • Sustain skills are reinforced. • Sustain oriented specialities gain authority. • Transform oriented specialities are encouraged to acquire sustain skills. • *Business likely to be stable.*
Business needs **Transform** activity	• Linkage between transform oriented specialties is strengthened. • Transform skills are reinforced. • Transform oriented specialities gain authority. • Sustain oriented specialities are encouraged to acquire transform skills. • *Business likely to succeed.*	• Linkage between sustain oriented specialties is strengthened. • Sustain skills are reinforced. • Sustain oriented specialities gain authority. • Transform oriented specialities are encouraged to acquire sustain skills. • *Business likely to fail to adapt to needed changes.*

Exhibit 4.4 Outcome Matrix for *Sustain* and *Transform* Needs versus *Sustainer* and *Transformer* Skills

Of course, businesses rarely need pure *sustain* or pure *transform* activity, and a general manager isn't purely a sustainer or purely a transformer. The model begins to shed some light, however, on why some excellent managers with proven track records fail in novel circumstances. It also has something to say about how to pick (or train) leaders.

In the last few pages we have been discussing in a fairly general way how mindsets, specialties, and skills influence linkage. We've concluded that it's easier to link people with similar mindsets. We've also observed that dissimilar mindsets are an inevitable feature of complex organizations.

I don't think that we've learned to cope with highly dissimilar mindsets even in situations where we've had centuries of practice (the salesman and the comptroller, for instance). Key to the present discussion is that business technology linkage is one of the tough ones and making it work has gotten to be important. The next section shows what happens as a result of poor business technology linkage.

How people behave

Within the information ecology there is often a tension between people who operate the existing set of systems and others who are trying to introduce new systems or new technology. They call each other names like "dinosaur" and "propeller head." The differences in mindset between sustainers and transformers is at the root of this tension. A quite different tension, however, animates the relationship between business people and technology people.

In Exhibit 4.5 they're smiling at each other. In their public statements, they are agreeing to an undeniable proposition. In their private thoughts they are both dissatisfied and blame each other. Benson, the business person, is on the left. Thomas, the techie, is on the right.

Exhibit 4.5   Public versus Private Attitudes of Business and Technology Experts

This cartoon sums up the situation.[3] In order for these people to succeed together they have to agree on strategy, tactics, roles, responsibilities, and measures. Divergent mindsets can make reaching these agreements very difficult. Let's reach back for some of the elements of typical business and technology mindsets and see how they interfere with getting things to work.

To Benson, ultimate responsibility means being in charge. This belief makes it difficult for Benson to see Thomas as an equal. To Thomas, ultimate responsibility means being to blame. This belief makes it difficult for Thomas to take risks. Benson tries to protect his position and Thomas tries to protect his rear. Discussions of strategy will never take place as long as neither thinks the other's participation in strategy is relevant.

Benson believes that his particular expertise constitutes the essence of the business. So does Thomas. These beliefs make it difficult for each to see the value of the other's expertise since that expertise is thought of as marginal to the *real* business or to what is *really* going on. They have different ideas of what is important so it is especially hard for them to agree on measures of performance that could apply to their shared work.

Benson believes that Thomas's job is to provide a service, that is, *to serve.* This belief makes Benson expect to be treated as Thomas's customer. Thomas believes that he and Benson both have jobs within the larger context of the company and they need to work together. This makes it difficult for Thomas to accept that he should act as if Benson is his customer and the customer is always right. It is also difficult to agree on roles and responsibilities when the relationship is viewed so differently.

Since Benson believes he is Thomas's customer and that the work they do together is a service that Thomas provides, Benson perceives it as Thomas's failure when things go wrong. Since Thomas believes that he and Benson have shared work, Thomas is likely to blame failures on Benson's lack of participation. They never agreed on roles and responsibilities, so it's never clear who is accountable for results.

Communication, cooperation, and mutual respect

Since Benson and Thomas have such different mindsets, it's hard for them to communicate effectively. Poor communications is part of a vicious cycle that can reinforce failure. The graphic in Exhibit 4.6 shows how poor relationships can get to be really bad.

Start anywhere in the diagram in Exhibit 4.6; for instance at the top left. As trust, communications, and understanding deteriorate, Benson and Thomas have less and less regard for each other. Their goals, methods, and understanding of roles and responsibilities continue to diverge. Cooperation drops off. Failure ensues causing Benson and Thomas to think even less of each other. Distrust grows and we're off around the circle again. The cycle reinforces itself and, without intervention, will create a worse and worse situation no matter how well intentioned and truly competent Benson and Thomas might be.

The cycle can start anywhere. For instance, failure to agree on goals, methods, and roles and responsibilities can lead to conflict, disappointment, and loss of mutual regard. Guarded or scanty communications can lead to misunderstandings, which diminish respect, which can undermine trust, and so forth. After a couple of cycles on the left, Thomas and Benson don't think enough of each other to even try to agree on goals and such.

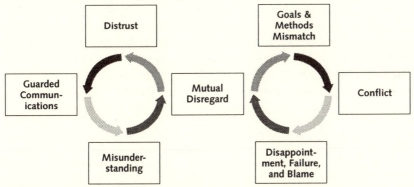

Exhibit 4.6   System Interaction Model Connecting Mutual Disregard with Poor Outcomes

Relationships which begin to run through this cycle don't stay the same, they get worse. The cycle behaves like an electric motor without a load, spinning faster and faster, absorbing energy, creating a hazard, doing no useful work. Fortunately, like an electric motor, which can be turned backward to make a generator, this cycle can be turned around to produce a better and better working environment. The revised version of the cycle is shown in Exhibit 4.7.

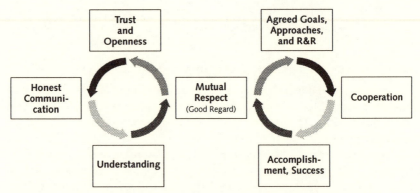

Exhibit 4.7   System Interaction Model Connecting Mutual Respect with Good Outcomes

This time let's start on the right. Good cooperation brings success and a feeling of mutual respect. Mutual good regard engenders trust and openness, which lead to good communications and good quality mutual understanding, reinforcing mutual respect. With sufficient mutual respect, goals, approaches, and roles can be reexamined and revised if necessary. And the loop begins again. Sometimes a relationship gets off to a good start and this cycle keeps making it better and better until something interrupts it or it runs down. Like the motor turned generator, however, we have to continue to put energy into the relationship to keep it going.

Based on this model of the way relationships improve or deteriorate, I'd like to assert that mutual respect is one of the key elements in business technology linkage. Furthermore I suggest that the relationship that was formed between business and technology when information technology was primarily a capital substitution game, started the cycle off with a low level of mutual respect, often resulting in a subsequent history of poor business technology linkage.

This chapter has investigated the need for business technology linkage.

- I introduced a definition: *linkage* is the condition wherein different people make choices while constrained by a common set of values and principles and a common vision.
- We said, *business technology linkage* can contain imperfections in our organizations and processes which hinder our ability to perform. Poor linkage; big imperfections. Good linkage; fewer imperfections.
- We examined the power of values, principles, and vision in coordinating people's actions.
- We said that linkage was central to addressing the *sustain* and *transform* issue and is a *permanent* challenge that requires a melding of expertise between the *traditional* business of business and the *new* business of business.

- We asserted that it is easier for sustainers to build linkage with other sustainers and transformers to build linkage with other transformers than it is for linkage to develop between sustainers and transformers.
- We began an examination of how people work together with an emphasis on mutual respect. We showed that working relationships tend either to improve or deteriorate depending on changes in the level of mutual respect.
- Historical forces have often tended to make our business technology relationships poor ones.

In Chapter 5 we begin the examination of relationships in general as a prelude to a detailed look at the relationships that exist between our business people and our technology people. When we understand the present relationship, we can begin to set out the specific steps needed to move to an effective linkage as we now understand it.

Notes

1. Principles-based management is explained and enthusiastically recommended in the early *Harvard Business Review* article by Davenport, Hammer and Metsisto (1989).
2. If you are uncomfortable with this approach, here's an experiment you can do to qualify this aspect. Ask each of your specialty areas to find out how much of their effort they spend in process activities and how much in project activity. Use these numbers as proxies for *sustain* and *transform*. Unless something very unusual is going on in your company, I bet you'll get similar results.
3. I'm dealing with generalizations here. I know that there are companies where the business and technology people work extremely well together. I know that even in companies where the tensions are the highest, there are still individuals from both sides who cooperate effectively. I believe, however, that the situation I describe is typical of many companies.

5

Relationships: They're Not Confined to Soap Operas

In Chapter 4 we examined linkage in detail, concluding that people, in pairs and groups, are linked when they make choices that fit together. Many of the important choices people make have to do with the other people they work with. The aggregate of these choices and the actions they engender constitute a *relationship*. This chapter introduces the basic concepts of relationships and investigates in detail the most common relationship between business people and technology people.[1]

Beliefs, expectations, perceptions, and actions

I'm sure that you can recall from your personal experience a situation in which someone else "just didn't get it." You put all the facts on the table. You drew the pictures. You made analogies. And they "just didn't get it!" You may even have said to yourself, This person is usually bright enough. What's going on? Why is he being so stubborn? It's very likely that you were experiencing a mindset mismatch. The logic of the situation was crystal clear to you when interpreted through your mindset and totally opaque when viewed through his.

You may have been on the other side of this situation, too, in which somebody explained something to you and the explanation just didn't make sense. The explainer was adamant, however, and your well-crafted objections fell, as they say, on deaf ears. Of course, the ears weren't deaf, the mind was. His explanation didn't fit your mindset and your automatic perception filter threw his information away. Your objections didn't fit his mindset and his automatic perception filter threw your information away.

This kind of thing is bad enough when it results in irreconcilable differences of opinion. It's often worse, however, when the result is apparent agreement. We both look at something or we say things that seem to us to be the same, but because of our different mindsets about the subject we don't really agree, even though we think we have. Based on this kind of misunderstanding you may interpret a subsequent action of mine as contrary to our agreement, even though what I did fits into exactly what I thought we had agreed to. After that you don't trust me.

Mindsets, like golf clubs, aren't right or wrong. They are more or less useful depending on the situation. It is a fact, however, that when people set out to co-operate, similar mindsets around the subjects of their cooperation are more useful than dissimilar mindsets.

Beliefs are important mindsets. For instance, I believe that people are basically good. This mindset makes it extremely difficult for me to understand how some people commit the awful crimes and atrocities that I know that some do. I suspect that my mindset about people and the mindsets held by victims of these awful crimes may be different. This understanding doesn't alter my belief, but recognizing the mismatch keeps me from saying or doing at least a few of the unhelpful things that I might otherwise say or do when I am dealing with victims. *Mindsets do alter perceptions and when it happens the process is automatic and unnoticed.*

It also happens that *perceptions alter mindsets.* When this happens, however, the process is usually conscious and requires effort. Mindsets usually get changed—if they get changed—spontaneously, by some relatively dramatic experience. Exhibit 5.1 is an illustration of how beliefs, expectations, perceptions, and actions are inextricably intertwined.

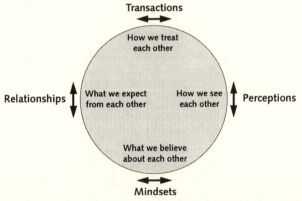

Exhibit 5.1   Interactions among Mindsets, Perceptions, Transactions, and Relationships

We've seen that mindsets, especially what we believe about each other, affect our perceptions and how sometimes perceptions can alter mindsets.

Perceptions, especially how we perceive each other's actions, exert a direct influence over how we treat each other. Each time we interact, the transaction joins with all the other transactions we have had with that person and a relationship is defined. Relationships are both the sum of all the transactions we have with another person and a collection of mindsets and behaviors. Discussing relationships gives us a suitably general place to start a program of change.

Interest and authority relationship grid

Relationships between individuals and, by extension, between organizations are influenced by perceptions and mindsets. Two important components are *perceived degree of common interest* and *perceived relative authority*. We are going to use one of the ubiquitous "consultant's grids" as a framework (Exhibit 5.2) for discussing relationships and how they vary depending on these two important components of mindsets. The vertical axis runs from low perception of common interest to high perception of common interest. The horizontal access runs from a perception of very unequal authority to a perception of completely equal authority. The grid is divided arbitrarily into quarters for simplicity in our discussion.

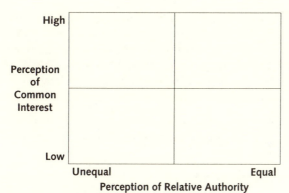

Exhibit 5.2   Relationship Framework

Perception of common interest

Perception of common interest between two people in a large organization is affected by lots of things, including:

- *Clarity of the organization's overall mission and values and the identification of the individual with the organization as a whole:* If you and I both feel like we are part of the company, not just incidental to it, we will be inclined to subscribe to the mission and values of the company, creating a perception of common interest between us. This doesn't work so well if the mission and values aren't clear. Just being attached to the same corporate charter doesn't give us much sense of being connected.
- *Organizational proximity:* We will perceive more common interest if we work in the same part of a big company. Our department, our division, our project team, our shift, and so forth, can serve as connections and contribute to a perception of common interest. For example, what's good for the department is good for me.
- *Physical proximity:* We perceive more common interest if we work close together. The office we share, the copier we share, the coffee room, and

water fountain all give us another bit of perceived common interest. For example, what's good for the people on the floor is good for me.

- *Degree to which reward systems are shared:* If we both get paid for performance, we have an interest in common. If we both get paid for loyalty or longevity, we will have different but still common interests. For example, what's good for the other contract employees is good for me.
- *Relationships between the individual's superiors in the hierarchy:* If my boss and your boss are friends or allies, we will perceive more common interest. For example, if it's good for people who work for my boss's friend, it's probably good for my boss and me. If our bosses are political opponents or if they just are indifferent to each other, we have less perceived common interest.
- *Degree of mutual understanding:* Anything else that contributes to our knowing each other and understanding each other—same educational background or home environment, shared minority status, common foreign language, same training courses or work experiences, etc.—will drive up our perception of common interest. For example, if it's good for other people I understand and respect, it's probably good for me.

You can easily imagine that perception of common interest can vary between two people over a wide range from feeling like they're "joined at the hip" to total mutual indifference.

Perception of relative authority

Relative authority is the same as balance of power. Our transactions with each other are subtly, and not so subtly, affected by how we perceive relative authority.

If I perceive you to have more authority (and hence power) than I do in a particular situation, I will accept your suggestions more readily, I will more likely defer to your judgments, and I will offer my suggestions more carefully. Our conversations will be mostly on topics of your choosing or topics which I carefully introduce. If I perceive that I have more authority in a given situation, I will expect you to behave accordingly.

If I perceive our authority in a given situation to be roughly equal, I will adopt a different set of behaviors and expect you to do likewise. In particular, I will expect that any actions we agree on will be based either on reciprocity or on common interest. Our conversations will be explorations of areas in which we can establish reciprocity or in which we can discover our common interests.

Like common interest, the perception of relative authority between two people in a large organization depends on a lot of factors. Perceived authority can be affected by things like:

- *Organizational hierarchy:* I perceive my boss and I to have unequal authority in general corporate considerations. She has more. I also perceive that her authority is unequal to her boss's. He has more.

- *Personality:* If I act as if I have a lot of authority, people will often perceive me that way. Some people just seem to be in charge. They have 'presence,' 'charisma,' 'stature,' or 'big cojones.' Likewise, there are people whose personalities tend to detract from our perception of their authority.
- *Political factors:* Being close to a person of power can lend you power and perceived authority. Being close to a person in trouble can subtract from your power. Your skills or background or style may be the "flavor of the month" giving you a temporary power advantage. The person you're dealing with may be very eager not to make waves and you benefit in perceived authority.
- *Relevant experience and expertise:* If I know or think that you have more experience and expertise in a situation, I cede you some perceived authority.

When individuals get together in any particular situation there is a netting out of all of these factors and a balance of power results. Power and authority may be perceived as unequal (the most common situation), each person realizes who leads and who defers, and they behave accordingly. Sometimes power and authority may be perceived as roughly equal and another set of behaviors is called into play. Pathological conditions may arise in which one person perceives the balance of power in one way and the other perceives it in another way. Such cases lead to deadlocks, misunderstandings, and conflicts.

Relationships develop in the presence of differing degrees of perceived common interest and different balances of power. These situations are common enough that we recognize all of them when they are pointed out to us.

The range of relationships

Let's start our review of relationship types with the situation in which the parties perceive little or no common interest and there is an unequal perception of relative authority. For example, we don't think we have much in common and we both perceive that you have a lot more power than I do. Exhibit 5.3 is the picture of all the kinds of relationships. The lower left-hand quadrant illustrates these low common interest and unequal authority relationships.

About the best kind of relationship that can develop out of this combination of perceptions is *indifference.*[2] This is the way a busy person and a newspaper vendor might relate to each other. This combination has the potential for the absolute worst kinds of relationships, *exploitation.* If the more powerful person perceives no common interest with the weaker person, the weaker person is effectively an object to be used. Very bad things can result.

The next situation we'll examine (the lower right quadrant of Exhibit 5.3) is where there is little perception of shared or common interest, but an equal perception of authority or power. This is the competition and contention quadrant. If there is any relationship at all between people who perceive each other this way they are going to be rivals, competitors, or enemies. There is nothing in it for one to help the other, but they have to be careful because they are equally powerful.

Exhibit 5.3   Relationship Matrix

In the top left quadrant of Exhibit 5.3 the parties have a significant degree of perceived common interest, but perceive each other as having unequal authority or power. This is the quadrant where the bulk of our human relationships take place in which one party directs or leads the other. Here is a partial list of the relationships that fall in this quadrant.

- Parent-child
- Liege lord-serf
- Leader-follower
- Doctor-patient
- Maestro-apprentice
- Master-slave
- Buyer-seller
- Senior partner-junior partner

You can see that common interest and unequal power produce a rich variety of relationships. The differences among the relationships reflect variations in the degrees of perceived common interest, variations in the purposes of the relationships, and variations in the kinds of transactions that are conducted. Each relationship type has its unique set of rules, traditions, expectations, and mindsets.

The final quadrant in the upper right of Exhibit 5.3 houses the relationships characterized by a high degree of perceived common interest and a perception of equal authority. These relationships are relatively rare and tend to be unstable. Example relationships in this quadrant are allies, neighbors, teammates, and partners. When these relationships are good, they are very good, but their tendency to instability is well known, and maintaining good relationships in this quadrant requires special effort and skills.

Instability results from the continual shifting of perceptions between the people in the relationship. In order for them to hold the perception of equal authority and strong common interest over time, their interactions must continuously reinforce these views. Partners must work at being partners or the relationship changes into some kind of directive relationship. Similarly allies, neighbors, and teammates need some rules or process to keep the sense of equality and common interest from changing into something else.

The business technology relationship

Now let's examine where the business technology relationship fits in the grid. A particular pair of business and technology people will perceive themselves to have common interest based on the degree to which they identify with or share common:

- Values and principles
- Goals, objectives, and mission
- Methods, processes, and procedures
- Performance measurements
- Organizational unit
- Reward structure

Our linkage elements—values, principles, and vision—cover the first four of these items. *In the absence of linkage, two people will perceive their common interest based primarily on organization and reward structure.*

The perception of relative authority is a more complicated matter. Business people hold a variety of attitudes including:

- I am totally in charge and in control of my technology.
- I am totally at sea about technology. When I can't avoid technology, I do whatever the techies tell me.
- I work with the technology people. There are some matters where I take the lead and some where they do.

The balance of power in a particular relationship might depend on the business. One might imagine, for instance, that more technology intense businesses would tend to have either equal perceived authority or a tilt toward the technology and, indeed, some businesses are like that, for example, technology businesses such as computer and software vendors. Many businesses, however, have grown into their technology intensiveness over a period of years and the perceived balance of power has not changed with the reality.

A typical mindset around the role of technology in such a business looks like Exhibit 5.4 This mindset has led most frequently to a version of *buyer-seller* as the relationship model for how people in business and technology relate to each other in our companies. The buyer-seller relationship is one from the upper left quadrant of the diagram in which there is perceived common interest and perceived unequal authority. The typical mindset indicates that the balance of power favors the "business" person in the relationship.

| There is a clear distinction between "business" and "technology." |
| Technology is what we use to control operational expense. |
| Technology serves the business. |
| Good technology management means displacing a lot of operational expense at a reasonable cost in technology. |

Exhibit 5.4   A Common Mindset that is No Longer Realistic in Information Intensive or Information Dependent Businesses

The buyer-seller relationship model is firmly entrenched in many of our companies. Details include:

- "Business" people are thought to buy services from "technology" people.
- Individual services are "purchased" by means of task orders.
- Whole groups of people and portions of people are "purchased" under level of effort agreements.
- Where "technology" people report in the same organization as the "business" people, the business "purchases" the whole seller and has a captive technology company.
- The arrangement is considered successful if the buyer is satisfied with *value received* for *payment rendered.*
- Transfer pricing, charge-out systems, and other administrative processes support this model.
- Occasionally this model has led to arm's length technology subsidiaries.

Buyer-seller is a familiar and totally legitimate model for governing transactions. It is one of the most common relationships we encounter in a free enterprise system. It's appealing, in part, because we understand it and everybody knows how it's supposed to work and how to act when in the role of either buyer or seller. Exhibit 5.5 reviews the characteristics of the buyer-seller relationship.

| **Transaction based and market driven** |
| Pricing is market based |
| Relationship purpose and duration are explicit |
| Self-maximizing behavior is assumed to motivate both parties |
| Buyer is motivated to optimize value |
| Seller is motivated to optimize profit |
| Opportunistic behavior is controlled by contracts |
| Significant contract specificity |
| **Arms length** |
| Individual transactions are designed to be independent |
| Clear and complete assignment of costs, burdens, and risks |
| **Contractual** |
| Specific peformance required of each party |
| Adapting to uncertain events is a litigation or arbitration process |

Exhibit 5.5   Characteristics of Buyer-Seller Relationship

Familiar as it may be, there are some serious problems involved in implementing the buyer-seller relationship within a company. For example,

- *Alternative sellers are usually excluded, resulting in no market pressure on the seller.* Internal suppliers of a service usually have a lock on the buyer because of expertise or corporate policy.
- *Seller is not allowed to profit.* It's unusual for an internal supplier of technology to be allowed to profit from internal sales. Without the profit motive, it is unclear what motivates the seller.
- *Obligations of the parties are often unclear.* The buyer-seller relationship is rarely explicit and implicit understandings are often misunderstandings.
- *Transactions are not necessarily entered into willingly.* Sometimes the business person will force the technology person to do something that the technology person opposes. Sometimes the technology person will do something, perhaps secretly, that the business person opposes but ends up "paying for" anyway.
- *Mutual benefit is assumed to motivate both parties, but reward systems may be inconsistent.* Different reward systems are the rule; *contradictory* rewards systems are not uncommon.

When so many key features of the buyer-seller relationship are absent from the way business and technology interact with each other, the relationship deteriorates into a more or less benign version of master-slave. The lower the level of perceived common interest, especially on the part of the more powerful party, the less and less benign the master-slave relationship is likely to be. If sufficiently little common interest is perceived by the more powerful party, the relationship drops into the lower left quadrant and benign master-slave turns into exploitation.

These badly deteriorated relationships are most often found when the business person perceives little common interest with the techie. "I buy your services, so do as I tell you" deteriorates into "Do it, damn it!" Occasionally the technology person will be in the more powerful position with respect to a particular business person and as perceived common interest drops, "This is the technology I think you ought to use… let me know how you like it" deteriorates into "I can't help you… I've got important things to do."

I believe that establishing the trappings of a buyer-seller relationship when, in fact, what exists is a benign or not so benign master-slave relationship is a major source of confusion, inefficiency, and bitterness. Technology people usually reconcile themselves to a service provider role without the motivations of being a seller. Business people usually reconcile themselves to the role of service recipients without recourse to market alternatives. The resulting relationship acts and feels just like a command economy. The popularity of outsourcing, at least as a topic for discussion, can be explained by the longing that some business people have for technology service that exhibits the characteristics of free enterprise. There is a parallel longing among corporate technology people for a business environment that rewards them for the value of what they do.

The attitudes that business people often develop about the relationship sound like this:

- I don't get what I'm paying for.
- They don't do what I tell them.
- I end up paying for frills and technology for the sake of technology.
- I know I could buy this service cheaper outside.
- These people just don't seem to understand customer service.
- If they had to do this for a living, they'd shape up fast enough.

On the other side, the attitudes that technology people often develop about the relationship sound like this:

- I have to do what I'm told even if it makes no sense.
- The business guys keep me working on stuff that's completely superficial and never let me get at the really important stuff.
- They get paid the big bucks when the company makes money. When the company's in trouble, I'm likely to lose my staff or my job.
- What they want is stupid and it'll never work, but "he who pays the piper calls the tune" so I'll do it anyway.
- When we pull off a tough project, the business guy gets a big bonus and I get a pat on the head (if I'm lucky).
- If I went to work for a consulting company, at least I'd get paid for all this grief.

I suggest that the unhealthy attitudes on both sides of this relationship result from trying to shoehorn the working relationship between business and technology into a buyer-seller model when the buyer-seller model isn't appropriate. The result deteriorates into a command economy model when it's good and an ugly version of master-slave when it's not. People play out their buyer and seller roles because they know it's expected of them. It's actually a surprise that things work anyway.

═══════════════════════════

In this chapter we took a look at a model for describing relationships in terms of the degree to which people perceive themselves to have common interests and in terms of the their perceived balance of power or relative authority.

Then we examined the relationship between business and technology people in terms of the typical mindset that exists and the buyer-seller model which is prevalent in most of our companies.

We observed that the buyer-seller model implementation that we use inside our companies was badly flawed and that it has led to a different kind of relationship, a version of benign master-slave. I suggested that a master-slave model masquerading as a buyer-seller model is the source of a lot of bad feelings and ineffective behavior.

In Chapter 6 we investigate an alternative mindset around the business technology interaction and alternative choices of relationship models, partnerships and teams.

Notes

1. The material in this chapter is original. Inspiration for the ideas came from various sources. (See Arnold 1993; Badaracco and Ellsworth 1988; Bergman 1990; Eccles and Noria 1992; Fritz 1989; Senge Fall 1990, 1990, and 1991.)
2. The relationships that I label as we go along are examples. Obviously there is a continuum of perceptions and a resulting infinite variety of relationships.

6

Partnerships for Linkage

In Chapter 5 we examined relationships and observed that the typical business technology relationship is a *buyer-seller* relationship in which the "business" person is the buyer and the "technology" person is the seller. We concluded that this relationship did not provide very effective linkage. The people know their roles, but the motivations don't work. In this chapter and the next we examine alternative relationships, which I suggest, are more effective for both *sustain* and *transform*, more suitable to the complexities of the information ecology, and provide much more effective linkage.

Partnerships

We'll start with partnerships, both equal partnerships and unequal partnerships. These relationships fall in the upper part of the chart in Exhibit 6.1, mostly on the right.

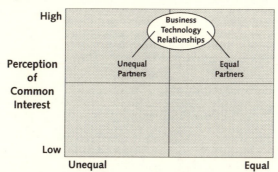

Exhibit 6.1   The Desired Position of Business Technology Relationships in the Relationship Matrix

I suggest that the target relationship for business technology linkage should be an equal partnership. Circumstances of the business and topics under considerations will require that the relationship shift into an unequal partnership (senior and junior partners) from time to time. The suggested mindset for both business and technology people looks like Exhibit 6.2.

The distinction between technology and the business is becoming increasingly blurred.
Technology is the key to achieving and sustaining competitive advantage.
Technology and business expertise empower and enable each other.
Good technology management means creating opportunities through appropriate investments.

Exhibit 6.2   Suggested Mindset for Business Technology Linkage

This is not necessarily going to be an easy mindset to establish in an organization that presently holds the more typical technology mindset we set out in Chapter 5.

- Some "business" people will be uncomfortable giving up power and sharing authority over the technology used in the business.
- Some "technology" people will be uncomfortable accepting the responsibility that comes with authority.

The *buyer-seller* relationship and its roles and rules are incompatible with the suggested mindset. A program to change the mindset will require a corresponding program to adjust the rules and roles in order to introduce a partnership model. To begin to understand the kinds of rules and roles we'll need, let's look at the characteristics of successful partnerships in Exhibit 6.3.[1]

Stability of the relationship
Sustained over time (no explicit end point)
Self maximizing behavior is not optimal
Opportunistic behavior controlled through processes rather than contracts
Significant contract ambiguity
Interdependence of the relationship
Stream of exchanges that are highly interdependent
Joint acceptance of costs, burdens, and risks
Flexibility of the relationship
Willingness to invest in the relationship
Mechanism for adapting to uncertain events

Exhibit 6.3   Characteristics of Successful Partnerships

These characteristics will translate into different sets of rules depending on the personalities and experiences of the participants, the objective of the partnership, and the culture of the company.

Establishing partnership as the model for business technology relationships within the company will have certain problems. For instance,

- *The partnership model is unfamiliar in this context.* People just don't know how to act.

- *Contract ambiguity is incompatible with most accepted planning processes.* Formal planning most often insists on knowing exactly *who, what, when, where,* and *how much.*
- *The buyer-seller model is the basis for transfer pricing and cost allocation.* Technology is often considered overhead to a profit center or product and internal charge-out processes frequently become extremely detailed as befits buyer-seller. These allocation models aren't suitable to partnerships.
- *The buyer-seller model is the basis for many existing processes in which business and technology interact.* Therefore, systems development methodologies, project life cycle methodologies, and service level agreement methodologies have to change somewhat to suit the partnership model.
- *In the absence of the buyer-seller model, there is no common understanding of how authority is established.* We need a substitute for *the customer is always right.*
- *Mutual benefit is assumed to motivate both parties in a partnership, but reward systems may be different.* For instance, if Benson and Thomas are working on the same project and Benson gets rewarded for the quality of the result and Thomas gets rewarded for timely completion, it's hard for them to see common interest in many transaction level details where time versus quality trade-offs are necessary.
- *Partnership requires explicit effort to maintain.* Buyer-seller is self-maintaining.

The rules governing partnership behavior and the processes necessary to establish the partnerships in the first place will differ from situation to situation. In the next couple of sections we describe, in general, how to establish and operate the partnerships at the strategic and tactical levels.

First we will examine strategic partnerships within the organization at two levels: corporate portfolio level and strategic business unit level. The corporate portfolio level is the highest level of business and technology linkage in the organization and we will deal with it in the next section by describing a strategic linkage partnership. Linkages within the portfolio, that is at the level of strategic business units, can be established by a tactical linkage partnership, which will be described in the subsequent section.

Strategic partnership

In order to have a business technology partnership at the corporate level there must be a CIO. Of course, it isn't necessary that that exact title exist in the company, but the role is required. If there is no person in this job, the CEO might play the role or might ask some other executive in the inner circle to play the role in addition to whatever other job he has. I don't think this is a very good idea. CIO is a big job and, if the role exists, there ought to be a person in it.

We are trying to ensure that there is a correspondence between how we position the company in the marketplace and how we position the company with regard to all the technology choices we might make. These concerns are external to the company. We draw the strategies after investigating the extent and quality of the market, the competition, the economic and political environment, the technological alternatives, and the pace and quality of change. The constraints include:

- How much leverage do we have?
- How much can we invest?
- How much risk can we tolerate?

Fundamental results of the strategic thinking are answers to these questions:

- What do we sustain?
- What do we transform and in what way?

It's basically the CEO's choice whether or not to involve the CIO in corporate business strategy. Even if the CIO isn't a partner, the company will get those strategic judgments that are the CIO's job explicitly, for instance:

- Will standards be open or proprietary?
- Will electronic connectivity be general and ubiquitous or specific and tailored?
- To what degree will technology in the company be uniform?
- To what degree will we attempt to use emerging technology?
- Will our technology infrastructure be reliable, highly reliable, or ultra reliable?
- Which parts of the technology infrastructure do we sustain and which do we transform?

We would expect to get the *technology strategy* whether we make the CIO a partner or not, but in order to make effective use of the CIO in the *business strategy* process, we need to make her a member of the corporate inner circle. Some important things will work better when a strong linkage is put in place at this level. For instance, better answers to questions like:

- How much should we invest and spend on technology overall?
- How should we allot our technology spending across our portfolio of businesses?
- What consideration should we make, if any, of the capabilities of our competitors and potential competitors to attack our customer base or our margins with improved technology?
- In what way does our technology strength or weakness affect our interest in strategic alliances, mergers, acquisitions, and divestitures?

Improving the quality of decision making on these sorts of questions is in addition to the technology strategic positioning one would expect from the

CIO. Partnering is a process that probably already has been extended to those we would consider the inner circle, perhaps, the COO, the CFO, and the group VPs. Imagine extending that level of trust and communication to the CIO. Behaving as partners, we would expect that basic assumptions and mindsets that support the *business strategy* will be challenged and eventually shared by the CIO just as the assumptions and mindsets that support the *technology strategy* will be challenged and eventually shared by all those in the inner circle. If we make the CIO a partner, we build a linkage between business strategy and technology strategy which is much stronger.

Here is a general recipe for creating a strategic linkage partnership that can be adjusted to the specific requirements of a given company.

- *Make sure you have the right people.* Each of the partners has to be willing to work with the others for an extended period of time. The relationship should not have an explicit end.
- *Make sure that everyone understands the features of the partnership model.* Take a course, attend a seminar, or have a group dialog around the partnership idea.
- *Establish partnership behavior guidelines.* What are the rules for your meetings and other interpersonal activities? Explicitly rule out self-maximizing behavior which comes at the expense of the partnership as a whole. Keep the rules general. Ambiguity is okay.
- *Agree on corporate mission and values.* The process of working these out as a group is important. Don't duck it and don't delegate it. It is not necessary for you to make the result public in order for benefit to flow from doing the work.[2] Emphasize a joint acceptance of costs, burdens, and risks.
- *Agree on a set of principles that will govern the partnership.* What general guidelines will you use for constraining your decision making?[3] Cover how you will deal with unusual situations that provide unexpected opportunities. Encourage interactions. Be explicit about your willingness to invest as part of your guidelines. Be explicit in recognizing uncertainty and spell out what you'll do about it.
- *Construct a shared vision.*[4] Go beyond numerical targets. What will the company feel like when it's right? What are the major pursuits? How do we measure progress? How do we measure success or failure?
- *Investigate how your reward structure fits with the mission, values, and vision.* Look carefully for role-oriented conflicts that might result from different reward schemes.
- *Work together on some regular basis.* Do real work together—the mission, values, principles, and vision work will get you off to a good start. If you don't have a history of group work skills in your company, get an expert facilitator to help you. Don't let your meetings be simply the presentation

of staff work. Make decisions on partnership concerns together. Don't let partnership decision making happen in another venue.

- *Review the state of the partnership.* Have a partners meeting regularly to decide: Do we need to adjust the membership? How good are the results of this partnership? How well are we working together? Are our mission statement, values statements, vision, and principles still working for us? Partnerships can deteriorate into a variety of other relationships that are built on inequality of perceived authority; it takes work to keep them healthy.

You may have noticed that this recipe for setting up a partnership doesn't have any mention of technology or any other expertise that the partners may have. The process is very general and it will work for all kinds of partnerships.

Every company has a hierarchy. If you and others in the company choose to enter into a partnership for the sake of linkage, the company hierarchy will be superimposed on the partnership. The result will be a complex of *senior partner-junior partner* relationships, which are subtly different from equal partners relationships.

Senior partners are deferred to as a matter of etiquette and senior partners break deadlocks should they arise. A wise senior partner will use this power very sparingly. Each use of authority that derives from position rather than expertise undermines the partnership relationship. For that reason, it would be best that a partnership designed to link business and technology strategy be comprised of members who are peers in the hierarchy or, at least, can behave as peers. As you think about establishing this partnership, it might be wise to give some consideration to the title and reporting structure of your company and how it might influence the ease with which the linkage partnership can be established.

Before we leave the topic of strategic linkage partnerships, we should consider the case of the company that doesn't want to link technology with strategy at the corporate level. Perhaps the company is a conglomerate and concludes that technology strategy is not relevant to its portfolio strategy. In that case, just apply the thinking to the operating companies. The rules for building a partnership at the corporate level may still be useful, but the conglomerate won't have need for a holding company level CIO.

Tactical partnerships

The tactical linkage partnership has different work from the strategic linkage partnership. Expect the tactical linkage partnership to undertake activities like:

- *Review and recommend technology budgets and capital investments.* The tactical linkage partnership should develop a continuing broad understanding of how technology is being employed in the company. They should act as the review and integrating authority for technology and related expenses.

- *Review and approve high-risk technology development projects.* If your company doesn't have an R&D function per se or even if it does, there will be applications of new technology to the business that carry substantial risk in regard to either cost or schedule. These projects can arise in any part of the organization but should come to the tactical linkage partnership for approval.
- *Develop shared procurement policies and procedures for technology.* Procedures concerning who buys what technology and how are developed by a subgroup and endorsed by the technology linkage partnership as a whole.
- *Endorse technology standards and processes.* Standard protocols, standard equipment and software configurations, standard user interfaces, design processes, maintenance processes, backup and recovery processes, information security processes, and reporting relationships and responsibilities for roles like system liaison, LAN administrator, information security administrator, and database administrator are developed by the CIO and suitable subgroups of the technology and business communities and endorsed by the technology linkage partnership.

The tactical linkage partnership has three overriding functions.

- *Provide completeness for the cross-linkages between business strategy and technology operations and technology strategy and business operations.* The partnership does this by examining operational level decisions in the context of business and technology strategy.
- *Provide validity for the cross-linkages.* The partnership does this by being a forum in which the assumptions and mindsets that underlie the strategies can be challenged, balancing the hierarchical linkages that provide the mechanism for challenging operational assumptions and mindsets in a strategic context.
- *Enable the horizontal linkage between business operations and technology operations.* By action and example the partnership provides a pattern and a motivation for improved linkage between *business operation* and *technology operation* people. The improved cross-linkage will minimize substantive conflicts and the leadership example will reduce perceived conflicts.

The membership for the tactical linkage partnership should represent the business and technology interests but probably one step down or so in the hierarchy from the CEO's inner circle. On the business side, the representatives are probably deputies, chiefs of staff, or senior executive assistants to the most senior business executives. On the technology side, the representatives are the reports to the CIO. Other representatives from functional areas, perhaps finance, human resources, or internal audit, may be necessary.

Use the same recipe to build the tactical linkage partnership (TLP) as you use for the strategic linkage partnership (SLP).

- *Make sure you have the right people.* The TLP will probably involve more people than the SLP and will probably experience more turnover. It's still important that the people explicitly agree to work together and that the duration of the partnership be open ended.
- *Make sure that everyone understands the features of the partnership model.* The TLP can use the same technique—a course, a seminar, or a group dialog—as the SLP.
- *Establish partnership behavior guidelines.* The TLP will probably use rules very similar to the SLP for inter-personal behavior in meetings. It is probably a good idea to be specific about how TLP members relate to SLP members. It's still a good idea to explicitly rule out self-maximizing behavior, which comes at the expense of the partnership as a whole. Remember, rules can be general and ambiguity is okay.
- *Agree on corporate mission and values.* The TLP will start with the results of the SLP work on mission and values. If the TLP feels that additions or changes are required, these should be cycled back for interaction with the SLP. Eventually both these partnerships must share (or, at least clearly understand) mission and values. Reemphasize a joint acceptance of costs, burdens, and risks.
- *Agree on a set of principles that will govern the partnership.* The TLP will start with the principle statements of the SLP. As with mission and values these must be shared or, at least, understood clearly. Because the TLP has a different kind of work to do the TLP partners will have additional principles to guide their activities.
- *Construct a shared vision.* Again, this is something that must be consistent with the SLP vision. The TLP members will almost certainly have additions to make in substance and detail. The TLP should be cycled back to the SLP and differences and misunderstandings should be worked out. It might be a good idea to do the shared vision work together originally if possible.
- *Review the reward structure.* The reward structure may be given to the TLP at its inception or it could work out its own and seek agreement from the SLP. It should be as explicit as possible. It should link to the vision's pursuits. Partnership performance should be most important.
- *Work together on some regular basis.* Same guidance as the SLP. Do real work together. Understanding a wide range of information is a key activity for the TLP so it is even more important that meeting not become simple a forum for presenting someone else's work. Make decisions on partnership concerns together; don't delegate either up or down.
- *Review the state of the partnership.* Same guidance as the SLP. Have a partner's meeting regularly to decide: Do we need to adjust the membership? How good are the results of this partnership? How well are we working together? Are our mission statement, values statements, vision, and principles still working for us?

We've now closely examined partnership as a mechanism in the overall framework of business technology linkage and I suggest another management principle.

Potential principle: **We will adopt the partnership relationship model as the primary organizational mechanism for planning and allocating resources and we will invest time, energy, and money to understand, establish, and improve partnership skills.**

The next section takes this recommended practice and puts it in the context of a theoretical framework that will help us understand how to evaluate the usefulness of any particular implementation.

The Henderson and Venkatraman strategic alignment model

I am going to introduce a framework for business technology linkage that was developed by John Henderson and N. Venkatraman while they were at the Center for Information Systems Research at MIT.[5] I'm going to use mostly different words in describing their ideas, but I hope to preserve the essence of their thinking, which I believe is excellent and will be helpful to us. Their work was focused specifically on planning, but I am taking the liberty of expanding it to encompass all the cooperative processes of the business including both planning and execution.

Exhibit 6.4 illustrates the top level of the model. Each block refers to an area of leadership, planning, decision making, and execution. Perfect linkage would result from adjusting the contents of each block so that the contents all fit together perfectly.

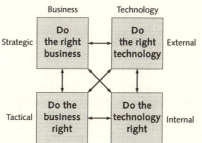

Exhibit 6.4   Henderson and Venkatraman Strategic Alignment Model

Here's what's inside the blocks:

- *Do the right business.* This is the *business strategy* box. These are our choices positioning the company in the product and market arena. Business strategy includes our selection of business scope (for example, total market, niche market, upscale, price sensitive, all sporting goods or golf equipment and clothes only, and so forth). Business strategy includes what we will do to differentiate ourselves from our competitors (for example, price, quality, image, delivery channels, and so forth). And business strategy also includes the extent to which we enter into value added partnerships, business alliances, or other collaborative mechanisms.

- *Do the business right.* This is the *business operations* box. It includes the management structure, work processes, and skills in our organization. Choices include: What organization structure do we use? What level of skills do we need? How will we do the work?

- *Do the right technology.* This is the *technology strategy* box. Will standards be open or proprietary? Will electronic connectivity be general and ubiquitous or specific and tailored? To what degree will technology in the company be uniform? To what degree will we attempt to use emerging technology? Will our technology infrastructure be reliable, highly reliable, or ultra reliable? Which parts of the technology infrastructure do we sustain and which do we transform?

- *Do the technology right.* This is the *technology operations*[6] box. Choices here include decisions about: application design (do we like stovepipes?); data (do we share it or isolate it?); hardware and software selections (terminals or PCs, mainframes or servers?); development methods (waterfalls? objects?); security procedures (single log on?); data center operations (lights out?); cost control (chargebacks?); people skills and values of the technology community.

In the real world, we would expect imperfections in whatever process we use to link these boxes but ideally linkage ensures that all details of all choices in all boxes fit together. They should fit together in a way that allows us the most flexibility to respond when things change and the most efficiency to exploit the situation when they don't.

Henderson and Venkatraman define four characteristics that give us dimensions of quality for any business technology linkage.

- *Consistency:* describes the degree to which details of the choices in one box fit together with the details of the choices in another box. Six distinct pairs of boxes, six dimensions in which the linkage can be consistent or not. Henderson and Venkatraman assert *the effectiveness increases in direct proportion to increases in consistency.* This seems reasonable enough. If the goals, approaches, and measures fit together better, the business will be more effective. For example, good linkage between business strategy and business operations is good; good linkage between business strategy, business operations, and technology operations is better.

- *Completeness:* describes the degree to which all four of the boxes are included in the linkage. If technology strategy is linked to technology operations and it stops there, there isn't much completeness. We can easily imagine a more complete process that produces good linkage from technology strategy to business strategy and then to business operations. This is called *technology exploitation.* Henderson and Venkatraman tell us that complete linkages, ones which involve specifically linking all four boxes, will be more efficient than less complete linkages even if there is a consistent linkage among three of the boxes.[7] This translates to an assertion that, if you have to trade-off, *completeness* is probably more important than *consistency!*

- *Validity:* describes the degree to which linkage is exerted to test the assumptions of the strongest set of decision makers. For example, complete and consistent linkage could exist in an organization but all be based on assumptions in, say, business strategy, that don't make any sense. *Validity* measures the degree to which linkage is a two-way street. An invalid linkage is one where the choices in one box drive the choices in the linked box without examination of why the choices in the first box were made the way they were. *Valid linkage* exists when the choices in each box are made with full understanding of and agreement on the principles, beliefs, and assumptions that underlie the choices in the other boxes.

- *Comprehensiveness:* describes the level of detail in which linkages exist. Both business operations and technology operations, for instance, are naturally concerned with lots of details. These boxes could be linked at the lowest level of detail or at a very high level of abstraction or someplace in between. Unlike the other dimensions of linkage quality, more *comprehensiveness* is not necessarily better. Here there is a clear trade-off between the cost and time necessary to create more *comprehensiveness* and the degree of effectiveness of the linkage. Henderson and Venkatraman tell us that when making a trade-off between *validity* and *comprehensiveness* in constructing linkages, favor *comprehensiveness* in a relatively stable environment and favor *validity* in a relatively unstable environment.

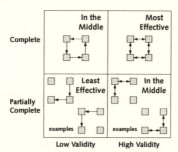

Exhibit 6.5   Relative Effectiveness of Partial Business Technology Linkages

As illustrated in Exhibit 6.5, Henderson and Venkatraman tell us that on average, linkages that are *complete* but *invalid* and linkage which are *incomplete* but *valid* will be equally effective and superior to linkages which are neither *complete* nor *valid*, even though they may be *consistent*.

The table in Exhibit 6.6 summarizes the important features of the Henderson and Venkatraman model as we are applying it to business technology linkage.

Linkage Consistency	Consistency is good if the details in the linked boxes fit together	There really isn't any linkage unless there is some degree of consistency Consistency does not guarantee correctness or efficiency.
Linkage Completeness	Completeness is better if more boxes are included. If all four are included, then the linkage is complete.	The quality of the linkage depends greatly on the number of the boxes which are involved. Linkage is best when they are all involved.
Linkage Validity	A linkage is valid if the assumptions and principles used to make choices in one box are understood and agreed to when making choices in the linked box.	If the rules, assumptions, and principles of one box drive choices in all the subsequent boxes, linkage can be complete, consistent, and comprehensive and the results may still be wrong. A situation could exist in which some linkages between boxes are valid and others not.
Linkage Comprehensiveness	A linkage is more comprehensive if the goals, approaches, and measures of two boxes fit together at a greater level of detail.	Comprehensiveness is subject to cost effectiveness considerations. More is not necessarily better. Comprehensiveness cannot substitute for validity in dynamic situations.

Exhibit 6.6   Summary of Henderson and Venkatraman Model Important Features As Applied to Business Technology Linkage

Making the linkages complete

Exhibit 6.7 is a summary of how strategic and tactical linkage partnerships build complete and valid linkage between business and technology. The other links in the diagram represent various kinds of tactical linkages.

Two of these linkages, business strategy to business operations and technology strategy to technology operations, are provided by the hierarchy and standard management practice. These links work best when there are mechanisms for encouraging dialog up and down the hierarchy. It is particularly difficult to ensure validity in the upward direction of these linkages without a specific process for getting operational level input into the strategy-making process.

Exhibit 6.7   Business Technology Linkage Framework Based on Henderson and Venkatraman Strategic Alignment Model

The tactical linkages on the diagonals, business strategy to technology operations and technology strategy to business operations aren't usually addressed in a traditional organization. The tool we suggest to build these linkages is tactical linkage partnership. The existence of such a mechanism is necessary for full completeness and it is particularly good for improving validity, especially between the assumptions and models of the business side and those of the technology side. Good quality work by this partnership is an important contributor to consistency in the planning and execution in the company as a whole. This partnership becomes more important as the pace of change increases on either the business or technology side of the linkage. The tactical linkage partnership becomes vital in making a shift from *sustain* to *transform*.

If the CIO becomes a partner in the CEO's inner circle, we build a linkage between business strategy and technology strategy that is not just more *consistent* and *complete*, but which is also *valid*. The *validity* comes from the nature of the partnership relationship. Behaving as partners, we would expect that basic assumptions and mindsets that support the business strategy will be challenged and eventually shared by the CIO just as the assumptions and mindsets that support the technology strategy will be challenged and eventually shared by all those in the inner circle. In general, I suggest that it is easier to adopt a techie into the CEO's inner circle than it is for one of the inner circle to successfully build a valid linkage between the technology strategy and technology operations boxes. The valid two-way linkage is most important here if a dynamic technology environment is anticipated. The only way the technology environment is going to be anything but dynamic is if the company is frozen, focuses on *sustain*, ignores *transform*, and doesn't reengineer. We have already talked about the fact that this choice is not likely. The bottom line here is: *if you're going to reengineer, make the CIO (or functional equivalent, maybe a "reengineering czar") a member of your inner circle.*

Exhibit 6.7 also has a bubble called "teams" as the linkage mechanism between business and technology at the tactical, get things done, execution level. The partnerships to link business and technology strategy and cross-link strategy and operations are absolutely essential for an effective organization, but they aren't the whole story. In fact, these partnerships will involve only a few people and, important as leadership is, it's performance we get paid for. I suggest that the central mechanism for performance in business should be the *team.* Chapter 7 explores the general nature of teams and the specific use we need to make of them in the information ecology.

===

In this chapter we introduced the desired mindset around the business technology relationship. We suggested that the partnership model was the relationship best suited to that mindset and most effective for linkage. Then we described the strategic linkage partnership and the tactical linkage partnership as the means for providing the upper level and cross function completeness and validity. Normal management process provides the vertical linkages. Chapter 7 deals with using teams to provide the remaining horizontal operational linkage.

Notes

1. This set of characteristics was documented by Boston University's John Henderson while he was with the Center for Information Systems Research at MIT.
2. A public version of the mission and values can be a big help to others in the company, but getting agreement on the exact wording that must withstand close scrutiny and still be meaningful is a lot of work.
3. Tom Davenport and Mike Hammer argue strongly for the use of management principles in Davenport, Hammer, and Metsisto 1989.
4. A strong introduction to shared vision as part of the leadership process can be found in Peter Senge's book, *The Fifth Discipline* (1990).
5. See Henderson and Venktraman August 1989 and October 1989.
6. "Operations" in this context is meant to include all the things we do in the information ecology, not just the data center and network operations piece.
7. They also say that in the real world, the four boxes may not be completely independent choices in which case this assertion might be wrong. For example, business operations and technology operation may be so connected that one planning perspective would work without a special linkage, perhaps as in the outsourcing business.

7

Teams to Sustain and Transform

I assert that the linkage between business operations and technology operations is best accomplished by the use of teams and we are about to go into the details. An important complication in the use of teams for the bottom horizontal linkage between business operations and technology operations is that the traditional functions of the hierarchy provide much of the vertical linkage on both the business and technology sides and there is a potential conflict for individuals who act both as part of the traditional hierarchy and as part of cross-functional teams.

Teams in a hierarchy

There is a debate among management theorists in which one side argues that the traditional management hierarchy is inappropriate to the circumstances of our modern world and that it must give way to something more flexible.[1] The other side argues that hierarchy provides the natural and most effective means to ensure accountability in large enterprises.[2] Rather than get in the middle of this fight, I propose to explore what I have to say on the topic of teams at the practical rather than theoretical level. We know two relevant facts:

- Every large company has a hierarchy and is likely to continue to have it.
- The information ecology demands work that can be performed best by teams that cross the lines of any hierarchy we are likely to construct.

The *team* is a group of individuals who work together to achieve a common purpose. When the group members are part of the same organization within the hierarchy and the team leader is the boss of that organization, there is no conflict within the hierarchy. If, however, we have a cross-functional team in which team members are drawn from several organizations within the hierarchy, team members may be uncertain about how to behave.

The teams we need to manage the information ecology effectively are increasingly cross-functional. The most useful work that can be done by teams working strictly within the hierarchy was done early in the development of the information ecology. After the initial wave of capital substitution work, "automating" traditional functions, the organization we built no longer fit the shape of the problem very well. Many companies have gone through waves of "decentralizing" and "centralizing" the information systems resource in response to the various symptoms of this poor fit. Most have not been too happy about the results.

My position is that we should work in teams that operate within our hierarchies. We won't expect that hierarchies will *wither away*. On the other hand, we should insist that the hierarchy not *get in the way*.

The standard model and the use of teams

The various team concepts that I introduce in this book assume that an individual often will work on a number of teams simultaneously and that the mix of teams a person will be part of will change over time. Also fundamental to the concept is the assertion that, properly structured and understood, there is no inherent conflict between working on a team and one's "real job"—that, in fact, the work of the teams *is* the real job. It's the purpose of this section to examine the reasonableness of these assertions:

- People can work in several teams concurrently.
- The teams don't have to be nested according to the hierarchy in order to succeed.
- The "real work" does not necessarily align exactly with the organizational hierarchy.

The standard model for organizations is something like this:

An organizational unit consists of a set of jobs or "slots" where each job is described by a job description stating what work is to be done by the person filling the slot. The unit also has some structure designating one slot for a unit leader, supervisor, manager, or boss and the slot to which each other slot reports.

A person is not only a member of the local unit but also a member of each organization in the hierarchy in which the local unit is nested. For instance, I might fill a slot in the day-shift section of the operations area of the computer operations department of the infrastructure management division of the information technology and operations group of the North American Region of the Global Business Company subsidiary of Worldwide Enterprises GMBH, making me in some sense at least a member of eight organizations.

Administrative teams and the "real work"

I'd like to elaborate the standard model to support the introduction of flexible teams. Let's start by designating the lowest level unit of traditional hierarchy in which I am a member as my *administrative team.* My administrative team is my immediate boss and my peers in the organization. If I'm a boss, I'm in two administrative teams—one, my boss, my peers, and me, and the other, my subordinates and me. I'm a member of one team and the leader of the other. Already I am in two teams.

Administrative teams are process teams. They exist primarily to *allocate* the organization's resources to the organization's work and to provide internal communications channels. They also carry out the organization's internal work: career counseling, attendance data collection, United Fund and Blood Drive solicitation and control, employee surveys, and so forth. The administrative team structure is useful in implementing processes that must include everyone in the organization. Information passes up and down the administrative team structure easily enough but doesn't move from one administrative team to another except by passing up the chain from one team to the lowest team connected to both and then down the chain to the other. Clearly, in the standard model, the work involved in the administrative teams doesn't take up much of the time of the organization. Administrative teams can be very stable; they only have to change when someone gets hired, fired, retired, or promoted.

In the traditional organizational hierarchy, all of the "real work" of the organization is assigned in various ways to the people who comprise the administrative teams. If I'm the customer service supervisor, my administrative team, comprised of my subordinates and me, is also the customer service process team. In practice, we don't usually distinguish between when the group is acting as an administrative team and when it is acting as a process work team, but the functions can be considered as distinct. This organization of the work is satisfactory as long as the numbers of people, skills, experience, and so forth of the administrative teams match up with the needs of the work assigned to them. When mismatches are small, we fix them by juggling work among departments, sharing staff, and moving people around. When the mismatches get large, we reorganize—that is, we rearrange the administrative team structure to more closely match the shape of the work. When the business changes rapidly, we reorganize frequently. Reorganizations have a heavy impact on the people involved because of the anxiety that accompanies the possibility of a new boss and the adjustments that follow.

Playing on several teams

As we saw in the standard model, simultaneous membership in more than one formal organization is a familiar concept, although it is familiar to most employees only in terms of this kind of hierarchical inclusion. Managers in many large organizations are accustomed to another kind of multiple membership— matrix management. In a matrix, the manager (and presumably the group he manages) reports to more than one other manager in the hierarchy. For instance, I may run a group of service providers and report to a product manager responsible for all the units like mine that provide our particular service and I report simultaneously to a relationship manager who is responsible for all the different products and service units, including mine, that support our particular customer set. This approach has been used with mixed results. Difficulties can arise out of conflicting priorities between the managers who are both responsible for a single resource. On other occasions, the combination of perspectives combine to create a powerful vision with positive results. As a matrix-managed unit, we experience being simultaneously members of two organizational units that are not nested hierarchically. In the example, the two units are a product organization and a customer segment organization. The two units we are part of may be in conflict, an uncomfortable situation, or they may be working synergistically, an exhilarating one.

If I am a manager in a matrix organization I may be part of, at least, four teams—the process team I lead, the administrative team I lead, and the two other administrative teams I am part of by virtue of my matrix reporting relationships. If I consider the nesting of administrative teams I can think of myself as a member of a fairly large number of different organizations in each of which I have different duties. We can begin to see that the idea of an individual playing many different roles in an organization is not such an unusual one.

Let's look at another familiar organization that calls on its members to play a variety of roles—the high school. A high school student in a class might be considered part of a "learning team." Throughout the day the student is a member of a different group of students each period. Most of these are academic periods in which the student plays a fairly consistent role but with different leadership and different subject matter (work). Typically, one period is a "homeroom," which serves many of the same functions as the administrative team in our model. During lunch periods, recess, study halls, and activity periods, the student plays a variety of different roles as leader, organizer, participant, independent contributor, and so forth. The entire school is reorganized each semester as students shift from one set of work to another.

From the student's point of view in the high school model, people work on a number of teams concurrently, the various teams are not nested in the school's subject matter hierarchy, and the nature of the work changes on a regular basis not strictly associated with the academic hierarchy.

How flexible do we need to be?

In a number of chapters in this book we will be discussing teams—*process teams* organized to carry out an on-going function like measuring the performance of a data center, and *project teams* organized to achieve a particular objective like consolidating two data centers. In general, process teams are more stable than project teams, that is, the number and definition of process teams and their membership and work patterns change less frequently than the number, definition, and membership of project teams. Both kinds of teams, however, require disciplines to organize themselves and change themselves when the business changes. It is useful to think of a scale of volatility for team structures like the one in Exhibit 7.1.

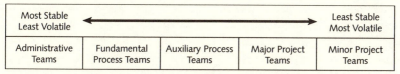

Most Stable Least Volatile				Least Stable Most Volatile
Administrative Teams	Fundamental Process Teams	Auxiliary Process Teams	Major Project Teams	Minor Project Teams

Exhibit 7.1   Volatility Scale for Group Membership and Work Patterns

If we organize an environment in which teams are formed, used, changed, and disbanded to suit the needs of the organization's changing pattern of work, we begin to put a lot more emphasis on the administrative team manager's primary responsibility to allocate the team's resources, that is, assign work to people and people to work. As long as fundamental process teams and the administrative teams are more or less identical, allocation is basically done once and then not changed until the next reorganization. When changing processes and doing projects becomes more important to the business, the leaders of the administrative teams (the organization's management group) need to spend more of their time and employ more formal disciplines in allocating people to a constantly changing team structure. This is a little like continuously reorganizing, except the negative effects of reorganizations are greatly diluted by maintaining the continuity of the administrative team—work and roles change, but your administrative boss is the same.

I have conjured the image of teams forming and reforming as the needs of the business change, eclipsing the traditional fixed working units of an organization. This is an extreme view. In the real world, some organizations (consulting companies, project engineering companies, and investment banking companies) use this model extensively, but few others do. To what degree should we plan to apply this flexible team organization model to a "normal" business?

Let's notice first that every organization uses this approach to some extent. Even the most rigid organization (for instance, an army) makes use of ad hoc teams for meeting special purposes. Most often in rigid organizations people in staff positions are the ones used as members for the ad hoc project teams. As the *volume* of business grows, the pressure is felt in the line units; as the *complexity* of the business environment grows, the pressure is felt first in the staff functions as they try to serve needs that the line units are not designed to fill.

In a large consulting company a rule of thumb suggests that 90% of the staff time should be spent in project related, flexible client teams—most of these people don't have any other "real job." This is one extreme. In a very rigid organization, perhaps 5% or less of the staff time is spent in flexible teams—practically everyone has some fixed responsibilities considered the "real job." This is the other extreme.

Sustain-oriented activities are less likely to require flexible teams than *transform* activities, but even *sustain* activities often benefit from spending some time in team activities that cross organizational boundaries. Think about stretching *sustain*-oriented organizational units (e.g., application maintenance, infrastructure operations, customer service) by using 10% to 15% of their staff time in flexible teams. These people will certainly still perceive their role in the administrative/process team as their "real job" and will have to be carefully coached in the importance of the flexible team roles they also play.

Transform-oriented activities (for example, application development, marketing) even in relatively stable business environments will benefit from a much higher proportion of flexible team work. Depending on the pace of change that drives the business, people in these activities could spend 50% to 80% of their time in different flexible team assignments. They will begin to see their team assignments as the "real work," and the challenge will be to allocate and reallocate the people to the needs in an effective way.

Key elements of teams

It's beyond the scope of this book to explore thoroughly the rich topic of how to make teams more effective, but, because I believe that mastering cross-functional teams and managing the creation, life, and termination of teams are key skills. I want to suggest enough about them to serve as a framework for evaluating how well teams are being used.

We're talking about groups of people working together to achieve a common purpose. The basketball team and the football team are these kinds of groups because the players must cooperate in order to succeed. The bowling team, the golf team, and the track team don't qualify because individual performance or the sum of individual performances are what counts with them—cooperation is not a major factor.[3]

If cooperation and coordination are the hallmarks of the team, then the degree to which the team members share common values, principles, assumptions, mindsets, vision, pursuits, and measures[4] will play a part in the effectiveness of the team. Call this quality *cohesion*. As a rule, the more cohesion in the team, the better.

People aren't born knowing how to work in teams. We get some experience as we grow up and in our jobs, but what we learn about working in teams is haphazard and often conflicting. Furthermore, we need to take specific steps to establish a set of rules about things like:

- Who can start a team?
- Who decides who the members are?
- Who decides what resources are available?
- Who determines the goals and objectives?
- How is the work planned, apportioned, and controlled?
- How does a team know when it's done and what happens then?

If we don't make this *team process* explicit, *cohesion* is insufficient and the team is less effective.

Everybody is willing to agree that people on teams play different roles, but after saying "team leader" and "team member" most of us run out of gas when we try to name and describe the roles. I'd like to complicate the situation a bit by suggesting that team members actually each play at least two independent roles.

- *A functional role:* that determines what part of the work the individual will do. My favorite list of functional roles is honcho, back-up honcho, scribe, worker, and wizard. Workers and wizards[5] come with a variety of subject matter skills, suitable, one hopes, to the work at hand.
- *A team role:* that determines what behaviors the individual will bring to the team work. My favorite way of looking at team roles is contained in the work of Dr. R. Meredith Belbin.[6]

Dr. Belbin tells us that there are nine team roles that make up a *balanced* team, that is, a team with all of the behaviors necessary to facilitate group work. The Belbin team roles are:

- *Shaper:* change agent and advocate... pressures colleagues, finds ways around obstacles. Challenges the status quo. Unites ideas into a single purpose.
- *Monitor evaluator:* analyst and evaluator... sees all the options, dispassionate and forthright. Critic; hardly ever wrong.
- *Coordinator:* orchestrator and facilitator... gets best out of team's resources—clarifies objectives, allocates work, promotes decision making.
- *Implementer:* practical organizer... turns ideas and decisions into practical actions. Does what needs to be done.
- *Plant:* radical and reformer... provides original ideas, suggestions, and proposals. Tackles difficult problems.
- *Resource investigator:* gatekeeper and ambassador... contacts outside world—explores, communicates, negotiates. Prevents introspection and stagnation.
- *Teamworker:* peacemaker and organizer... counterbalances discord— oiler and lubricator. Promoter of harmony, cares for people on the team.
- *Completer:* finisher and worrier... relentless follow-through—searches out errors and omissions and keeps colleagues on alert.
- *Specialist:* technical or professional expert... source of rare skills and knowledge.

Belbin tells us that a balanced team has all or most of these roles represented and few of them duplicated. This would only be a mild curiosity except for three things.

- Belbin has established experimentally that *a balanced team is more effective* than one that isn't *balanced.*

- He has designed a *means for measuring* the inclination of individuals to play these various roles.
- He has established a *method to forecast the effectiveness of teams* based on the team members' inclination to play these roles.

This set of knowledge gives us the means to engineer a team that is better balanced and, therefore, more effective. I can offer from my personal experience that knowing your own inclinations in regards to these team roles and working with others who are also aware of theirs can lead to much more effective allocation of work. This leads to another suggested management principle.

Potential Principle: We will use teams as the primary organizational mechanism for carrying out processes and projects and we will invest in understanding, establishing, executing, and evaluating team activities.

Exhibit 7.2 gives an example of a balanced five-person team. Each person has a functional role and most have two team roles. We could expect this to be a highly effective team.

	Honcho	Back-up Honcho	Scribe	Worker	Wizard
Plant					Edward
Resource Investigator	Alan				
Coordinator		Betty			
Shaper	Alan				
Monitor Evaluator		Betty			
Teamworker			Carol		
Implementer				David	
Completer			Carol		
Specialist					Edward

Exhibit 7.2   An Example of How a Balanced Small Team Might Embody Five Functional Roles and All Nine Team Roles

To summarize, we evaluate the quality of our teams based on:

- *Cohesion:* how well do the team members think together? Are our people comfortable with the concept of mindsets? Do we have mission and value statements and broad-based principles. Do we take steps to ensure that team members have a common vision, pursuits, and measures?
- *Process:* do the team members know what is expected of them? What do we do to teach people how to work in teams? Does our planning process deal in terms of teams? Do we have corporate processes and procedures for working in teams? Do our evaluation and reward structures accommodate work performed in cross-functional teams?
- *Balance:* are all the necessary team roles covered? Do our people understand the difference between functional and team role? Do we try to measure the team role inclinations of our people? Do we try to design our teams?

These general criteria are broadly applicable to work in teams. Let's focus now on teamwork as it applies specifically to the business technology linkage.

Teams that do systems

Exhibit 7.3 shows us another framework for thinking about the activities that enliven the information ecology. The picture is sending several messages:

- There are *sustain* and *transform* activities in both the business operations and technology operations parts of the business.
- Typically the largest amount of activity is *sustain* activity, which provides maintenance and continuous enhancement in support of the on-going business processes.
- Maintenance activity always requires both technology and business skills and frequently requires a variety of each.
- There is the possibility of *transform* activity that produces discontinuous change in business processes. Today's jargon for this is "business reengineering." It almost always requires a mix of business operations and technology operations people.

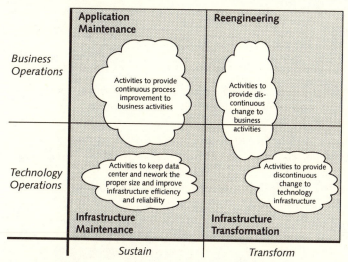

Exhibit 7.3   **The Activities in the Information Ecology Cross All the Boundaries of Business and Technology and *Sustain* and *Transform***

- Some *transform* activity also occurs in the pure technology operations activity as we make discontinuous changes to technology infrastructure.

Infrastructure maintenance work involves:

- *Fix systems problems when they arise.* For example, if the overnight account processing fails, work with the application maintenance people to fix it.

- *Maintain adequate computing capacity to ensure acceptable response time for on-line systems and acceptable running time for overnight applications.* For example, make sure that the additional computer memory or mass storage or telephone lines are in place exactly when the growth of the business requires them, but not sooner. These upgrades should be invisible to any user.
- *Make sure that terminals and associated devices are added, removed, moved, and changed as the business requires.* For example, when the customer service center moves to its new location make sure that the customer service workstations are all working when the service reps get there.
- *Update or replace equipment and software for computing and communications when cheaper, faster, or more reliable versions become cost effective.* For example, replace the two old Whizbang 1000's with one Whizbang 2000, saving 10% of the cost and doubling the capacity. This should be invisible to any user of the system.
- *Maintain and test procedures to ensure infrastructure support to disaster recovery continuity of business plans.* For example, make sure that all the applications running in the data center will also run in the backup data center and that all the phone lines running to the data center can be switched to the backup data center.

Application maintenance work involves:

- *Fix systems problems when they arise.* For example, if the overnight account processing fails, work with the infrastructure maintenance people to fix it.
- *Make regulatory changes to application systems when required.* For example, when the tax law changes, change the payroll application and the HR system and, maybe, the general ledger system.
- *Make enhancements and modifications to application systems to change business operations.* For example, when we introduce a new product, change the order entry system, inventory system, customer billing system, customer service system, and the product profitability system.
- *Make enhancements and modifications to application systems to improve cost of operations and cost of application maintenance.* For example, write a clever program that makes the overnight processing take eight hours instead of ten hours or rewrite an especially complicated program so that the next time it has to be changed it will be easier to understand and faster to fix.
- *Maintain and test procedures to ensure that disaster recovery continuity of business plans work.* For example, let the order entry clerks run for a day using the backup terminals and data center.

Reading over the range of tasks involved in these activities, these things seem to be connected. Tasks aren't easily slotted into one kind or another. Projects overlap. Roles and accountabilities overlap. We sense the complexity and continuity of the information ecology. For instance, fixing problems is everybody's work. Taking advantage of efficiencies is everybody's work. Accommodating changes in the environment and the business is everybody's work. Ensuring continuity of business is everybody's work.

True, different tasks require different mixes of expertise, but the continuity of interest translates into continuity of participation—it's mostly the same groups of people from technology operations and business operations who tend to be involved. Even in a crisis, we know that we have to "round up the usual suspects." Whether we like it or not, plan for it or not, recognize it or not, *the real work gets done by teams.*

The teams that do the *sustain* work are relatively stable and, over time, people get to know each other. The work gets done.

Does the work always get done as well as it should? Probably not. Some of these informal teams work together better than others. We already know the reasons.

- Some have more *cohesion* because of similar values, principles, assumptions, and mindsets.
- Some have worked out *team processes* that are more effective than others.
- Some are better *balanced* in their mix of team roles.

Sustain work usually gets done. It gets done in spite of the fact that the teams may not have much cohesion or team process or balance because individuals, given enough time, find ways to make things happen. If we make somebody accountable, that person will chew on the problem until either it's solved or the person is fired, transferred, or promoted. The ingenuity of the individual makes up for the poor process design.

Now let's take a look at the *transform* side of the diagram starting with what we mean by *infrastructure transformation.* Let's look at some examples of infrastructure transformation:

- *Computing machines:* Substituting computers for human labor was a infrastructure transformation, the one that started the information ecology as we know it.
- *Teleprocessing:* Attaching terminals to computers through telephone lines was an infrastructure transformation that freed from geographical constraints the process of getting data into and out of computers.
- *Microcomputers and the PC:* Building cheap small computers is an infrastructure transformation that expanded the range of the problems that could be addressed economically by machines and amplified the effectiveness of individuals.

- *Network computing:* figuring out how computers can cooperate with each other is an infrastructure transformation that will remove most of the remaining constraints on the range of problems that can be addressed by machines and will amplify the effectiveness of work groups.

There are many more infrastructure transformations that have been less visible, especially in software, such as the introduction of compilers, the concepts of layered protocols, and the ideas of database management. Among the most modern of these are reusable software component systems and the introduction of objects.

It seems to me that the early infrastructure transformations were handled more smoothly and effectively than the more recent ones. For instance, the shift to teleprocessing was difficult both as a technology and management problem, but all in all it went reasonably well. The PC revolution, on the other hand, is a monumental example of failed vision and management. The introduction of PCs and other micro-computer based machines into our information ecology has been bungled in nearly every large company, resulting in outrageous costs, deep organizational scars, and embarrassingly modest benefits. The shift to network computing isn't going much better; in many companies it's barely going at all.

I think that what's happened is that the technology operations part of the management process has grown large and complex enough to suffer from what we suffer from in the business at large—processes and skills in *sustain* that have frozen out processes and skills to transform. Technology operations is filled with people who

- Sustain the data center
- Sustain the network
- Sustain the applications

and pitifully few who know how or are inclined to transform anything. I think that technology operations began to have trouble with *transform* in the late 70s and early 80s when the information ecology was growing at a very rapid rate and things were breaking from the strain. Enough of the critical business of the company had been computerized by that time that system failures could no longer be tolerated. Stability and reliability became much more important values than flexibility or adaptability. The gung ho, shoot from the hip style of the early computing industry was almost completely extinguished in most large companies by 1985, giving way to management for stability even in the midst of growth. *Sustain* won the day.

If any *transform* inclinations or skills remained, they probably were to be found in the application development groups rather than in the data center or the network group. But, even among the development people, *sustain* was the dominant cultural driver. People who wanted to do *transform* left the company to work for software vendors or consultants or they transferred to an adventurous business unit to "work in PCs." There was no love lost between those who stayed and those who left. The chasm between *sustain* and *transform* deepened.

The activity on the *transform* side of the diagram is reengineering. The reengineering events in an organization are idiosyncratic to an industry, if not to a specific company, but may include things like:

- Integration of order processing with inventory and shop floor automation in a manufacturing company.
- Integration of asset and liability accounts transaction and safekeeping accounts in a financial services firm.
- Integration of point of sale transaction, inventory control, and cash management in a retail company.

It's reengineering because:

- It didn't start that way. There was large-scale discontinuous change.
- It focused on integrating and sometimes eliminating previously separate functions.
- It depended on information technology.

No matter how big a company may be, there haven't been many of these reengineering successes.

Reengineering, even more than infrastructure transformation, has been inhibited by our lack of appropriate attitudes and skills. The few successful reengineering activities we have pulled off have come at great effort and usually were led by an unusual champion. The reengineering successes are outnumbered by the reengineering failures, most of which died stillborn when some executive said to himself, "It's a great idea but we'll never pull it off." Many startups and small companies skipped the old ways and by good fortune or good planning went directly to the best new technology in support of a new, clean integrated process. These competitors will constitute a significant threat as they grow up, but we may not see them coming until it's too late.

The *transform* activities, technology infrastructure transformation and business reengineering, depend much more than *sustain* activities on good teams and are less likely than *sustain* activities to have them.

Reengineering, in particular, requires the strongest teams because:

- The stakes are larger than most *sustain* activities.
- Change management is a set of skills unto itself and *sustain* oriented activities don't build them.
- Many different points of view must be represented to build and sell a successful concept.
- Each reengineering project is a new program with new people and new points of view.

Imagine trying to do a reengineering project with a poor team.

- *No cohesion:* values, principles, assumptions, mindsets, and vision all different, ill-fitting, and undocumented... misunderstandings, lack of trust, indifference or hostility... split loyalties... conflicting agendas.
- *No process:* make it up as we go along... assignments get confused... things fall through the cracks.
- *Unbalanced:* everybody decides what to do, nobody does it... or too many people get lost in the details... or things get started, nothing gets finished... or misunderstandings and conflicts get out of hand... or nobody thinks about what's outside the team

Worse even than such a bad team, however, is trying to do reengineering with *no* team—just hand the project to an operating manager and stand back. Stand back and watch the other managers kill the project with benign neglect, frontal assault, or whispers, whichever is the corporate culture's preferred style. If it crosses the hierarchy, the hierarchy will get cross in return. *To do reengineering, set up a cross-functional team. To make a cross-functional team work, design in high-quality cohesion, process, and balance. Neither the team nor the team quality happen by accident.*

A high-quality cross-functional team is an absolute precondition to success in reengineering. And, by the way, a suitable cross-functional team is the key to technology infrastructure transformation too. And, while we're at it, high-quality cross-functional teams will make all the *sustain* activity work better too.

In this chapter we examined teams as the mechanism for providing linkage within and between business operations and technology operations. We said that these teams were an essential coordinating device. We recognized that although teams must operate within the context of established management hierarchies, it is cross-functional teams, those that cross hierarchy lines, that are the most valuable.

We said that teams may be measured in three dimensions:

- *Cohesion:* How well do the team members share values, mindsets, vision, and so forth?
- *Process:* To what degree have the team members formally agreed on how to do things?
- *Balance:* How well have the team members been selected to fill, not only functional roles, but team roles as well?

We observed that *sustain* teams and *transform* teams have different requirements.

In the information ecology infrastructure maintenance and application maintenance are best conducted by *sustain*-oriented teams but if the teams are not explicitly established, it is likely that over time informal arrangements will evolve to support the work anyway.

Infrastructure transformation and business reengineering, on the other hand, require *transform*-oriented teams and nothing is likely to happen until the right teams are established. Business reengineering requires the strongest teams we can build.

Notes

1. This position, for example, is persuasively and energetically argued by Tom Peters (1988).
2. This position is argued elegantly by Elliott Jaques (1990 and 1991).
3. Team spirit is an undeniable phenomenon and these kinds of teams often succeed or fail based on how much esprit they can forge. The same phenomenon can provide value in our business, for instance, in a sales team. This, however, is not the focus of our discussion.
4. This is the same list used for partnerships.
5. The primary job in the worker role is to get the work done. The primary job in the wizard role is to add expertise to the workers.
6. See Hemingway 1991 for a practical guide to applying Dr. Belbin's theoretical work.

8

Measurement—Changing the Rules of Rewards

The last couple of chapters have proposed we make heavy use of partnerships and teams as fundamental parts of our business. This chapter takes on the question of accountability in the proposed mix of partnerships, hierarchy, and teams.

Two fundamental business activities

Exhibit 8.1 illustrates a simple mental model of business activity in which I suggest that practically every job at every level in the company is involved with either allocation or execution.

- *Allocation:* choosing which things to do and choosing how to do things (planning)
- *Execution:* actually doing them.

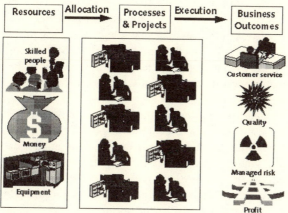

Exhibit 8.1 **Simple Model of Business Activity in which Allocation of Resources and Execution of Processes and Projects Produce Business Outcomes**

Front-line jobs tend to be dominated by execution, doing things well. Sales-men, customer service representatives, production line workers, programmers, sales clerks, traders, draftsmen, and so forth tend to focus on the execution part of their jobs while retaining, at least to a modest degree, power of choice over what things to do.

Management and executive positions tend to be dominated by allocation, making the right choices, especially resource allocation choices. CEOs, VPs, di-vision heads, department heads, and supervisors tend to focus on allocating re-sources so that the right things get done while continuing to have some amount of task execution to do.

People high in the hierarchy tend to have *allocate* dominated jobs and people low in the hierarchy tend to have *execute* dominated jobs.

Available company resources are allocated to processes and projects by a va-riety of planning and controlling activities. Once allocated to specific purposes, the resources are consumed in execution. The purpose of both the allocation activities and the execution activities is to produce a desirable set of business outcomes. Presumably, if we allocate well (do the right things) and execute well (do those things right), we will produce good business outcomes and prosper.

If this sounds a little familiar, it is. In Chapter 6, we introduced the simplifi-cation that strategy was *doing the right business* and operations was *doing the business right*. We have the sense that correctly choosing the work to be done from all possible alternatives is a higher order decision than correctly choosing how to do the work from all the possible alternative approaches and both are higher order than actually doing something. Strategic planning is higher order work than tactical planning and both are higher order work than execution. We tend to hold some people accountable for their choices of what work to do and others accountable for the way they do the work they are assigned.

Unfortunately, real jobs aren't quite so simple. Every job is a mix of allocate and execute activities. Although the top and bottom of the hierarchy tend to-ward pure allocate or pure execute, in between there is a great deal of both, es-pecially in supervisory, middle management, or professional positions. Even an individual contributor allocates the resource that he, himself, represents. The mental model that tries to support clear accountability, breaks down when carefully examined. Accountability tends to blur, measurement systems are fuzzy, and rewards are inconsistent.

To further complicate this mental model we are building, we need to observe that a mix of allocate work and execute work exists for both *sustain* activities and *transform* activities. *Sustain* activities involve work to allocate resources to various possible *sustain* uses and work to utilize the resources and actually ex-ecute the *sustain* work. Likewise, *transform* activities involve work to allocate resources to various possible *transform* uses and work to actually execute the *transform* work. Exhibit 8.2 illustrates the point.

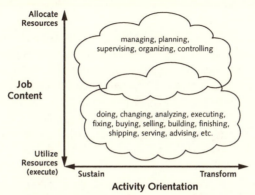

Exhibit 8.2   There Is a Continuum of Job Content from Allocation to Execution and from *Sustain* to *Transform*

Two points made by the picture are:

- Jobs vary in a continuum from almost totally resource-allocating jobs to almost totally resource-utilizing, but all jobs do some of each.
- The continuum of *sustain-* and *transform*-oriented activities also has a full range of these jobs.

Accountability in fundamental business activities

Accountability is a term much used in hierarchies. The theory is that when an individual knows he will be "held accountable" for an action, decision, or outcome, he is more concerned with a successful outcome than he might otherwise be and will therefore work harder to achieve one.[1] I think it's clear from the way we use these words that accountability is a little scary. Accountability seems to be associated with motivation by fear and negative reinforcement. Accountability is rarely associated with reward. Let's overlook that aspect of the term and assume that accountability means responsibility for an outcome and will lead equally to reward or punishment.

So, assigning accountability is all about figuring out who to reward when we get good outcomes and who to punish when we get bad ones. Fairness suggests that there be some symmetry in this assignment of accountability. That is, if I'm accountable for a certain process, I will be rewarded for a good outcome and punished for a bad one. If the situation doesn't have this symmetry, strange behaviors result. Imagine, for instance, I am rewarded for successful outcomes and you are punished for failures. That would tend to make me quite a risk taker. It would probably make you seek employment elsewhere. Accountability tends to be slippery this way and, frankly, it seems to me that the organizations that are very focused on accountability are most likely to focus on it after something goes wrong. Let's look at some situations where accountability is an issue.

Balaclava, whose failure?

I'd like to ask some questions about the battle of Balaclava... you know, where the "Light Brigade" rode "into the valley of death"... an incident in the Crimean war that Alfred Lord Tennyson turned into a poem.

The date was October 25, 1854. The British and French had pushed the Russians back into a line of old Turkish artillery positions (old positions, new artillery). Colonel Airey, the British quartermaster general, sent Captain Nolan forward with a written order for the Light Brigade, one of the units under the command of Lord Lucan, to charge along the southern line of heights and drive the Russians from the gun positions. Lucan transmitted the order to the earl of Cardigan who was the leader of the Brigade. Cardigan couldn't see the position of the Russians from where he stood and thought he had been ordered to charge through the valley. He did. Twenty minutes later 247 of the 673 mounted men were dead or wounded.

Who's accountable? The man who gave the order? The man who transmitted the order? The man who carried out the order?

Being memorialized in a poem doesn't change the fact that this was a group failure. In the rules of a hierarchy like this one where accountability is clearly assigned (at least in theory), someone must be at fault.[2] Clearly, however, pinning the blame on one of the possible scapegoats doesn't do any good for any one.

From our distant seat, we might conclude that what was really needed was modern intelligence, weapons, and communications. Given such a modern "process," this incident would never have occurred. Given the processes available at the time, however, the failure was very likely. This is consistent with a philosophy of continuous improvement, which suggests that we look at each failure or problem as an opportunity to examine our processes and determine what improvements in the *process* will prevent similar problems or failures in the future.

This "no fault" approach has the healthy feature of focusing attention on the right issue, fixing the problem rather than fixing the blame. Extreme adherents of this approach don't hold anyone accountable for failures. Given the extreme position, I think it's fair to ask who, then, is rewarded for success? If the *process* is the only thing that can fail is the *process* also the only thing that can succeed? I suggest that complex situations demand a more complete understanding of roles and responsibilities than the strict adherence to a no-fault approach usually allows.

Accountability problems in group work

When you and Bob and Betty and I cooperate to produce an outcome, several things can happen, as illustrated in Exhibit 8.3. Clearly there is a continuum on both axes so the four boxes are for simplicity of discussion. The question is who's accountable?

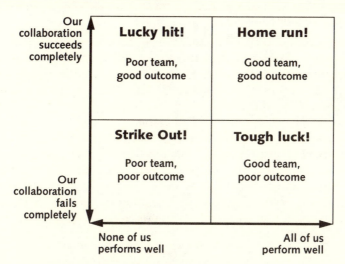

Exhibit 8.3   How Well We Work Together and How Well We Do as a Group Are Separate Dimensions of Performance

In *Home run!* and *Strike out!*, both individual accountability or collective accountability seem fair. Everybody did well and we succeeded or everyone did poorly and we failed. If a mixed team succeeds, we say they succeeded in spite of a poor performance from some team member. If they fail, we say they failed in spite of a good performance from a some team member.

In *Tough luck!* it doesn't seem right to hold the team members individually accountable for a failure when they all performed well. And in *Lucky hit!* it doesn't seem right to give credit for the good outcome to the team members, all of whom performed poorly. If we have a mixed team with one poor performer and we have a *Tough luck!* outcome, that one person becomes the goat. If we have a mixed team with one good performer and a *Lucky hit!* outcome, that one person becomes a hero. Should the goat or hero be held accountable? Should the others?

Someone might say, "The team leader is accountable! After all, the team leader is supposed to do whatever is necessary to make the team succeed. If the team has poor performing members, it's the team leader's job to reform of replace the miscreants."

Given that view, we are forced to ask two questions.

- *What about the poor performing leader with a good team?* Surely you've seen or heard of situations where the team carried the leader. Who's accountable for the success if they succeed?
- *What about the impossible project?* If the nine women don't produce the baby in a month, is the team leader accountable for the failure?

In order to sort this out we need another picture.

Accountability and rewards

The diagram in exhibit 8.4 is logically similar to the one at the beginning of this chapter where we observed that business has the two fundamental activities of allocate and execute. We've added a bit of complexity this time by showing how the feedback loops work. We measure the outcomes so we can reward (or punish) the people who do the work.

Usually, we can measure how well we execute. We can measure the output of a process in terms of efficiency (minimized waste material, maximize output per unit time, and so forth) or a project in terms of project deliverables. This is the *science of management.* We can work to perfect execution by optimizing the things that we can measure, but we rarely can connect these execution measurements with specific business outcomes. And we know that even with perfect execution, we must choose the right processes and projects and assign the right resources to succeed.

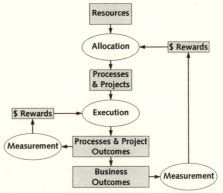

Exhibit 8.4   Model of Business Activity with Measurement and Feedback Added

Usually we can't measure, directly, how well we allocate. Once we've decided on a particular set of processes and projects and a particular assignment of people, equipment, and dollars, we can't take it back and do it over. We do "what if" studies up front, but we never really know for sure how well we chose compared to some theoretical optimum set of processes, projects, and resource assignments. This is the *art of management.* Allocation decisions usually take a relatively long time to affect business outcomes and, even then, other factors that we can't control tend to obscure the consequences so we can rarely connect allocation decisions directly with specific business outcomes. And we remember that even with perfect allocation, we must execute expertly to succeed.

Over the long term, we compare our business outcomes with those of our competition and get either a pat on the back or a kick a little lower. If we've executed well and we get good business outcomes, we can infer that our allocation decisions were at least okay. If we executed poorly and our business outcomes are still okay, we either made great allocation decisions or were lucky. If we executed well and our business outcomes were poor, we may have made poor allocation decisions or we may have been unlucky. If we executed poorly and our business outcomes were poor, there's not much we can say about the allocation decisions.

We pay execute work for performance. We tend to measure the performance of people doing *execute* work and pay them based on how well they do their jobs compared to some standard or formula. Piecework pays more the better you are at it. Sales pays more the better you are at it. Likewise, building houses, overhauling carburetors, and mowing lawns.

We pay allocate work based on overall business outcomes. We tend to measure the performance of people doing *allocate* work by judging the overall business outcomes. The more senior the manager the more likely he is to be measured on the profit or market share or return on equity of the business.[3]

So who's accountable?

With this discussion behind us, let's revisit the question, who's accountable?

I am accountable to the company that employs me for the use of resources entrusted to me. If I am the CEO of the company, I am accountable for all the company's resources. If I am a department head, I am accountable for the people, equipment, and company funds (my department budget) entrusted to me. If I am an individual contributor, I am accountable for how I use the resource that I, myself, represent.

I am accountable for resources that I allocate. Multiple accountability is an important consequence of this rule. If I allocate a resource, it is a resource allocated to me by my boss to whom it was allocated by her boss, and so forth, and we are all accountable. This is, in fact, a primary function of the organizational hierarchy.

What you measure is what you get

The value of the information ecology to the business is one of the very difficult things for us to measure. CEOs often are reported to believe that their companies are not getting sufficient value back for their technology investments, but a measurable relationship between information technology investment and expense and business outcome (profitability, return on equity, return on investment, market share, etc.) has been extremely elusive.[4]

Since we can't measure information technology contribution directly, we have tended to manage it by optimizing some *proxy*, something we can measure and that a reasonable person would expect to be related somehow to overall contribution.[5] Various companies have chosen to manage IT in order to optimize proxies like unit costs, user satisfaction, or competitive spending. Their thinking was something like this:

- If unit costs of technology intensive products trend down, that's probably good.
- If business users of information technology are "satisfied" with the quality of their information systems, that's probably good.

- If it costs us less to own and operate our information ecology than it costs our competition, that's probably good.

One might say, "These proxies have hidden assumptions" or "Aren't these a little too simple minded to model the real world?" I agree.

- *Are low unit costs good?* I can drive the unit costs of technology intensive products way down by investing in high-capacity plant and equipment. This is entirely reasonable if demand is stable or growing. If demand is volatile and subject to abrupt down turns, high fixed costs can be disastrous.
- *Are happy users good?* Having satisfied users may mean that I've catered and pandered to their idiosyncrasies at the cost, perhaps, of something they are less interested in, say, infrastructure investment. I've optimized a *master-slave* relationship.
- *Is spending less than the competition good?* I may have brought our cost to own and operate the information ecology way below our competitors and failed to provide competitive quality or flexibility.

Focusing on the wrong proxies for overall business outcome and holding inappropriate mental models of how technology and business interact is a very bad combination because if we set up to measure what we think we want and it isn't what we need, the outcome can be very unfortunate. Horror stories abound. Sometimes companies get what they measure and regret it.

Centralize versus decentralize, an example

I am familiar with an organization that had a history of extremely poor performance by the central IT system developers in terms of meeting schedules and budgets. The techies would propose projects saying it would take x months and y dollars. When the business side agreed to the original numbers, the developers would take 1.5x months and spend 2y dollars. Of course, the business people grew increasingly angry and frustrated and blamed centralized IT management for being insensitive to the needs of the business, arrogant, and basically incompetent.

Eventually, there was a major reorganization and the developers found themselves working inside the business groups—they'd been "decentralized." The leaders of the old centralized organization were fired.

It was made clear to everyone concerned that these "executions" and the decentralization were driven by the poor budget and schedule performance of the old centralized organization.

Guess what happened to project performance. *No project was ever late or over budget again...* not even after cost pressures forced the company to centralize all the system developers again!

What happened here? Did IT in this company get suddenly better because a few middle managers were fired? Certainly not. In fact, the *quality* of the information ecology actually declined. Here's why.

Under the old guard, the important values had been craftsman's values. It was important to the system developers that work be done to a given level of quality no matter how long it took. The business people with whom the developers had to work were often unavailable or uninterested in systems work, so getting all the details of a new project clearly enough defined to implement was a tedious and time-consuming chore with lots of frustration for the developers. Schedules slipped, but the system developers were dogged in the pursuit of enough information about the user's requirements to meet their perception of quality. The systems that were produced were complete and "to spec," even though they were late and over budget.

When heads rolled and organizations were split up and reassigned, the techies got the message. The values that mattered in the new regime were the ones associated with meeting schedules and budgets.

The business people with whom the developers had to work now felt they "owned" their developers, but they were no more interested than ever in working on the details of systems. The reaction from the developers was reasonable enough, given their perspective. They decided that they would consider budget and schedule fixed and adjust the scope of their work to fit. Since the business people weren't paying much attention to things like the details of what new systems did or the degree to which the new systems were tested, it was easy for the developers to "declare victory" at the appointed time and explain that anything that wasn't exactly what the business needed would be corrected in phase two!

The business made it clear to the system developers that they would be measured on budget and schedule performance—and budget and schedule performance they got.

Biases in measurement

Because "you get what you measure" and activities are not equally easy to measure, we get some performance bias toward things that are more easily measured. Specifically, more energy and attention is devoted to execution activities than to allocation activities simply because it's easier to measure execution. We tend to establish systems that measure execution kinds of work, but we rarely measure (or even record) much of the allocation activity.

This combination results in a bias toward action and a focus on the near term at the expense of the longer term. This near term bias is simply an outcome of measurement. We are more likely to establish measurement programs to examine short-term results than long-term results—more measurement of short-term events, more focus on the short term. We get what we measure.

This bias toward the short term is also a bias toward *sustain* at the expense of *transform*. *Sustain* activities not only persist for a while so we can set up measurement systems for them, they also tend to show their results in the relatively short term, so they are measured more. *Sustain* is better measured than *transform*, hence we get more *sustain* activity than *transform*.

Allocation and execution in teams

Teams are groups of people working together for a specific purpose. The purpose, in theory, could be either allocation or execution. In practice, teams are almost always formed with some execution focus. Most often, the team is conceived as a tool for performing a process or carrying out a project. The resource represented by the team is allocated by some appropriate authority in the hierarchy. That authority then is accountable for the resource represented by the team. At the beginning of the team activity, however, allocation continues when the team decides who does what, what the processes will be, and what resources outside the group will be required.

Traditional teams think of the team leader as the one responsible for the team's allocation activity. Self-managed teams deemphasize the team leader role and share the allocation activities more broadly. Self-organized team participants, at least in theory, allocate their own resource as the team organizes itself. It is only in the traditional team where a team member has a functional role primarily focused on allocation. So, a traditional team leader may be accountable and, more obscurely, individual team members may be accountable as well, depending on the team process.

It is just about here in the description of team function and accountability that some people begin to be nervous. What does "more obscurely" mean in the last paragraph? Are team members individually accountable for the results of the team or aren't they? More specifically, when we measure team work outcomes, do we reward or punish all the members equally for the success or failure of the team? My specific answers about measuring and rewarding teams are the topic of the next section.

Measuring team performance

Remembering that we get what we measure, let's start by determining what it is we want to get from a team.

- *Team result:* We want the team to perform some process or project that an individual couldn't do alone. That's why we set up the team.
- *Functional role performance:* We want each team member to perform his or her functional role well (leader, worker, expert, scribe, etc.) because individual excellence is an ingredient of team excellence.
- *Individual adherence.* We want each individual to behave according to the values and principles of the organization as a whole because we believe that this improves decision making and cooperation (effectiveness) within the team and improves the quality of interaction (hence effectiveness) between the team and the rest of the organization.

We're going to look at these desired outcomes one at a time.

Team result

Measuring team result should be easy. We shouldn't set up a team unless we know what we want it to do.

A process team should have performance goals (e.g., answer customer calls before the third ring 95% of the time... open at least 25 new accounts per quarter with a minimum order of $1000... manufacture 2500 units per month with customer complaints less than 1 per 100,000 units shipped).

A project team needs specific project objectives too (e.g., build a stout barn in a single day that will house 30 head of cattle and feed for a long winter... design a 8" X 10" book cover to appeal to teenagers and have it photo ready by Thursday... implement a reengineered accounts payable function this year that will operate with 10% of the present staff).

Teams should be set up in the context of a shared vision that includes a common understanding of the desired future state, agreed-to pursuits for bringing about the desired future state, and agreed-to measures for determining progress along the pursuits toward the desired future state. Team goals and objectives should be tied to the pursuits and team performance measures should be tied to the measures of the vision. If we find ourselves setting up processes and projects that don't tie into the vision, we are doing the wrong things or we have an inadequate vision. In either case, alarm bells should go off.

Functional role performance

The functional roles that we need in our business depend on what business we're in, on what technology we use in that business, and on the specific processes we use to apply that technology to our business. For each functional role we establish, we should describe what work needs to be done. Exhibit 8.5 gives examples of functional role descriptions for the very general roles of process team leader, project team member, and expert.

It's not difficult to see how any particular role could be measured according to these desired behaviors. The measurement could be carried out by the person playing the role, by the person in the hierarchy who allocated the resources and established the team, some third party measurement group, or one or more members of the team. The best measurement might, in fact, include several or even all of these. We have to be very careful in drawing up these functional role descriptions because what we measure is what we get and if we begin measuring an individual's role performance against a specific set of desired behaviors, we will get those behaviors.

The functional role descriptions look like job descriptions, don't they. The differences between a functional role description and a classic job description are not so much in what they say but more in our expectations about how they will be used. It is a difference in mental model. Differences in the mental model include:

- We may expect a person to fill more than one functional role in a team.
- We may expect a person to fill different functional roles on different teams
- We may expect a person to fill the same functional role on different teams
- We may ask a person to move from one functional role to another and back with no sense of promotion or organizational change.

So functional roles contain the details of what we want a person to do as part of the team. When we measure the degree to which people behave in the desired way, we will more and more get the desired behavior. Functional roles describe *what* we want people in our teams to do. We measure *individual adherence* to determine to what degree they display the personal traits and behaviors we want them to.

Process Team Leader.

Establish a clear statement of the purpose, functions, internal processes, external connections, and overall context in which the process takes place.

Establish and communicate to all stakeholders and participants desired operational goals such as level of production and quality.

Plan and practice for continuity of process in the face of internal or external disruption.

Establish plans, projects, and processes to safeguard corporate resources.

Direct, measure, monitor, and document the use of corporate resources.

Establish functions which measure the quantity and quality of process results.

Contrast process input and output with standards, preferably external standards.

Communicate process performance to all stakeholders and participants.

Adopt and use any relevant methodologies and tools.

Establish projects to improve the performance of the process.

Resolve conflicts with other leaders over the availability of participants and other resources.

Cross train participants.

Enlist and use the experts.

Take appropriate steps at regular intervals to evaluate participants on their performance.

Project Team Member.

Understand and be able to articulate the objective of the project and the context in which the project is being undertaken.

Clarify, when necessary, the amount of the participant's time available for the project and identify, when required, all alternative activities competing for the participant's time.

Carry out assigned tasks using relevant methodologies and tools.

Consult and enlist the aid of experts.

Document and report the use of resources including the participant's own time.

Communicate promptly to the project leader significant events, unexpected results, and new ideas.

Make a best effort to resolve conflicts with other participants over the availability of resources and escalate the conflict promptly to the project leader when resolution fails.

Expert.

Maintain knowledge and skills at an expert level.

Understand the competitive and other external environment as it concerns the area of expertise.

Understand the internal environment as it concerns the area of expertise.

Build skills, techniques, and materials for sharing the expertise and transferring the expert knowledge.

Establish links with leaders and participants so that the expertise is known.

Seek out opportunities to contribute based on the expertise.

Undertake concrete tasks in projects to facilitate both the completion of the task and, if possible, transfer of the expert knowledge.

Communicate promptly to the appropriate leaders significant events, unexpected results, and new ideas.

Exhibit 8.5   Sample Role Descriptions for Process Team Leader, Project Team Member, and Expert

Individual adherence

In order to measure individual adherence we need a framework of desired behaviors that is consistent with our values and principles. Exhibit 8.6 is a sample of the kinds of things we might settle on.

Honest and Fair. We have a responsibility to be truthful and straightforward in our dealings with other people and to conduct our business fairly.

Empowered and Empowering. We are expected to understand our empowerment, that we are each responsible for the overall success of the enterprise in which we work and to exercise prudently the authority that accompanies that responsibility. We have a responsibility to help our colleagues understand their empowerment as well.

Competent. We have a responsibility to be good at what we do. We are expected to be able to articulate what our skills are, to work to improve them, and to be able to communicate a realistic view of our relative expertise in each.

Involved. We are expected to contribute our full professional effort to our work, to understand the context in which our work is performed, to seek out and solicit involvement from all stakeholders, and to exhibit a sense of responsibility for the success of the corporation, our unit, and our team.

Cooperative. We are expected to contribute to every group effort in which our participation is enlisted by communicating openly, sharing information freely, and undertaking an appropriate portion of shared work.

Adaptable. We are expected to be able to fill any major role (leader, participant, or expert) in either process or project groups, to be able to operate effectively in a climate of rapidly changing resources, constraints, and priorities, and to be tolerant of ambiguity. We are expected to learn new skills when needed.

Customer Focused. We are expected to recognize we are vital links in the service chain that leads to the customer and contribute value accordingly.

Exhibit 8.6   Example of Desired Behaviors to which Individual Adherence Could Be Evaluated

It is not too difficult to imagine how we might evaluate an individual according to these desired behaviors and measure to what degree that person adheres to these values. The evaluation might come from the person's superior in the hierarchy, from a third party evaluation group, from other team members, from randomly selected colleagues with whom the person works, from the person himself, or from some combination of any or all of these.

As we begin to measure behavior against the values of the organization, we begin to get those behaviors so, again, it's vital that we choose carefully. Obviously, the values to which we wish people to adhere should be consistent with the values on which our shared vision, its pursuits, and its measures are based.

Everybody plays

I asserted earlier that cross-functional teams were the method of choice for effectively linking business operations with technology operations. Let's look at an example of how this might work.

Let's imagine a project team set up to build a new customer service system The new system will support three product areas: grass widgets, cloud widgets, and pavement widgets. The systems organization assigns four people to work on the project, the grass and cloud product groups assign a single person each, and the pavement product group assigns two people. Let's say that the team decides on the functional role assignments displayed in Exhibit 8.7.

Functional Role	Organization
Data expert	Systems
Infrastructure expert	Systems
Implementer	Systems
Implementer	Systems
Testing expert	Cloud Widgets
Documentation and training expert	Grass Widgets
Customer service expert	Pavement Widgets
Project team leader	Pavement Widgets

Exhibit 8.7   Example of Cross Organizational Assignment of Functional Roles

Who's accountable? Well, the resources were allocated by responsible managers in Systems and in the three widget product groups. That is, four managers in various places in the hierarchy allocated company resources to this project. They are jointly accountable. If this is just one of a continuing series of common projects, perhaps, they should think of forming a partnership around their shared interests. As a minimum, their shared accountability should encourage them to consider themselves some kind of oversight group or steering committee.

Because the skills needed to do this work are quite varied, the project team leader, if she's wise, won't try to be too directive, so the team members will be allocating a lot of their own resource and they all share in the accountability too. Maybe the steering committee ought to consider the entire project team to be members too.

As the project takes shape, specific goals and objectives will be agreed on by all the stakeholders. Plans will take shape. Work assignments will be made. Work will be started. Project reviews will occur. Work will get done. Ultimately the project is complete.

Let's imagine that the project is a modest success. It was completed a month late, but under budget. The first few weeks of operation were not smooth, but gradually improved to the point where everyone was willing to say that the poor start was just growing pains. On a scale of 1 to 10 this new system project gets an eight.

Let's also assume that we have in place some measurement systems that let us score each of the team member's functional and individual adherence performance. Exhibit 8.8 is a summary of the scores.

Team Member	Functional Role	Organization	Team Performance	Functional Role Performance	Individual Adherence
MariLou	Data expert	Systems	8	9	7
Su Cheong	Infrastructure expert	Systems	8	8	7
Rachel	Implementer	Systems	8	10	8
Kevin	Implementer	Systems	8	8	9
Alice	Testing expert	Cloud Widgets	8	6	4
Ruth	Documentation and training expert	Grass Widgets	8	9	9
George	Customer service expert	Pavement Widgets	8	5	9
Cynthia	Project team leader	Pavement Widgets	8	8	9

Exhibit 8.8   Example of a Multi-Dimensional Team Member Performance Evaluation

Before the team disbands, let's ask some questions about how it is rewarded for the success.

We can see from the scores that most of the team members were both strong performers in their functional roles and strong adherents to the values of the organization. That accounts for why the project was a success. Two of the team members, however, were problems to the team to some extent.

George, the team member who was supposed to be the customer service expert, just didn't know enough about the topic and couldn't perform as well as the team needed. He knew pavements widgets and their customer service problems, but he'd never been in either of the other two product areas. But George is the kind of person we want in our teams, as pointed out by his high adherence to our shared values. The problem here seems to be that the allocation process might have been better if it had selected a person with broader knowledge of the various widget products for the key role of customer service expert. The right thing to do is improve the allocation process for the next time.

Alice, the team member who was supposed to be the testing expert, is a different case. She didn't perform well and she didn't behave in accord with the values of the organization. In some sense this could be considered another allocation problem, but the fact is that Alice has the necessary credentials to do a good job in the testing role; she just didn't. Even in a tolerant organization, she wouldn't be allowed too many repetitions of this kind of performance.

Cynthia, the team leader, has learned a lot from this experience and next time will know better how to deal with problems like the ones presented by George and Alice.

The company thinks that this important project was done well enough to deserve a bonus. In my opinion, the total bonus amount ought to be decided in accord with the importance of the project and the quality of the result and that amount should be divided among the team members according to their relative functional performance. No bonus should go to a performance like Alice's. It is a matter of principle whether or not George's performance should share in the bonus at all.

When it is salary increase time, *improvements* in the scores that these people get on their individual adherence ratings as they move from assignment to assignment should be combined with any *improvements* in their performance in various functional roles and these should influence the amount of salary increase. The rationale is that better role skills or better adherence make a more valuable employee. Once the increase in value is built into the salary, however, other factors come into play for further extraordinary increases.[6]

Here are the things I'd like you to take away from this example.

- This was a cross-functional project. It didn't belong to either Systems or to any of the product areas.
- All the stakeholders were represented on the project team.
- All the team members had real functional responsibilities.
- The accountable managers were clearly identified.
- The result was a team result.
- Results were measured individually.
- Both the team result and the individual performances were rewarded.

I don't know about you, but this is the kind of environment I'd like to work in.

For contrast, think how damaging it would be if Alice went back to Clouds and got a big bonus because Clouds had a great year; George and Cynthia got little bonuses because Pavements had a mediocre year; Ruth wasn't bonus eligible because the Grass Widget product business only gives bonuses to VPs; and MariLou, Su Cheong, Rachel, and Kevin got no bonuses at all because Systems is a cost center and doesn't have a bonus program. *If we want cross-functional teams to work, everybody plays and... everybody plays by the same rules.* I suggest as a management principle the following.

Potential Principle: **We will arrange our evaluation and reward systems so that members of a given partnership or members of a given team are subject to compatible compensation schemes.**

Note that *compatible* is not the same as *identical.* Since people can be in several group efforts, partnerships, or teams, at the same time, it isn't reasonable to put everyone in exactly the same compensation program. Compatibility, however, is possible by ensuring that alternative patterns of reward are not contradictory.

A practical concern

If we use cross-evaluation for both functional role performance and individual adherence (and I think we should), each team member rates the performance of each team member. For a team with eight members, this means 128 evaluations are required to include both measures. If you add in some ratings by the hierarchy or a third party, it's easy to get to a very large number of individual evaluations. You may be thinking about now, that it's tough enough to get a performance appraisal filled out on each employee every year, much less something like this. Are we talking about an impossible dream or a paper blizzard?

This concern is real. A paper-based system of evaluations of this magnitude would be very difficult to manage. Help, however, is on the way for this administrative roadblock and many others. We will bring our technology to bear on this part of our business as we have on others.

This chapter took on the task of reconciling the concept of accountability in a hierarchy with the notion of teams to do important work.

We said that all our activities fell into either *allocation* or *execution*. Allocation activities assign resources to processes and projects. Execution activities do the work. We said that every real job was a mix of these two kinds of activities.

We showed with several examples that accountability is a slippery concept especially when group work is involved.

I pointed out that we can usually measure execution work fairly well but measuring allocation work was very difficult, and we usually looked to overall business outcomes to infer how well we had done the allocate tasks.

I asserted that a member of the hierarchy who allocates a resource is accountable for the resource. This leads to a hierarchy of responsibility and accountability for the successful use of the company's resources.

Execution should be measurable and the reward mechanisms of the company should be linked to those measurements. I asserted that the measurement process itself strongly influences behavior; what you measure is what you get. As a consequence, there are biases toward execution activities and *sustain* activities built into our most basic business processes.

I proposed that team execution be subjected to three independent measures:

- *Team result.* Did we get what we wanted?
- *Functional role performance.* Did each person do what was expected of them?
- *Individual adherence.* Did each person behave according to the values of the organization?

We examined how these three independent measures can give insight into the workings of a team and useful information to guide both process improvement and personal growth.

In Chapter 9, we examine how we can use technology itself to enhance the way our people work together.

Notes

1. See Carson 1992 for a typical use of the concept of accountability.
2. Tennyson's poem was published in late 1854, shortly after the incident, but it wasn't until late the following year that the phrase "someone had blundered" was included in a second edition of the poem. By then the military had decided to blame it on Lucan. Curiously, Lucan became the goat but almost certainly would not have been the hero if the charge had gone as originally conceived. What does that suggest about the real role of middle managers?
3. Often we pay some senior allocators in stock options. Stock options tie reward not only to company performance, but to how the company performance compares to the competition and to other businesses in which the capital alternatively might be deployed.
4. An important result of this inability to directly connect technology investment with business outcome is that businesses usually don't know how to decide how much to spend on the information ecology.
5. See Eccles 1992.
6. This assumes a bonus system to implement pay for performance.

9

Technology Makes It Better

We have been examining the business technology linkage for the last few chapters. We've talked about the nature of linkage, relationships, partnerships, teams, measurement, and reward. We've hardly mentioned technology. In this chapter, we are going to take a look at how we can use information technology to make the business technology linkage work better.

Stakeholders, especially those in linkage partnerships and teams, can use technology to:

- Know more about what is going on in the information ecology.
- Exchange information more effectively
- Make group decisions more effectively.

These desirable results require some imagination, some will, some planning, and some technology.

Process instrumentation

I am going to argue in this section for an all out effort to instrument the information ecology. Specifically, I will talk about measuring and keeping records of an enormous number of details about how the information ecology works. In general, the purpose is to have available when needed a wealth of information about how our processes presently work so that from time to time we can test our mental models of these processes against their realities.[1]

Infrastructure and infrastructure management processes

Infrastructure is usually pretty well instrumented. Data centers measure capacity and utilization to an exacting degree. Networks are commonly monitored in detail. In many companies the information infrastructure is the only part of the business subjected to rigorous measurement.

Good measurement of infrastructure comes about for a small number of healthy and not so healthy reasons. For instance,

- *The computer is considered to be a scarce, expensive resource and its use must be carefully tracked so that waste does not creep in.* Of course, this is an old idea no longer relevant in our present era of very cheap computing.
- *Careful monitoring of utilization is necessary to protect the business from sudden breakdown.* Mainframe computers and many other infrastructure devices exhibit a threshold effect in which performance remains essentially constant until the machine's capacity reaches a critical point beyond which performance deteriorates drastically with even small additional workload.
- *The data center and networks are usually shared resources and charge-out systems require detailed records of which business units used which parts of the shared resource.* This perfectly reasonable idea has serious consequences when the information is misused as it often is.
- *Infrastructure needs instrumentation for control and optimization.* Much of what actually happens in the information infrastructure takes place electronically and only detailed instrumentation can reveal what is going on. Without instrumentation, the data center and networks appear to be just so much wire plugged into a bunch of refrigerators. With sufficient instrumentation technicians can tune the various pieces of equipment to improve performance or efficiency.
- *Mainframes and network reliability get measured for the protection of the people in charge.* Computers and networks occasionally fail. When there are many users, some of them will—because of bad luck, bad timing, or bad attitude—believe and say very loudly to anyone who will listen, "The @#$%& computer is always down!" or "The @#$%& network is so unreliable I never use it!" The fact is that the mainframe and the networks are probably 97% to 99% available and the folks in charge of the infrastructure better be able to prove it!

It shouldn't be too much of a surprise that the instrumentation and measurement activities in the infrastructure are focused on *sustain*. After all, that is the principal focus of the entire infrastructure.

Transaction processing applications and processes

Almost all of the useful work done by the information ecology is done by our transaction processing systems. Consequently, one might imagine them to be a particular focus of instrumentation and measurement, but alas, it isn't so.

The infrastructure people usually keep some records about the transaction processing systems, largely in self-defense. Actual measurement of response time and so forth are often necessary to counter the subjective impression of unhappy users. Such measurements, however, don't help us to understand what is going on in our business processes.

I'd like to be able to identify in detail all the things I think you should be measuring about your transaction processing systems. Unfortunately, I can't because your transaction systems are unique to your business. I think I can give you an idea, however, of the general kinds of things you ought to be measuring. For instance,

- *Measure system flux.* Transactions enter your business for processing (new orders, claims, requests for information, payments, and so forth). Ideally, each transaction is processed immediately and then closed, but it doesn't always work that way. I suggest that you build instrumentation into your systems to measure how many transactions come in, how long they stay in your process, and how many go out. Measure how long it takes for the typical transaction to flow all the way through your process. Make a special effort to find out how many transactions must be held over each shift, day, week, month, and so forth.

- *Measure the division of effort.* Instrument your processes so that you know how much of the work required to process a transaction is done by a person and how much is done by a machine. You may want to use some cost allocation model to translate the different elements of work into commensurate terms.

- *Measure exception processing.* Transactions typically have a normal path and one or more exception paths. Pay particular attention to the transactions that flow through the exception paths because these are the transactions that require something other than what the designers thought was "normal." Significant divergence from what was expected suggests that the system designer's mental model doesn't fit the facts of the business.

- *Measure errors that stump the system.* Information systems have two kinds of error handling. In one kind, the system encounters something it just can't cope with. In that case, a good system will put the transaction aside and go on; sort of a last resort exception process. These are truly outside the mental model of the process and require careful examination. A gradual buildup of these kinds of errors may be signaling a major change in the underlying nature of the business.

- *Measure errors that don't stump the system.* The other kind of error handling happens when the system figures out what is wrong and takes or requests some action to fix it. For example, a terminal input routine may check account numbers as they are entered to see if they are real account numbers. If they don't match the pattern, the program rejects the number and makes the operator enter it again. Keeping track of this kind of error handling can give you insight into how well the interface between the user and the system is working. An occasional rejected account number is probably just a slip of the fingers; lots of rejected account numbers may mean a bad input form, a sloppy screen design, too much pressure on the operators, or something else that needs attention.

Try to establish a measurement regime for transaction processing that goes beyond the computer application and encompasses as much of the entire business process as you can. Measurements like these are not usually part of your information ecology. The main reason is that these measurements are not usually perceived to be necessary for *sustain* activities.[2] Whether or not this perception is correct, transaction processing instrumentation and measurement become vital and even seminal for *transform* activities.

Is the P&L an MIS report?

I am very positive about the ability of the information ecology to produce information that will help us manage our businesses. The more that we know about the transaction processes the better and using the power of information systems to collect and refine data about themselves is clearly the way to go. We need more of this rather than less.

On the other hand, I am wary of much of what we call management information reporting because of an almost universal lack of rigor in our thinking about it. At the risk of alienating my friends in the accounting profession, I have to assert that it is the overwhelming influence of the "accounting mentality" on management mindsets that has so often confused our concepts of management information.[3] The entirely rational emphasis of business managers on the "bottom line" has been the jumping off place for a logical leap that is just wrong. We have looked at the accounting process in a business and, at least unconsciously, concluded that since the bottom line is the ultimate measure of our success, the mental model of the business that allows us to compute the bottom line must be the ultimate representation of our business. This thinking is not only wrong, it's dangerous. The P&L does not provide information on how to manage a business.

If we think of the revenue and expense lines of our operating statement as the levers by which we control the business, we will have a warped and largely useless mental model.[4] Revenue is not a lever; product quality, price, advertising, and sales calls are. Expense lines and cost-of-sales ratios are not levers; product design, design changes, purchasing power, inventory turnover, and manufacturing technology are. Ultimately it's things like transaction flux, exception and error handling, and infrastructure utilization that underlie many of the business measures. None of these have more than a distant connection to charge-backs and allocations that are the usual stuff of MIS systems.[5]

How many processes does it take to change a light bulb?

Of course, management and administrative processes themselves are in theory subject to instrumentation and measurement, but in fact, they rarely are instrumented or measured.

Does an executive know how many process teams are allocated in his company? Does he know how many projects are underway in his company? If he knew something about these basic activity measures, he might begin to get a better handle on allocation. The only traditional allocation tool, the organization chart, is the focus of endless scrutiny, conjecture, and debate, but everyone knows that the organization chart is often irrelevant to the way resources are allocated and the way things actually get done.

Wouldn't it be useful to know, for each accountable manager, how many process teams and project teams are active? How many teams are changed and how much? How many process teams are started and how many disbanded? How many project teams are set up, how many succeed, how many fail, and how many are disbanded without result? On the average, how many teams is a single person part of? Does this vary from one accountable manager to another? How many people in the company don't seem to be on any process or project team? What do they do?

We have to be careful here, because we will begin to get what we measure. Therefore, we have to have a firm grip on what allocation behavior we want from our accountable managers before we decide what part of the management process we want to instrument and measure. If we ever wish to measure and manage our allocation process in order to balance *sustain* and *transform*, we will have to think deeply about our allocation activity.

The system development and maintenance processes

System development and maintenance is just one of a number of key business processes, but I'd like to give it special attention for four reasons:

- System development is a relatively new process as company processes go and, consequently, poorly measured and modeled by practitioners.
- System development is almost totally mysterious to most corporate executives.
- System development is the key enabler in business process reengineering.
- System development is the pivotal process in balancing *sustain* and *transform*.

I think the three key questions that instrumentation and measurement of the system development and maintenance process might help us answer are:

- What work is being done in the system development and maintenance process?
- How well is it being done?
- Who is it being done for and why?

In Chapter 2, we observed that NatNec's development staff distributed their efforts about as shown in Exhibit 9.1.

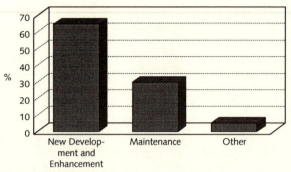

Exhibit 9.1   Estimated Allocation of Development Resource

System developers spend a lot more time doing new development and en-hancements to systems than is customarily believed. In NatNec, this means more than 200 professionals working on the company's systems. Do we really know what they're doing?

I suspect that much of this resource is being allocated at a very low level in the hierarchy. In fact, I suspect that often low-level system liaisons or even the developers themselves are choosing the work to be done. Developers and low-level liaisons are not necessarily choosing bad things to do, but they certainly are unlikely to be implementing much strategy! Most likely the work selected at this level in the hierarchy is detail improvement and fine tuning with a strong bias toward *sustain*.

If you ask developers to report their time according to the steps of a typical system life cycle development methodology, you get something like the distri-bution displayed in Exhibit 9.2.[6]

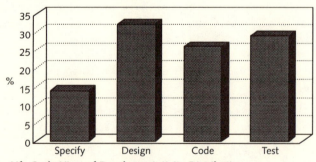

Exhibit 9.2   Life Cycle View of Developer Activity Distribution

If you watched one of these system developers work, however, you couldn't tell most of the time which of these steps you were watching and you definitely couldn't tell whether the work you were seeing was development, enhancement, or maintenance. No matter what the objective of the developer's work, it looks pretty much the same. If you watched developers and their managers for a while you would see something like the activity distribution displayed in Exhibit 9.3.[7]

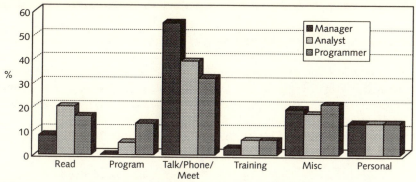

Exhibit 9.3 **Work Content View of Developer Activity Distribution**

The mental model of a system developer as a person who sits at a terminal all day and writes code is not true and not useful. The work of these people is dominated by *communication* activities. Half or more of what they do involves communication. Another rather unexpected observation about the way these people work is that they most often work in groups. Take a look at the numbers in Exhibit 9.4.[8]

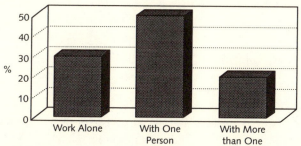

Exhibit 9.4 **Developers are Twice as Likely to be Working with Others as to be Working Alone**

More than two thirds of the system developer's time is spent in group activities! A new mental model begins to emerge of the system developer:

- Most of the time spent figuring out exactly what to do, how it should be done, sharing that information, and determining if the results match the expectations.
- A lot of meetings, conversations, written and spoken communications.
- A lot of team and small group interactions.
- A modest amount of time actually spent coding.

The old mental model led many IT executives to introduce lower CASE tools to make coding more efficient. Upper and lower CASE has given us some truly amazing power tools for putting computer programs together. We should make use of them and continue to pursue ever better versions.[9] Given this different mental model of a developer's activities, however, we can see that no matter how efficient we make the coding part it will have only a small influence on overall productivity. It's a little like trying to speed up air travel by making escalators in airports faster.

If we want to do something serious to improve developer *productivity* we have to improve their group work and communication processes. If we want to do something serious to improve developer *effectiveness*, we want to improve the allocation of this resource—better linkage.

At the beginning of this section, I said that I thought that instrumentation and measurement might help us determine:

- What work is being done in the system development and maintenance process?
- How well is it being done?
- Who is it being done for and why?

The first two of these questions focus on the productivity of the system development resource, and good system development managers have begun to measure their activities aggressively to improve productivity. Good development managers measure the dimensions and details of the various parts of the information ecology for which they are responsible:

- *Application systems:* How much code is there? How much work does it do? How complex is it?[10] How old is it? How well was it made? How well has it been maintained? How much do the different parts of a system get used? Which parts have failed in the past?[11] Which parts take longest to fix?
- *Developers:* How many developers are there? What are their skills and experience with particular technical tools? What are their skills and experience with particular systems? Which developers are good builders?[12] Which are good fixers?[13] Which are good changers?
- *Development and maintenance activities:* What new systems are under construction? What changes are in the work queue for each existing system? What are the present priorities for these changes? How many releases are scheduled for each system and when? What changes are planned for each new release? What test plans are in place for each release? What infrastructure changes are associated with each release? What operational changes are associated with each new release?

We can expect that questions focused on development process productivity and the associated resources are in the purview of the system development leadership. The third question, however, "Who is the work being done for and why?" is concerned with the efficient use of the resource in the business and it falls into our broader responsibility. In most large companies, the knee jerk reaction to this question is a *project tracking system.*

The typical project tracking system is some variant of a timekeeping system for the developers.

- The administrative manager sets up a project code for each active project and a set of pseudo projects to account for other acceptable activities (vacation and so forth).
- Every period (day, week, or month) each developer fills out a timesheet assigning hours worked to one or more of the project codes. Often the hours are required to be classified as to what part of the standard project life cycle they belong (design, coding, testing, etc.).
- The timesheets are entered into a computer system, which adds up the hours worked on each project.
- Reports are generated.

This seemingly innocent timekeeping activity is one of the most misleading and corrosive things that goes on in the information ecology.

These systems are misleading because they are interpreted according to inappropriate mental models by most of the people who use the results. They are corrosive because they almost invariably demand a certain amount of dishonesty on the part of the people supplying the information. These, I suggest, are very bad outcomes.

Invariably these bad outcomes will result from any effort to use timekeeping information in support of the *buyer-seller* relationship model between business and technology. Although it seems simple, since we are already collecting hours worked on a project, to multiply by cost per hour and get costs by project, it is almost always the wrong thing to do.[14] Here's why.

- The accountants will insist on some scheme that involves *full recovery* of *actual costs.*
- Recipients of the costs will insist on *auditability.*
- The mental model that says developer's activities can be cleanly assigned to a step in the project life cycle or to a particular project is always wrong.
- The mismatch between the mental model on which the project tracking system is built and what actually goes on will require someone to "fudge" the numbers.

Here are examples of the way the real world intrudes into the project tracking system to produce results that are easily misinterpreted or are in some way dishonest.

- *Developers don't always work on projects.* Some developers are experts who assist others by creating examples or giving advice. Some developers work on shared technical subsystems that are later used by many projects. Developers often spend time helping users understand their systems: training, user support, or problem identification. These activities aren't on the project list, so somebody has to decide to add them to the list (who pays then?) or just charge the time to the nearest thing.

- *Developers don't always work a standard day or week.* Often developers work odd hours because of the pressure of the work, the availability of good computer time, or just natural inclination. Overtime and undertime produce anomalous charges. Usually, somebody decides that the individuals ought to report straight time regardless of what was actually worked.

- *Developers don't always know what project they are working on.* A programmer gets an order to make three changes in a program. He has to analyze the code, get questions answered by the last guy who worked on the module, find all the places that will be affected by the changes, find out if the test routines have to be updated, code the changes, document the new code, run the test programs, and fill out the paperwork for change control so that the new program can go into production. The programmer doesn't know or care that the three changes came from three different projects. The manager isn't quite sure how to deal with the fact the all three changes benefit two users of the system, two of the changes only benefit one of the users, and the other change benefits one user now and another user next year. Somebody has to tell the programmer how to charge his time.

- *Emergencies aren't neat.* A senior developer gets a call in the middle of the night. A data input program had a bug in it and bad input got through into the nightly posting. The developer spends all night and all the next day helping the data-center people correct the major posting run. This developer has to charge his time but he never did any work on the input program (other people fixed it) and there wasn't really anything wrong with the posting program. Where does the charge go?

- *Getting it right isn't possible, so why bother to make it close?* Very quickly the people filling out the time sheets learn that the system won't accommodate the truth even if they know it. Compromises are made with the truth. The developer never sees the output anyway so why sweat it? Some people refuse to sign timesheets that aren't right, but nothing happens; somebody else puts in what is expected. Gradually only the administrative person responsible for producing the report cares any more.

- *Maintenance is the catchall.* When in doubt charge it to maintenance. Everybody knows maintenance is necessary, but nobody knows what it is. And, besides, maintenance people never get laid off.

Defenders of timekeeping for cost allocation will argue that any example I can find can be handled by some elaboration of the timekeeping process. I assert that the reality of the work being done is infinitely richer that the mental model that we try to impose on it and significant exceptions will always arise.

Furthermore, this mess just gets worse and worse the more detail we try to include. Recipients of the costs dig deeper and deeper to try to uncover errors. Accountants want to reconcile. Developers know the time reporting is some-place between wrong and fraudulent. System managers know the entire process is useless but are afraid they will be accused of being "out of control" if they don't play the game. Executive managers see high-level summaries of this data and believe it, misplaced faith that can lead to disastrous decisions.

Before I get off this topic, I'd like to ask you to consider one more question. Are there any professionals other than system developers in your organization who are asked to account for their time at this level of detail? If there are no oth-ers, why not? I suggest that the *buyer-seller* business technology relationship is at the heart of these timekeeping schemes and the schemes themselves are in-tended to serve a purpose analogous to a collar and leash. Here's the thought I'd like you to take away from this discussion: *don't use a time reporting system for charge-backs!*

So, if the usual approach to the third question "Who is the work being done for and why?" is a project tracking system and I'm warning you against time re-porting for charge-backs, what do we do instead?

If we look back to the team processes we described before, we can find an approach to determining how the system development resource is being allo-cated that doesn't require time reporting or anything else that compromises in-tegrity.

Each team has a set of team goals and objectives. These goals and objectives are the finest level of resolution that we need for determining our allocation of resources. Since it is one of the responsibilities of a process or project team leader to be able to account for the team's use of resources, he or she will be able to report resources assigned and consumed. Simple rules are fine. The details don't matter. The important idea is, if teams are the fundamental device we use for execution, then teams are the appropriate level at which to manage and re-port allocation, which suggest another management principle.

Potential Principle: We will track and report our use of resources at the team level.

Good technology is available to help us support this team level record keep-ing for management purposes. The same technology will help us resolve the concerns we raised in the last chapter about the amount of work necessary to keep track of all the evaluation processes we would like to do for teams. The technology I'm referring to falls under the rubric of *groupware* and is the topic of the next section.

Communication in support of linkage

Picture the cockpit of a modern fighter plane—LED displays, computer synthe-sized voice, image screens, heads up displays projecting information in front of the pilot's eyes—the full complement of modern communications. Now picture, just to the left of the throttles, two 9" x 12" trays marked IN and OUT.

TILT! It just doesn't fit, does it. Fighter pilots don't get memos in the cockpit. If they did, they wouldn't read them, and if they read them they'd get shot down.

Let's take this one step further. Try to imagine in the second seat behind the pilot a person who answers and places all the pilot's calls, opens the mail and drops it in the IN box (presumably between missions), picks up the contents of the OUT box, and does the pilot's typing and filing (filing? in a jet?).

I know this sounds silly; it's supposed to. The point is that modern communications is not a frill, it is an option that becomes more and more important as the environment increases its rate of change. Paper based communication was perfectly satisfactory when the pace of change was slow, but modern business runs on electronics.[15] You know this already. Nothing really important ever comes in the mail—certainly not the interoffice mail. If it's important you get a call or a fax.

You may be surprised to know that your information ecology runs on paper. Feasibility plans are on paper. System specifications are on paper. Flow charts are on paper. So are program listings, user documentation, test plans, backup and recovery plans, development methodology, project plans, status reports, project files, change requests, production change requests, performance reports, terminal moves and changes requests, change order confirmations, data models, data definitions, capacity analyses, and Christmas party invitations, to name just a few.

This is enormous folly. Experience with transforming the development and infrastructure management to electronic communications has shown 30% to 1000% increases in productivity and associated hard dollar saves. Quality goes up, speed goes up, costs go down. So why hasn't the electronic flow of information already taken hold in the information ecology? Two big reasons:

- *Buyer-seller thinking makes it difficult to identify benefits.* As sellers, the systems people don't feel free to initiate these changes by themselves. As buyers, the business people don't see as much benefit to overhauling the communications environment for linkage as they see in alternative functional changes to their applications. The systems community sees the need for a company wide change; business units see the relationship in much narrower terms.
- *Buyer-seller thinking masks the symmetric nature of the function.* If you apply electronic communications to the systems side alone you get benefits in the 30% to 50% range. If you apply electronic communications to the systems and business side together, benefits grow to astronomical sizes. *Buyer-seller* thinking makes it difficult for the business (buyer) side to see why *they* should change anything.

For the rest of this chapter I'm going to illustrate how today's electronic communication could support the business technology linkage.

Team Member	Functional Role	Organization	Location
MariLou	Data Expert	Systems	Denver
Su Cheong	Infrastructure expert	Systems	Denver
Rachel	Implementer	Systems	Denver
Kevin	Implementer	Systems	Denver
Alice	Testing expert	Cloud Widgets	Dallas
Ruth	Documentation and training expert	Grass Widgets	Atlanta
George	Customer service expert	Pavement Widgets	Detroit
Cynthia	Project team leader	Pavement Widgets	Detroit

Exhibit 9.5 **Example of a Geographically Dispersed and Organizationally Dispersed Team**

Exhibit 9.5 is a familiar team roster. Remember these people? Let's take a close-up of some of the things that happened during their project work together.

Cynthia's boss at Pavement Widgets, Clark Kent, walked into her office late Friday afternoon and dropped a thick notebook on her desk. "This is a consulting study," he said, "that has convinced us that we need a new integrated customer service system for all three widget companies. Starting now you're the full time team leader for the North American Integrated Customer Service Excellence System… get it?… N.I.C.E.… You're going to be a NICE project manager.

"And, it will be a NICE project," concluded Cynthia with a crooked smile. Clark wished her a nice weekend with an ironic chuckle, waved airily, and departed. Cynthia's gaze fell to the notebook which suddenly looked a lot heavier than it had just a moment before. She sighed, picked it up, and started reading.

Four days later Cynthia and her project team were gathered in a pleasant high-tech conference room in the Denver Systems Center. The out-of-towners had flown in the afternoon before and the group had assembled for dinner at a local cowboy style restaurant where men's ties are against the rules and violators have their neckwear amputated. The bottom halves of hundreds of neckties were nailed to the rough wood walls, evidence of violations past. The dinner had been strictly social, a way to break the ice and start some team spirit. It seemed to work pretty well but the atmosphere in the room this morning was still expectant.

Cynthia started the meeting by welcoming everyone to the NICE project team, thanking the Denver Systems Center for the use of their facility, and outlining the work for the day.

"This is probably the only time we will meet in person for the duration of the project. The next time we are all in the same room will be for the victory party!

"This physical meeting has three purposes. The first is team building. We all know that teams work better together over communication nets if the people involved have had at least one face to face meeting. Well, this is ours. So feel free to put your face in everybody else's.

"The other purposes of the meeting are to rough out the system design and project plan. We'll work from now 'til lunch on the system design and after lunch we'll do the project plan. One of the reasons we came to Denver is that they have a lot of these nice design rooms with the best group support software we can find.

"First thing tomorrow morning we'll have a video meeting with the steering committee and show them the design and planning results. After that, the out-of-towners will hit the road for home.

"Before our first topic here's the list of organizational steps I've taken since I got this project."

She touched the keyboard at her side and the large screen behind her lit up with a list of topics. She used the electronic pointer as she went down the list explaining that she had registered the project with the Corporate Controller's office, established a project NICE group file, assembled short biographies including hers and full contact information for each of the team members, and had the consulting study and all the associated work papers scanned. She'd added the personnel information and all background material to the project group file.

"As usual, the project group file is organized to give the steering committee access to the finished products only. Our working documents and messages are available only to the team members. Ruth is the documentation specialist and sysop[16] for the project group file.

"By the way, I am assuming that all of you will register as full-time team members. Does anyone have a problem with that?"

Cynthia looked around the room at the attentive faces. She was pleased that in the circle people hadn't grouped themselves by either location or function; the dinner must have helped. She continued.

"I'm proposing we adopt the standard corporate values statement and incorporate the usual development team principles. Are you all familiar with these?" A pause while heads nodded. "Well, be sure to review them and, if anything needs to be changed, put up a message in the project group file and we'll discuss it.

"Well, I think that about covers the team organization stuff. If you don't have any input on the general subject of how we'll work together, we'll get started," she glanced from face to face.

"Now," she said, "You guys know the drill. We brainstorm desirable design features first. No judgment, just get the ideas out. Comments on other ideas that extend them are fine, but don't try to fine tune things. Let's go to work."

All the team members turned their backs to the circle and moved their chairs up to one of the workstations placed on tables around three sides of the room. Each person settled into a comfortable posture in front of the screen but nobody touched the keyboard yet.

"First topic," said Cynthia as she pulled herself up to her workstation, "is related to problem scope. Imagine you're a customer. What questions would you want answers to when you call customer service? Why else would you call?

"Okay, the topic is live. Get started."

Team members turned to their workstations and began responding to the topic. Each screen had two parts. In one part the team member could compose his thought, typing, editing, and changing what he'd written until it suited him and he released it. In the other part of the screen, the shared part, he could see the entries of the other team members. Slowly, at first, and then more and more quickly ideas appeared in the shared portion of the screen as team members completed thoughts and released them.

Some team members ignored the shared screen at first, simply typing their ideas as fast as they could and releasing them. After exhausting their first rush of ideas, these members began reading the shared list, finding new inspiration in some of the entries and adding to the list.

After ten minutes the initial furious pace of new ideas had passed and slowly people reviewed the aggregate list of ideas, from time to time expanding an idea. There were nearly 200 statements in the list describing what a customer might want when he called customer service.

Cynthia called for the group's attention and as everyone swiveled around to form the group circle again, Cynthia began. "I've put the list up on the big screen. As I scroll down the list, anybody who doesn't understand one of the ideas, speak up." Quickly, the group ran down the long list of ideas, clarifying the few that weren't completely understood. "Everybody ready to rank?" asked Cynthia. The team members bustled back to their screens.

Now each team member went through the ideas one at a time and entered a number from one to ten for each idea. Ten indicated a most important potential function and one an unimportant function. Each team member had a section of the screen in which to work on the ideas at his own pace and another section available, if desired, to see the average score and distribution of scores for each idea as the team process continued. Some team members went charging ahead without regard for what others were doing. Some held back to get a feeling for what others thought important before scoring the list themselves. Some looked at what the group as a whole was doing and went back and changed their own scores.

In another ten minutes, the 200 ideas were weighted and ranked by the whole group. Cynthia called the group to order again. She pointed to the list on the big screen.

"There's a clear split here after the first 35 ideas. After that the average score drops way off. Let's take these 35, then, as the first cut of the functional requirement.

"Okay, so those are the things that customers will want when they call. The second topic goes like this: imagine you are a customer service representative; what are the features that you will want to use to answer these calls? We'll take a ten minute break and brainstorm the system as viewed by the customer service representative when we come back."

The morning passed quickly. By lunch the team had a preliminary conceptual design for the new customer service system. They added a full set of operational and technical considerations to the customer and service rep requirements. Then they brainstormed all the things that might go wrong.

In the afternoon, they used a similar group work approach to come up with all the steps that would have to be taken to complete the project. Another tool helped them work out which activities had to be completed before others could begin and to assign skills to the various tasks. They used a group estimating tool to make a first cut of the time required to do each task. By mid-afternoon the team had organized itself around the outline they would use for the teleconference with the steering committee.

One team converted their planning results to a project management system. The other put together parts of the presentation to describe the conceptual design they had developed. All the work was done on-line in the same high-tech design room using the corporate standard software for presentations.

By 6:45 they had a complete presentation. They ran through it, critiqued it together and wrapped it up before 8:00 PM. The out-of-towners arranged to eat together ("At a real restaurant this time—no cowboys, please") and the Denverites headed home.

You'll be happy to know that the teleconference the next day with the four managers who made up the steering committee went very well. Afterward, the team had a long lunch together and then headed in their various directions back to work or the airport. We pick up the story about a six weeks later.

"Maybe vacations just aren't worth the trouble," Cynthia thought to herself as she set down her first cup of coffee, squared her shoulders, sighed loudly, and started back to work. Two icons glowed with urgent red in the center of her workstation screen. One was the icon that represented the NICE project group file; the other was her electronic mail. Little numbers next to the icons told her that 286 items had been added to the project file while she was on vacation and there were 312 items unread in her electronic mail.

She pointed at the e-mail icon and clicked it. A window opened on her screen with a list of e-mail titles waiting to be read. The most recent item in the list was from George. "He must have mailed this from home" thought Cynthia, "it's dated last night. He really takes being acting team leader seriously." She clicked on the message line and as the text of George's message opened on her screen her workstation speakers let loose with the first four bars of "Hail to the Chief." Cynthia laughed out loud.

The note welcomed her back, assured her that all was well, and directed her attention to a report in the project group file on the simulated user interface focus group results for the customer service reps. She considered clicking on the link button that George had thoughtfully included in this mail note. The link button would take her directly to the place in the project group file George mentioned, but she decided to wait until she'd seen more of her mail. She closed George's note and asked her workstation to select new mail items from her boss Clark and other members of the steering committee. There were seven items. One by one she clicked them, read them, and closed them. One of them was an attaboy on the functional spec from the President of Clouds. Before closing it, she forwarded it to the team group code, sending a copy automatically to each of the team members and to the project group file.

As she worked through her e-mail, Cynthia found the usual patterns.

A lot of the messages were from her voicemail system, which she played by clicking on them. She searched out the ones that might be interesting and left the long ones or the ones likely to be dull for another time.

There were a lot of administrative messages: the security administration standard procedures has been updated, highlights include...; due to tax law changes the reimbursement parameter in the expense reporting system for personal car use has been changed...; pictures in the human resources system will be updated at least every three years....

There were a lot of forms to be approved. As NICE team leader, the steering committee had asked her to assume approval responsibility for all the hardware, software, and physical plant procurement. More than 100 of her e-mail messages were various requisition forms for her approval. She examined each one for a suitable link to the NICE project group file, which would supply the purchase justification. Most of these she knew without actually referring to the group file; on one requisition she clicked the link and a window opened into the part of the NICE project group file that justified the request. Quickly satisfied, she clicked back to the requisition and approved it.

After approving all the new requisitions, Cynthia clicked an icon that she had customized to take her to the part of the NICE project group file that kept track of resources committed on the project. The requisitions she had just approved had updated the portion of the file, which showed "committed but not received." She noted the numbers and moved back to her mail.

The next item she accessed turned out to be from the Marketing Department. It was a sample of the latest television image ads, which stressed the full line of widgets. She clicked on the icon embedded in the message and a window opened and played the full video and audio of the new ad. Cynthia thought to herself that the Marketing people were really exploiting multimedia capabilities very well. She typed out a quick congratulatory note to her contact in Marketing and linked the note and the ad to the project group file before she sent it.

One of the more interesting new mail items was an employee attitude survey. She had been selected to answer a bunch of questions to "help executive management stay in touch with the feelings of all staff members about important corporate issues." The survey was a simple set of questions with choices to be clicked on. She rapidly worked through the survey form and then clicked the part of the form that caused it to be returned automatically. She noted that the survey results were going to be available in about a week, so she made a note on her electronic personal calendar to remind her to see how it had come out.

Finally, with her e-mail under control, Cynthia turned her attention again to the NICE project group file. When she clicked the icon, she found that almost every major category of the project file had items marked unread. She slowly worked her way through the new entries.

Changes in functional specification were very minor. The additions to the file were mostly e-mail notes from some of the stragglers indicating their approval.

Project plan updates were plentiful, but thankfully nearly all represented task completions.

There were a lot of technical updates to the file: interface specs, new code references, hardware compatibility test results, and so forth. Cynthia just skimmed these.

The on-line staff meeting section of the project file took most of her time. In this section, each team member made comments on topics of general interest that all team members could read. It was like a continuous conversation. The entries varied from deep to trivial, from technical to social, and from serious to humorous. "They're great people," she thought. "This team is really shaping up. And, it's a good thing too 'cause this project is half done." She added a note to say that she was back, had enjoyed her vacation, and had read the project file up to date.[17]

We already know that the project turned out pretty well. Cynthia had some problems with Alice and George, but all in all the result was considered a modest success. Let's look in on the team just once more to see what happened at the end of the project.

Rachel pondered her workstation screen. The window that had her attention was a simple survey form. It asked her to evaluate how well MariLou had performed as data expert for the recently completed NICE project. The actions required of the data expert role were listed and a place existed where Rachel could enter her evaluation score for each action. It also asked her to give a confidence weighting for each of her scores. The form had an option for each action entry where Rachel could put in a link to someplace in the NICE project group file to support or illustrate her evaluation. The form was simple—fifteen actions, two numbers to enter for each—but Rachel took her time. She knew that these evaluations were important and she wanted to give them the same degree of care that she hoped the others in the team would give to her evaluations.

In a couple of minutes, Rachel had completed the functional role evaluation form on MariLou and went on to the individual adherence form. This one was the same for everybody. It listed the values of the group and asked for a score for the individual's adherence to the value. Again there was also a confidence weighting and a place for any supporting links. This was easier for Rachel because she had formed clear impressions of the other members of the team as they worked together even though she had met half of them in person only once.

With the functional role evaluation and individual adherence evaluation done for MariLou, only two more people on the team remained to evaluate, Cynthia, the team leader and Rachel herself. Rachel thought to herself, "The easiest and hardest left… I'll do the easy one first" and then she called up the forms for evaluating Cynthia as the team leader. Click, click, link, link… this one was a snap. The adherence form was just as easy. Click, click and it's done. "Now for the tough one," she thought, "Why are self-evaluations always so hard?"

While Rachel struggled with the last of her team evaluation forms, at the other end of the Denver Systems Center, Kevin opened the e-mail message from the team evaluation system which said his results on the NICE project team were complete and clicked on the link that took him to the team evaluation system itself. There were his scores. Next to each required action for an implementer was the weighted score that he'd been given by the members of the team and next to that was the score he'd given himself. As he stepped down the report from action to action, he was very pleased and a little surprised. His teammates had consistently rated his functional performance better than he had rated himself!

He clicked quickly into the e-mail system and sent off a quick note of thanks to all the people on the team. "I'm very pleased," he wrote, "that you think so highly of my work. I'd love to work with all of you again. Good luck!"[18]

The close-up look we have taken in the last few pages of the workaday mechanics of the NICE project team is not science fiction. Everything described and implied in this scenario is today's technology.[19] Not bleeding edge, most of it just ordinary stuff we can do with products off the shelf. I have worked in an organization where all of these things could be done and most of them were. I believe that this topic is important enough to prompt another management principle.

Potential Principle: We will invest in understanding, implementing, and using technology to support group work.

This chapter has been about how we can use technology itself to improve the business technology linkage. The important ideas I would like you to take from this chapter are these.

- Infrastructure and associated processes are usually pretty well instrumented and measured for a combination of healthy and not so healthy reasons. Most of the focus of this measurement is on *sustain.*
- Transaction processing applications *and the associated processes* need a lot more measurement than they usually get.
- MIS applications should provide measurements about our allocation of resources but usually don't do this well. We need to improve our mental models of how allocation works before we can effectively instrument MIS processes and measure useful things.
- The system development and maintenance resource is the key enabler of business process reengineering and is pivotal in balancing *sustain* and *transform.*
- System development and maintenance is primarily a communication activity and improving its productivity and effectiveness requires a focus on communications.
- There are a lot of things good system development managers measure that produce improved performance, but the key thing to measure about system development and maintenance is how the resource is allocated. We don't do this well.
- Don't use time reporting systems for charge-backs!
- If teams are the fundamental device we for execution, then teams are the appropriate level at which to manage and report allocation.
- The information ecology is largely paper based and there is an enormous potential increase in productivity and effectiveness possible by converting to modern communications technology to support the system development and maintenance process.

- In order to get the benefit, the *buyer-seller* model of the relationship must give way to partnership and team models and all members of the teams must share in the new technology.

This chapter brings to a close the section of the book that describes the business technology linkage and how it might be improved. The next four chapters integrate all of the topics we have covered in the book so far and attempt to lay out a coherent approach to managing the information ecology. We start with infrastructure.

Notes

1. There is a very large literature on the subject of measuring things in the information ecology. It stretches from broad issues like trying to figure out what we get for our investment (see Dejarnett 1992, Gold 1992, Kaplan and Norton 1992) to very narrow issues like the internal use of system resources or the productivity of programmers (see DeMarco 1982, Jones 1986, Rubin April 1992, Weinberg 1991). The topic is not often covered in a broad , integrated way.
2. I happen to believe that thorough instrumentation of transaction processing systems is just as important to healthy *sustain* activities as to *transform.*
3. For a view similar to mine see Johnson and Kaplan 1987.
4. I say largely useless, not completely useless. Financial engineering, the only activity that should draw on this mental model of a business, is occasionally a useful thing to do.
5. Eccles 1985 puts the entire transfer pricing and allocation process in a theoretical context that makes it much easier to deal with. He emphasizes the arbitrary nature of any particular solution and provides some extremely useful material for avoiding "religious wars."
6. See, for example, Fairley 1989.
7. The estimate for developer activity combines information from Jones 1986 with a diary study I did as part of the work of Citibank's Advanced Technology Office Program in 1978.
8. See DeMarco 1982.
9. See Rubin April 1992.
10. Complex systems are more expensive to build and maintain than simple ones.
11. Intuition suggests that the more bugs we've found in a system the fewer would be left. The exact opposite is true. The best predictor of the likelihood of a program failing is the number of times it has failed in the past (see Weinberg 1991).
12. Good system developers can produce working programs 100 times faster than average developers using the same tools (see Jones 1986).
13. The best builders are not usually the best fixers. Perhaps, it's because poor builders get more practice finding and fixing defects than good builders.
14. The only time such a system can be used without damaging your systems organization is when you decide to let them charge business units a price for their services rather than a cost. If you allow the systems unit to actually profit on these transactions, you will introduce the correct incentives on the sell side for a buyer seller relationships. Captive buyers, on the other hand, might become a problem.
15. I have a certain nostalgia for a world of fine calligraphy, wax seals, and the stately pace of carefully crafted letters exchanged between thoughtful correspondents. After

all, I chose to write a book here, not a music video. On the other hand, I don't want any business I depend on to run that way.

16. Sysop is electronic communication jargon for the person who takes charge of house-keeping for a shared on-line file like the ones described here. The term is a contraction of system operator and came into general use in the area of on-line bulletin board systems. The sysop is generally responsible to see that members play by the rules, that the structure of the information in the shared file is reasonable, and that junk is excised periodically.

17. Some of the cultural impacts of this kind of technology are discussed in LaPlante May 1993.

18. The process and impact of peer and superior reviews are discussed in Bernadin and Beatty Summer 1987 and English 1992.

19. Tom Davenport and Jim McGee specifically call "groupware," as described in this scenario, "the prototypical product for the ecologically-oriented firm" (see Davenport and McGee 1994).

10

Sustain and Transform Infrastructure

This chapter is about how to *sustain* and *transform* infrastructure. We always think of infrastructure as *under* something or, perhaps, under *everything*. It's that which must be there for anything else to flourish. The simplest view of the information ecology infrastructure equates it with the bottom blocks in the diagram in Exhibit 10.1: data centers, networks, and their equipment and connections. We might think of infrastructure as the portion of the information ecology analogous to a park's terrain—the earth, molded and contoured to our needs, the river dredged and manicured, the artful pond, the paths, the roads, the bridges, and all the carefully engineered barriers, ditches, drainage tunnels, and pumps.

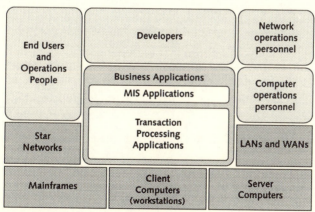

Exhibit 10.1 Components of the Information Ecology

Whether we talk about the infrastructure of companies, cities, buildings, or governments, most people find infrastructure dull. This is actually the key fact about infrastructure. It's dull—we don't care much about it. *We don't have to care much about it!* Infrastructure is all that stuff that is essential, important, and vital, and to whose details we are indifferent.

Think about the electrical power in your house. The power grid is part of the community's infrastructure and the distribution to and within your house is part of the house's infrastructure. Most of us would agree that we don't know or care how the power is generated, controlled, and distributed; we don't have any particular understanding of or interest in how the power comes to the wall sockets; we expect that the power will always be there; if the power goes out, we wait for an expert to fix it; if the expert fails, we're in big trouble; we want the power to be as cheap as possible—good power is cheap power; all we need to know is how to plug things in; we are perfectly willing to share the power service as long as we get the service we need; and, we are happy to agree to standards for voltage, frequency, wiring, grounding, and power outlets as long as we are completely free to use the power without interference from the power company.

A similar list of feelings and expectations could be made for the water or sewer systems in our house or for the air conditioning or elevators in our office buildings or for the bridges, roads, and tunnels in our cities. The common elements are:

- We don't know much about it and we don't much care.
- We expect it to always be there.
- If it breaks, we expect an expert to fix it, and if it isn't fixed, we're in trouble.
- Using it is very simple.
- It's better when it's cheaper.
- We are willing to share it.
- We are willing to accept the discipline of standards to keep it simple and cheap.

That's how we think about infrastructure, including the information infrastructure. Let's try to get into the mind of the person who *manages* the infrastructure. His perspective is very different. He would probably think thoughts like these.

- Nobody knows much of anything about what I do and they don't much care.
- The only time they ever think about what I do is when it breaks or when they have to pay for it.
- The way I do a good job is to make the service reliable and cheap.
- I will design the service so that all of the complication is on my side; I can trust my team to deal with the complexity, but I can't trust my user not to screw up.

- I can get the unit price down by getting as many users as possible.
- My business is so complicated and the user's attention span so short that my billing scheme has to be very simple.
- Only the occasional emergency gets people to think how important this function is but I don't mind taking charge of emergencies, especially if the emergency obviously isn't my fault, because it is my opportunity for recognition.

It seems to me that the values of such a person naturally would be stability, consistency, and safety. Interpersonal skills that build loyalty and trust would be important. Careful calculation, shrewd negotiation, clarity of purpose, and a firm grasp of key facts would seem to suit such a role. It would be easy for this person to forego flexibility. Marketing skills would be essentially useless. In my experience, this is a good description of the people who run the information infrastructure.

What might such a role and such a mindset mean for the balance between *sustain* and *transform*?

Clearly, *sustain* is the key activity. Stability, consistency, and safety suit *sustain*. *Sustain* is very comfortable in the world of infrastructure. On the other hand, the technology of which the information infrastructure is made is the very essence of *transform*. No technology has ever evolved as quickly and dramatically as the technology of computers and communications. The price performance of computers has improved by a factor of ten every 36 to 48 months for 30 years. Similar price performance improvement has occurred in data communication for nearly 20 years.[1] Information infrastructure managers couldn't ignore the effects of these dramatic changes, so they learned to adapt within the context of *sustain*.

The most significant adaptation made by information infrastructure management to this pace of change was to regularize and institutionalize the introduction of the next generation of equipment. Since the early 1970s, major computer upgrades have been frequent events in every data center. Most data centers have mastered this drill so well that the changes occur without anyone noticing. This is a feat not unlike changing the engines on a plane in flight.

Of course, in order to make these changes invisible, there are strict constraints. The new machine must be very like the old machine in important ways. This encourages an IBM data center to remain one, a tendency so strong that an industry has been built on it.[2] IBM's design standards became de facto industry standards for mainframes. It has taken extraordinary forces to break the absolute lock these standards have had on our data centers.

Information infrastructure managers learned to perform a kind of transformation that fit firmly with their values. They mastered the art of replacing the old IBM mainframe to take advantage of the technology's dramatic improvement in price performance. They applied the values of *sustain* to a very specific transformation and, as a result, made this continuing radical change a part of *sustain.* Information infrastructure management has adopted a similar strategy for managing the continuous change in data communications. A torrid pace of price performance improvement can be maintained as long as the new equipment corresponds in important ways to the old equipment. Much as the data center has tended to be *frozen* into the IBM design standards, so have the data communication networks been frozen into the standards of the IBM-style network.

And so our information infrastructure learned to accommodate radical change within its culture of *sustain… as long as it was the right kind of change.*

This strategy succeeded without serious challenge until the consequences of the PC revolution were seen clearly and network computing was recognized as a fundamental transformation. Since the mid '80s the price performance of mainframe style computers and star networks has continued to improve but not nearly as fast as the potential price performance of network computing. The other benefits of network computing—flexibility, small investment increments, superior software concepts, inherent reliability, and low cost of entry— along with the massive and growing price performance advantage, have led start-up enterprises to adopt the new technology, but not so the large company.

The information infrastructure manager in the established large company does not know how to manage a transition to this technology and is disinclined by personality and experience to learn. The values, attitudes, and skills of *transform* are totally foreign to the typical information infrastructure manager. Hence, the hostility between the dinosaurs and the propeller heads.

As if this weren't enough, another powerful force tends to keep infrastructure management tightly focused on *sustain.* This force emerges from a combination of influences.

- *Performance focus:* Having achieved a satisfactory level of service and reliability, the only way an infrastructure manager can distinguish himself is by improving the price performance of the infrastructure.
- *Slow, difficult upgrades:* Infrastructure upgrades are difficult and require careful planning and implementation… and time.
- *Demands on capital:* Infrastructure is capital intensive and useful upgrades often require large capital outlays.
- *Management indifference:* Since infrastructure is of no interest to most people, it is very difficult to attract management attention to improving it.
- *Low priority:* Competitive pressures on expenses and the relative obscurity of infrastructure combine to make infrastructure maintenance a very low priority investment area.

These influences combine to produce a high probability of deteriorating infrastructure. We've seen the effect in our physical infrastructure—deteriorating roads, bridges, tunnels, and water and sewer systems. Deterioration in physical systems is decay. Deterioration in information infrastructure is obsolescence. The results are roughly the same; after a long period of neglect the systems become suddenly useless or nearly useless. Deteriorated physical systems break; deteriorated information systems can't meet new requirements or can't be maintained. The result in both cases is a sudden urgent need for a large capital investment that users are reluctant to make but are impatient to have.

It's easy to see and understand this problem as it has impacted our physical infrastructure. Suddenly bridges fall down, huge holes open up in the roads, and water mains burst and flood whole neighborhoods. Things got this bad because maintenance was neglected. Support of the infrastructure didn't compete effectively for funds and the infrastructure rotted invisibly. We know this just isn't right. A rational person would say that infrastructure maintenance is a special class of expense to which we commit ourselves unconditionally when we acquire an infrastructure asset. The maintenance is not optional, it's obligatory if we want to continue to get the benefit of the asset.

The information infrastructure is subtly different. It doesn't physically wear out[3] but it "wears out" functionally. The purpose for which the infrastructure was conceived and constructed changes over time and the unchanging infrastructure is ultimately unusable for the altered purpose. The computer system originally intended to support 10 transactions per second is unsuitable when the requirement changes to 1000 transactions per second. The network intended to support data communications between terminals and the mainframe is unsuitable when the requirement changes to audio, video, and image messages between workstations.

The answer to keeping the information infrastructure usable is the same as the answer for keeping the roads and bridges usable… keep spending the money for necessary maintenance.

Any manager needs help to do this part of the job. An information ecology infrastructure manager needs *special* help. The information infrastructure is special because routine maintenance (patching and painting) isn't enough to deal with the pace of change. Even the super high-tech "patching and painting" that information infrastructure managers have learned to do to upgrade mainframes and networks isn't enough. The infrastructure manager needs to learn to deal with *transform* and general managers need to learn to deal with *transform* in the infrastructure.

There are two things we need to learn in order to deal with *transform* in the information infrastructure. Specifically, we must:

- Manage appropriate and consistent investment in information infrastructure.
- Link transform in business processes to the information infrastructure.

Let's look at these one at a time.

Capital use in the information infrastructure

The information infrastructure consists mostly of tangible equipment and associated software. There are few consumables aside from paper and electricity. Drawing on our representative company from Chapter 2, we see that NatNec's information infrastructure expenses look like Exhibit 10.2.

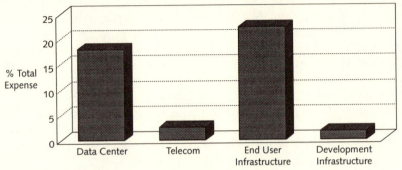

Exhibit 10.2 Infrastructure Components of Total IT Expense for Representative Company

Information infrastructure represents about 45% of the total cost of the information ecology. That's certainly an important portion of the entire information ecology cost, but knowing the cost does not tell us much about how to manage it. Exhibit 10.3 takes another slice of the $79.8 million that makes up the infrastructure 45%.

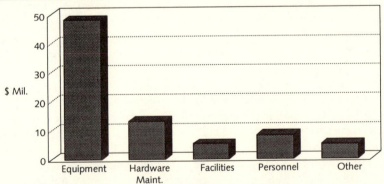

Exhibit 10.3 Line Item Breakdown of Representative Company's Infrastructure Expense

It's not hard to see what the information infrastructure manager spends his time on. The equipment, the equipment maintenance, and the housing for the equipment constitute 83% of the total infrastructure expense. Clearly it's equipment expense that the manager focuses on. We, on the other hand, are focusing on the use of *capital* in the information infrastructure, so let's ask, how much of the company's capital are we using?

Does anybody know what this stuff costs?

If we assume a five-year replacement cycle for the equipment and 20 years for the facilities, we can estimate that the information infrastructure represents about $350 million in equipment and buildings. We don't make decisions about buildings too often, so let's take the facilities costs out of the discussion. That leaves us with $242 million in equipment that the company is paying for in some way or another. If these were all straight purchases, we'd see the expense in the depreciation line and the asset on the balance sheet. If these were capital leases, we'd see the expense in the lease payments line and the leasehold asset and future payments liability on the balance sheet. If these were operating leases, we'd see the expense as equipment rental but there might not be a balance sheet entry. These three options alone suggest why it's difficult to pin down the amount of capital in use. Add to that the fact that when you are prepared to spend a *quarter billion dollars* on anything, there are a lot of options about how to go about it.

A major occupation of most information infrastructure managers is attending to the details of buying much of this equipment. His major preoccupation is buying it in such a way that the overall expenses of the information infrastructure are reduced from year to year. With all the different individual purchases, with all the changes in product price performance, with all the options available for financing the purchase, and with all the flexibility the vendor will have on terms and conditions, this objective is usually met but in the process, it becomes very difficult to develop a clear understanding of how much of the company's capital is in use in the information infrastructure.

Does anybody know what this stuff is worth?

It's even more difficult to get a clear understanding of how much infrastructure we get for the capital in use. Let's try an analogy.

Imagine we build a $20 million widget factory. It took three years to plan and build and was finished last year. The factory is on our books now as an asset worth $20 million. As a new factory we can expect it to build modern widgets in a modern way and, assuming we didn't over pay to build it, its *functional value* is probably about its asset value, $20 million. If there is a good market for widgets and we want to be in the widget business and we know how to operate a widget factory, its *useful value* to us is probably the same $20 million.

Imagine now that our $20 million factory is five years old and the value on our books is now $15 million. Since we built the factory, a new process has been invented that has revolutionized the manufacture of widgets and our factory can no longer compete. Its functional value for anything other than scrap has disappeared. Since we can't use it to compete effectively even if we want to and know how, its useful value has disappeared too. Our factory is obsolescent and essentially worthless.

Now imagine instead that there has been no new process for manufacturing widgets. Imagine that the bottom dropped out of the widget market and you can't give the things away. The asset and functional value of the factory may still be $15 million, but the useful value is zero.

Or imagine that there is still a pretty good market for widgets, but it's impossible to get anyone to work in our widget factory. Again, the asset and functional value of the factory may still be $15 million, but the useful value to us is zip!

In these two cases, our factory isn't obsolete but it's essentially worthless to us.

In information systems infrastructure the same things happen, but faster. Information system products, like all products, change from one product cycle to the next in response to changes in buyer requirements and technical innovation. The influence of technical innovation is more important to information system products than to many other kinds of products and it is fair to say that much of the buyer requirement is response to innovation per se. It's there because they'll buy it and they'll buy it because it's there. As a result, the product cycle is a good proxy for the rate of change of the functional requirement.[4] Product obsolescence results as the functional requirement diverges from the product's features.

Useful value, on the other hand, begins at a low level for a new product (rarely higher than the useful value of the preceding generation of the product) and grows as we acquire knowledge of how to use it. Then it begins to decay as functional value obsolesces. The asset value of the product may also be undercut by very rapid price reductions that are characteristic of information technology products. *Asset value, as reflected on our books, is a poor measure of either functional value or useful value.*

The time required for large-scale computer and communication equipment planning, procurement, acquisition, and deployment is about the same as the equipment's product cycle time. Consequently, anything that is actually in use is probably out of date; not useless, but probably less useful than originally considered to be. Someplace between two and three product cycles, obsolescent becomes obsolete. Functional value rapidly diverges from asset value.

Vendors keep large customers informed of the details of the next product cycle or two by giving "nondisclosure" briefings in which the tentative features of the next generation products are disclosed. By the time the product is announced, it's old news. By the time it is in service, it's at least partially obsolescent. If we could—in a single day—understand, plan, purchase, and put into use a complete information infrastructure of computers and communication gear, wires and workstations, we would have an information infrastructure the functional value of which is exactly its price, but functional value decays from the day the requirements are set. By the time the equipment is installed and in use, a portion of its value is already lost to obsolescence.

Useful value follows a bit more complicated curve. When a product is first disclosed, neither the vendor or the customer has a complete knowledge of its potential application. It takes about a year of real use before a true understanding develops. Over the life of a typical information system hardware product, the market price drops by a factor of three to six. Buying into a new product early minimizes the functional obsolescence, but at the risk of purchasing at a premium price before the usability of the product is well established.

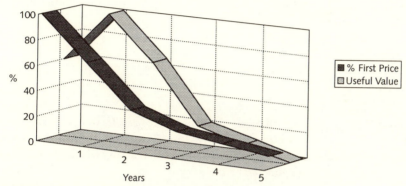

Exhibit 10.4 Typical Price Value History for Information System Products

The curves in Exhibit 10.4 suggest a strategy—buy the new product after it has been in use for six months to a year then shift to the next generation product before the product is three years old. This "rapid follower" strategy is, in fact, a popular one for many technology-aware companies. It is rarely carefully articulated, however. Few companies spend the time to understand the price value relationships of their information infrastructure components.

Managing information infrastructure value

I have made some very broad generalizations in the last couple of sections and it should be understood that we can't wish away the complications of this topic and expect to manage it. On the other hand, I believe that what is important in infrastructure management is pretty clear. Information infrastructure must:

- Meet the needs of the business.
- Perform at an acceptable level of reliability.
- Be appropriately secure from compromise and appropriately recoverable in the event of business disruption.

These requirements, consistent with the needs of *sustain*, are usually well met by our existing infrastructure management policies and practices. In addition, however, I believe that the information infrastructure must meet the needs of *transform*:

- Limit obsolescence to a degree consistent with the needs of the business to change rapidly.
- Identify and adopt infrastructure transformations that enable the business to compete effectively.

Both of these objectives are in conflict with the basic values and principles of the usual information infrastructure manager. Different values and principles will have to be introduced from outside the information infrastructure management—in a hierarchy, this means new values and principles from the CIO and the rest of executive management.

In Chapter 2, we spent time analyzing how much money to spend on the information ecology as a whole. I suggest that it is important not only to plan the *expense* of the information infrastructure but also to plan the amount of the firm's capital we will put to use as information infrastructure. Consider the following management principle.

Potential Principle: **We will determine the level of capital that we wish to devote to the information infrastructure and maximize the useful value of the infrastructure within that level of capital over time.**

In practice it makes sense to apply this principle to subcategories within the information infrastructure. For example, we might decide to manage the information infrastructure in these parts.[5]

- *Computing devices:* mainframe computers, minicomputers, transaction servers
- *Mass storage devices:* disk, drum, and tape systems attached to mainframes and minicomputers, file servers
- *Data communication devices:* front-end computers, controllers, switches, routers, bridges, gateways, modems, multiplexers
- *Data communication lines:* wiring, leased and rented communication services arrangements
- *End user terminal devices:* terminals, workstations, point-of-sale terminals
- *Infrastructure control equipment:* monitoring equipment, alternative routing switches, capacity analysis equipment
- *Dedicated facilities:* data centers, communication closets, microwave towers
- *Operating capital:* capital equivalents to support-related expense streams

Imagine that we have some kind of analysis that supplies the information for a table like the one in Exhibit 10.5. The idea of the table is conceptual. It would probably require a sizable report to present all this information in a usable level of detail.

	Five year History of Capital Employed	Functional Value	Useful Value	Potential Transform Involvement
Computing devices				
Mass storage devices				
Data communication devices				
Data communication lines				
End user terminal devices				
Infrastructure control equipment				
Dedicated facilities				
Operating capital				
Total Information Infrastructure				

Exhibit 10.5   Conceptual Layout of MIS to Support Information Infrastructure Capital Investment

Assembling this information doesn't make decisions on information infrastructure for us, but it does make informed decisions possible. Let's look at the uses of the information.

- *Five-year history of capital employed.* The total capital employed for the information infrastructure combined with the history of various corporate dimensions (sales, offices, employees, earnings, total expenses, capital base, etc.) gives us insight into whether or not the capital in use in the information infrastructure has tracked with changes in the company. It alerts us to any unexpected buildup in the infrastructure and to any potential deterioration. The details show us where these changes are taking place.

- *Functional value:* Each cell gives information about how well the present array of equipment in the category meets the functional needs of the information ecology as a whole. This requires input from both infrastructure management and knowledgeable developers and users. We are trying to get an impression of how fast functional requirements are moving and how well we are keeping up.

- *Useful value:* Each cell gives information about how well the information ecology as a whole is using the array of equipment in the category. Judgments include an evaluation of the ability of the users to use the products, of the developers to exploit the features, and the infrastructure personnel to operate and maintain the equipment. This category also includes information on where the present equipment falls in the product life cycle. Information comes from experts in the functional area and the products.

- *Potential transform involvement:* Each cell gives information about the degree to which the infrastructure and product experts see this area as possibly involved in infrastructure transformation and the degree to which informed developers and users see this area as necessary for business process transformation.

An assembly of information like this supports information infrastructure allocation decisions in which executive management, financial management, infrastructure management, developers, and business users are all informed participants.

When is it infrastructure?

The discussion of infrastructure has dealt so far largely with equipment—typically boxes full of electronics. The trends toward network computing and radically different ways to build applications are complicating the notion of information infrastructure.

The PC revolution was transformational in a lot of ways, not the least of which was in information infrastructure. It was *transform* outside of the boundaries of the established infrastructure manager's comfort. The end users and some of the application developers built a new and competing information infrastructure. LANs, servers, and workstations—arguably infrastructure— were not embraced by the "infrastructure establishment."

To this day, the typical information infrastructure manager considers the LAN, server, and workstation world as a problem to be solved. He talks about "controlling the spread of PCs" and "solving the PC problem." As it has become clear in the last few years that this phenomenon is not going away, more information infrastructure managers have decided to try to regain control of network computing. The strategy is to point out the ways in which network computing fails to adhere to the values of infrastructure; it's not sufficiently cheap or sufficiently reliable or sufficiently simple to use. They are, of course, often right. The values of *transform* tend to be different and, ultimately when the work of *transform* is done, the new order must adopt the ways of *sustain*. How do we manage this shift?

Let's take a real example. Computers in a network exchange data by means of a series of communication protocols layered one upon another. Agreements must be made on all the levels of the protocol stack in order for communication to take place. If the layers are carefully selected and the boundaries between layers are standardized, then we are indifferent to the particular choices of protocols. The key word is *indifferent*. It's not that we are indifferent to the *existence* of these protocols. We care very much that they exist (without them the computers couldn't communicate), we just don't care about the *details*, as long as the interface is standard, the protocols (whatever they are) work reliably, and the whole thing is economical to operate. We would prefer, in fact, that some expert take over the management of these details providing, of course, that the expert is there promptly to fix any problems. This is infrastructure.

Exhibit 10.6 is a simple look at the layers of agreement that are required for computers to talk to each other. I've split the table to make a point about infrastructure. As long as the agreements in the bottom part of the table exist (including any necessary interface standards), the people making decisions about how to do the functions in the top part of the table are indifferent to the details of the lower level agreements.

Agreements about what can be talked about	Agreements on the kinds of messages which can be exchanged between computers
	Agreements on displaying and accepting information from people

Agreements on redundancy processing	Agreements on error handling
Agreements on language and usage	Agreements on codes and characters, message formats, and error correction
Agreements on flow control	Agreements on setting up and completing communication sessions
Agreements on signaling	Wire standards, electrical pulse standards, and connector standards

Exhibit 10.6 Simplified Model of the Network Protocol Stack (Agreements Required for Computers to Communicate) Illustrating the Split between Infrastructure and Non-Infrastructure.

Choices and standards in the lower part of the protocol stack become infrastructure from the point of view of the people working in the upper level of the stack. Just like any other infrastructure, the lower levels of the protocol stack are uninteresting to people working on the higher levels. In fact, people who are involved with designing the interface between people and computers (top level) are bored to death with the details of something like wiring or electrical signaling (bottom level). They will go out of their way to turn lower levels of this hierarchy into infrastructure and be grateful to whoever is willing to undertake the infrastructure's management.

There are relationships among many of the modern software component subsystems analogous to the layering of communications protocols, although somewhat more complicated in that these subsystems are related to several other subsystems, not just to ones above and below in a stack. A common element, however, is the role that standards can play. Given a good set of standards, the choices of software subsystems can become a matter of indifference to application developers. That is, the right set of standards and choices can turn many software subsystems into infrastructure. Here's another suggested management principle.

Potential Principle: **When a system component's relationships with other system components is specified by a suitable set of standards so that one product meeting the standards can be freely substituted for another and the standards are acceptable to all stakeholders, then we will manage the system component as infrastructure.**

This principle puts a heavy burden on the selection and adoption of standards. The people in our organizations that understand and follow the development of standards must be given a position of much more prominence than has been the case in the past because a primary key to simultaneously managing *sustain* and *transform* is to make as much of the information ecology as possible part of infrastructure without trading away flexibility and the ability to change radically and rapidly. The heart of such flexibility is the wide-scale adoption of well-defined standards.

With the best modern technology, system development can be 10 to 100 times more productive than the best 1980s technology by using reusable components. This dramatic improvement in productivity is critical to a permanent increased emphasis on *transform*. In order for this very responsive environment to be stable, usable, and safe, it must embody the virtues of *sustain*. The best way to achieve that is to push software subsystems and the bulk of network computing into the infrastructure. The key element to turn these things into infrastructure is good standards. Hence, the long-term success of a shift in the balance toward *transform* depends on intelligent management of standards in our information ecology.

This chapter has introduced the key ideas of how to balance *sustain* and *transform* in information infrastructure.

- We started by describing the common aspects of all infrastructure: it's dull; we want someone else to take care of it; we want it reliable and cheap; we're willing to share it and adhere to reasonable standards.
- We saw that infrastructure management has a strong culture of *sustain* and strong forces combine to put information infrastructure at risk of functional obsolescence.
- I proposed two principles to add to the culture and values of information infrastructure management to allow us to balance *sustain* with *transform*.
    1. The first suggested we determine the level of capital that we wish to devote to the information infrastructure and maximize over time the useful value of the infrastructure within that level of capital. I suggested an analysis that will provide the necessary quantitative and qualitative information on which well-informed allocation decisions in the area of information infrastructure can be made.
    2. The second principle provided a way to reassess continuously those aspects of the information ecology that should be managed as infrastructure and suggested that when a system component's relationships with other system components is specified by a suitable set of standards so that one product meeting the standards can be freely substituted for another and the standards are acceptable to all stakeholders, then the system component should be managed as infrastructure.
- This principle puts a dramatically increased emphasis on standards and the people and processes involved in adopting them.

The migration of major new portions of business application software into the infrastructure where they can be managed with the values of *sustain* frees the system development resource to shift toward being the agent of *transform*. Finding the right balance for system developers in this new role is the subject of Chapter 11.

Notes

1. See Tapscott and Caston 1993.
2. Companies, notably Amdahl, NEC, and Storage Technology build machines "just like IBM, 'cept better" so that the ease of upgrading could be maintained while reintroducing some market pressure.
3. Some things actually do wear out. Circuit cards, for instance, need to be replaced from time to time. This kind of maintenance is rarely neglected, but when obsolescence sets in, replacement circuit cards first become scarce and then ultimately unavailable.
4. A critic might be tempted to say that much of the change from product cycle to product cycle is technology change for the sake of technology and that changing business requirements have little to do with the design of new products, therefore the product change is not a proxy for need as much as a reflection of a desire for novelty. I suggest that, although information technology does have its "styles" and it's important to some techies to be "stylish," changing technology styles are truly meaningful and embody profound potential improvements. Early adopters, regardless of motive, get a head start in learning how to realize the new style's potential.
5. The breakdown of infrastructure components in this section is illustrative, not exhaustive. Any practical application of this MIS process should include an analysis of the pertinent infrastructure components, including consideration of software infrastructure.

11

Sustain and Transform in System Development

In Chapter 10, we talked about information infrastructure, the terrain of the information ecology. Our analogy suggested that infrastructure is like the earth, hills, valleys, and streams that shape a park. In this chapter, we look at how to manage system development—the landscapers, the gardeners, construction crews, and maintenance workers in the park.

The park takes on a different character depending on the choice and quality of walks, playgrounds, skating ponds, sailing ponds, an outdoor theater, a zoo, a carousel, a croquet lawn, a cricket pitch, a river for rafting, or a formal garden for contemplation. Likewise, our information ecology takes on different character with the choices and quality of the business applications which we support.

We estimated in Chapter 2 that 65% of the system development resource in a typical system development organization is devoted to building and changing business applications. In most large organizations, these changes are made mostly at the margins of business function. Friends of this process call these small changes "functional enhancements"; those less kind call them "tweaks." It is clear that these many small changes are made by a resource allocated at a very low level and that they are part of the culture of *sustain*.

The system development staff has enormous leverage on the mechanics of our business. Ultimately these experts and the business applications they have built define to a very large extent *how* we do our business. They made it the way it is, they keep it the way it is, and they can change it to anything we choose to make it. If we devote this resource to tweaks, we have voted to keep things the way they are. We have endorsed *sustain*. If we devote this resource to supporting business reengineering and changing the way we work, we have voted for the future. We have endorsed *transform*.

A central challenge to executives and leaders is to balance *sustain* and *transform. Adjusting the allocation of the system development resource is the highest leverage point in the company for striking this balance.* Most of our large companies are deeply stuck in *sustain* because:

- *Executive management takes little or no interest in the allocation of the system development resource.* Although executive management is likely to be intensely interested in some resource allocations at the detail level, advertising for instance, the details of allocating the system development resource are rarely of interest.

- *Infrastructure management is driven to support sustain and resist transform.* This puts an important constraint on anyone in the business or in the system development area who wishes to employ new technology in support of *transform.*

- *The buyer-seller model pushes system development resource allocation below the strategic level in the business.* Under the *buyer-seller* model for business technology relationship, the detailed discussions of how the system development resource will be allocated take place at a low level. Often a systems liaison function acts as a purchasing and quality control agent for the business unit. *Transform* is very likely to cross business unit lines, making potential for *transform* invisible or unapproachable to any single business unit.

- *No clear distinction exists between the sustain and transform duties of the system development resource.* The system development resource is most often organized to face off against specific business units or, where applications are shared among business units, the system development resource may be focused on the application. Either way, the focus is on the applications as they exist. Rarely is the system development resource organized to focus on a *business process*, the likely focus of *transform.* Consequently, system developers don't think of themselves or their work as either sustaining or transforming.

- *The system development resource itself is not well skilled in transform.* System development groups in large companies rarely build new systems. They automated the major functions of the business years ago and the job since then has been *sustain.* By and large, the system development staff has not mastered the new tools and techniques that characterize *transform.*

At NatNec, this pivotal system development resource costs about $20 million a year, 1% of their operating budget. Balancing *sustain* and *transform* requires allocating this 1% in a new way. In this chapter, I advocate allocating the system development resource dynamically to teams that focus on the various aspects of both *sustain* and *transform.* As the requirements in the business change, the balance between *sustain* and *transform* can be adjusted by changing the mix and emphasis of these teams. Let's start the description with a new way of looking at teams to do *sustain.*

SAM teams

We rarely have assets in our business that are unmanaged. Financial assets such as loans and accounts receivable are managed. Physical assets such as office buildings and factories are managed. System assets other than infrastructure, however, are not managed. Even though a company the size of NatNec may have paid a *half billion dollars* for their system assets over a period of years, no one has the job of making sure that they get full value from these application systems. This omission is significant.

I propose that we organize teams with the specific mission to maximize the value the company derives from a set of system assets. Call these *system asset management teams*, SAM teams.

The initial organization of SAM teams probably will follow the existing organization of system developers, although the membership will have to encompass a number of people outside the current development organization. Some SAM teams will be established for the business applications that support a business unit and others will be established for shared systems.

The team will be required to determine how its system assets add value to the business and put in place plans to maximize this value. For example, the SAM team responsible for the new customer service system that Cynthia and her team built in Chapter 9 might identify customer satisfaction as the value added they wish to maximize. They might establish overall results measures like customer survey results and repeat and lost customers. They might establish operational proxies for these measures like incoming calls abandoned, call resolution time and cost, number of *I'll have to get back to you*'s and so forth.

The SAM team will design a model of the process supported by the system asset so that all of the relevant components are within their consideration. For example, the SAM team is certainly interested in the NICE system that Cynthia's team built, but they are also interested in the performance of the customer service reps who use the system and the marketing activities which connect the customer to the service.

The SAM team is responsible for continuous improvement in all parts of the process including system performance, design and program defects, risk control, security, operator performance, connections with other systems, and suitability to the business process. It's clear from this scope that the team members need more than straight technical skills. The SAM team should include software people, infrastructure people, business operations people, and representatives of any other significant stakeholder (in the case of the NICE system, this might mean including a person from market research on the team). The managers accountable for allocating resources to this team form a steering committee that, depending on their degree of mutual interaction, may wish to consider forming a partnership around the process.

SAM teams are process teams. They continuously improve the process that the system assets support. The team performance is measured by their success in improving their process measures. Although there may be rotation of individual members within the SAM-team roles and of people in and out of the team, the SAM team overall will be managed for stability, continuity, and reliability. SAM teams are the mechanism of *sustain* in system development.

Process reengineering teams

The strongest step a company can take toward *transform* is to reengineer a business process. Business processes—product development, marketing, sales and order fulfillment, customer service, and so forth—are the fundamental stuff of every enterprise. Industry, environmental, and company idiosyncrasies modestly change the list of fundamental business processes from business to business, but no matter what set of business processes a particular company might choose, the lists have things in common. No matter how you break down your fundamental business processes,

- *There are relatively few fundamental processes.* You may find it useful to have a substructure within the fundamental processes, but at the top level, 20 is probably too many.
- *The set covers all the things that the company does.* It should be relatively easy to categorize all of the company's activities into the set of processes. If it is very hard, the set of processes or their definitions may be ill chosen. If there are only a few business functions that don't seem to fit, don't try to invent business processes to pick them up. Keep track of them and eventually it will be clear where they fit or, perhaps, that they needn't be done at all.
- *Looking at your business as a set of fundamental processes is one of the most powerful conceptual steps you can make toward transform.* The mindset that involves a model of interlocking processes is much more useful to analyzing value added than a mindset built on an organization chart model of business units plus corporate functions.[1]

Given a process-oriented mental model, the question, How can we improve this process? becomes enormously powerful. Answering this question is the work of the *business process reengineering team,* the BPR team.

A BPR team must be allocated at a high level in the hierarchy, high enough to include accountability encompassing all the stakeholders. Often this means allocating a BPR team at the CEO or management committee level. I've known a couple of cases where oversight of whole corporate processes has been delegated to various senior executives who then act on behalf of the corporation to establish BPR teams. This seems to work. So does the idea of a "reengineering czar" who takes responsibility for BPR teams. The central idea remains that authority flows ultimately from the very top of the allocation pyramid.

The mission of a BPR team is to involve all stakeholders in optimizing the business process by designing and implementing:

- Policies and procedures
- Quality and performance standards
- Organization structures and job definitions
- Information systems.

It is extremely difficult for a BPR team to succeed without a suitable context of corporate values, principles, and mission. A full-blown corporate vision with desired future state, pursuits, and measures would be an enormous boost to a BPR team and would provide an important coordinating mechanism if more than one BPR team is active at once. Usually politics will suggest that the leadership of the BPR team come from the business side of the business technology linkage.

The very large scope of a BPR team suggests that much of its work is coordination of other teams who work on the details of the reengineered process. The BPR team must have a suitable mechanism for allocating the resources involved in these subordinate teams. This means either direct authority or good access to suitable authority.

A BPR team is a project team with the objective of assessing potential and achieving it by instituting a reengineered process. Ultimately the BPR team is judged on the effectiveness of the new process.[2] In the short term it is judged on its ability to produce a set of interim deliverables that shape the new process. Specifically,

- Process concept description
- New procedures and operating guidelines
- Revised organization structure and job definitions
- New managerial frameworks and performance measurement disciplines
- Information systems
- Reengineering project plan

The process concept description is the *personal* work of the members of the BPR team. They should seek information and assistance from any and all possible sources, but the process concept design itself must be the direct result of the team members working together. The process concept addresses policies, procedures, organization, measurement, and information systems in sufficient detail to support mission statements and other guidance for subordinate teams. It remains, then, for the BPR team to coordinate the work of the subordinate teams and carry out the project plan.

Systems reengineering implementation teams

A BPR team is highly likely to produce a new process concept that requires extensive information systems work. This work is likely to be some combination of new applications and revised applications. It is likely to require new technology and new information infrastructure. This information systems work should be carried out by a *systems reengineering implementation team,* an SRI team.[3]

Before setting up the SRI team, however, the BPR team should sponsor the creation of a new SAM team that will eventually take charge of the new system asset producing the flow illustrated in Exhibit 11.1. The SAM team may be largely pro forma until a new system asset is completed, but it will serve to represent the interests of on-going support while the design is being created.

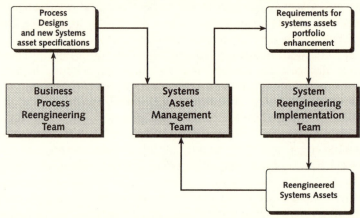

Exhibit 11.1   The SAM Team Has a Central Role in the Development of a New or Replacement System.

The mission of an SRI project team is to implement the systems environment necessary to support the BPR team's process concept and turn over to the new SAM team a system asset to manage. In reengineering, many of the system development activities involve systems that already provide some of the functions although perhaps in a very different way. These existing systems will have SAM team members who have a great deal of functional knowledge and irreplaceable conversion support expertise, which the SRI team will call on. The SRI team is likely to have a lot of skills and, perhaps, even people in common with the SAM teams. There will be software implementers, data experts, functional experts, and change management experts.

In very large process reengineering efforts, the SRI team may need to serve more of a coordinating function and spawn other SRI teams to do implementation. Regardless of how the allocation and execution of the systems work is organized, it must be clear that SRI work and SAM work are distinct. This separation must be held to even in a situation where the SAM team and the SRI team have exactly the same membership.

It is a matter of negotiation between the BPR team, the new SAM team, and the SRI team to determine who has responsibility for the actual implementation of the new process. Most often this responsibility would fall to the BPR team, but if the changes necessary to the new process are mostly systems events, it might be appropriate for the new SAM team or even the SRI team to take implementation responsibility, as was the case in Chapter 9. So the performance of the SRI team is measured either on its production of a suitable new or altered system asset or on successfully placing the new or altered system asset into service.

We have indicated that SRI teams are the system implementation arm of BPR teams. This is the most powerful application of an SRI team. These teams, however, can arise in another way as well. It is common that legacy systems grow complex and difficult to maintain after years of patching and patching the patches. From time to time, it is cost effective to replace an old system with a new one that does essentially the same thing. The cost of this replacement development is paid back through subsequent operational or maintenance savings.

When such an overhaul is needed, an SRI team should be constituted to do the work even though there may be considerable overlap with the SAM team responsible for the old system (and which will become responsible for the new system asset). The mission of such a project team is to build a replacement system with new technology. Its measures of performance are concerned with meeting project objectives and providing a new system with target performance.

Balance

Balancing SAM teams with BPR and SRI teams is the underlying mechanism for balancing *sustain* and *transform*. Exhibit 11.2 illustrates a mental model of the *sustain* and *transform* balance. BPR teams have enormous leverage on the company's *sustain* and *transform* balance. It doesn't take a lot of BPR teams to introduce as much change as an organization can tolerate.[4] SRI teams have leverage on the organization too, but not as much. Relatively little new allocation to *transform* brings the company into balance with *sustain*. Of course, this mental model is just a metaphor. Balancing *sustain* and *transform* in a real situation has to be done by feel, but it is a sufficiently important concept to be embodied in a management principle.

Potential Principle: **We will invest time and resources in balancing our efforts to sustain our business with our efforts to transform it. The primary means for striking the balance will be an adjustment of resources among cross-functional teams which manage our systems as assets and other cross-functional teams that reengineer our processes and implement discontinuous change.**

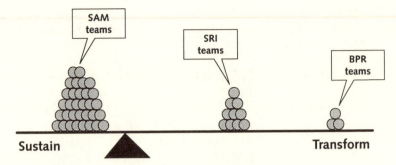

Exhibit 11.2 BPR Teams Exert The Most Leverage For *Transform*

Reengineering and reusability

SAM teams, BPR teams, and SRI teams don't necessarily have to think about the leverage to be had from network computing and reusable components. The introduction of these technologies to the information ecology is a major decision and a major commitment. The decision and commitment, when made, should be embodied in the culture at the level of principles like

Possible Principle: We will invest in information infrastructure and evolve our business applications toward a goal of completely converting to network computing within five years.

Possible Principle: We will invest in skills, tools, and retrofitting to maximize our use of reusable components in infrastructure software, data, and business applications.

If the company decides to make a commitment to network computing, information infrastructure knowledge and skills play a larger role in BPR and SRI teams. The overall shift to network computing might be thought of as business process reengineering for the information ecology.

If the company decides to make the commitment to reusability, there is a strong interaction with the work of the SAM, BPR, and SRI teams, which we will investigate shortly. In addition, two new types of teams enter the picture associated with reusability.

Parts makers and parts keepers

Reusable components don't magically appear. Defining and building them is a complex, challenging, difficult job requiring knowledge of standards, system development techniques, hard core computer science, and the application domain in which the reusable components will be employed. The job also requires a certain artistic turn of mind that makes it possible for the component designer to make crucial, but intuitive, decisions about exactly how much functionality should be included in a given component. Reusable component design is in its very early days—still as much a craft as an engineering discipline.

Teams that build reusable components (*Parts* teams), while they usually work from the specific to the abstract, approach their task from two directions.

- *From small details:* A programmer, for example, may express a need for a bit of code that allows a user to draw circles on the screen. The Parts team looks at the requirement and designs a reusable software component that allows a user to draw ellipses which may be forced to be circles by holding down a certain key. The component also lets the user move the ellipse around, make it larger or smaller, and fill it with the user's choice of color or pattern.
- *From large concepts:* A BPR team, for example, may express a need for software that deals with loans. The Parts team analyzes the requirement and designs reusable software components that store the pertinent data about an interest earning asset (that is, a generalized loan), compute the value of the asset as various events occur (draw downs, interest rate changes, payments, and so forth), and report the asset's current details when asked.

It is most likely that, as the art and science of reusable components develop, the components themselves will be manufactured by third parties. Few companies will build their own. This will serve to bring down even further the cost of components and improve the productivity of an enterprise that builds with them. There will be an interim period during which many companies will build some and buy some. Positions on the Parts teams will be much coveted by the best software people and eventually these people will tend to migrate to companies that specialize in building reusable components.

As the use of reusable components matures, the number of these components will grow large. Hundreds of thousands (perhaps more) individual reusable components will be available to implementers. Quickly, a real problem develops around how implementers select reusable components for inclusion in their new systems. Confronted with thousands of choices, important questions arise:

- *How does an implementer know if a reusable component exists that does what he needs done?* There has to be some very efficient way to describe the behavior of reusable components so that it is easy for an implementer to compare his requirements to the capability of the components.
- *Having selected a reusable component that appears to do what is required, how does the implementer know that the behavior of the component is exactly what is needed rather than almost what is needed?* Software components are notoriously complex and their behavior is subtle. The requirement must be expressed in a way that compliance can be tested.
- *How do we know if any particular component, designed to be reusable, is actually being reused?* If every bit of code written by every implementer is designated reusable, but none of it is ever reused, we have added only

complexity with no benefit. There need to be good records of what is reused and good analysis to learn what makes some components more
likely to be reused than others. And we must avoid indiscriminately adding to the collection components which are very nearly the same as
others.

Dealing with these problems is the work of the *reusable component library*
team (*Library* team). The library team is a process team whose mission is to establish and manage the library of reusable components and whose effectiveness
is measured in terms of the extent to which reusable components are used in
working systems and the degree to which components in the library are actually
reused. This team

- Acquires reusable components
- Organizes, indexes, and stores reusable components
- Assists SAM teams in selecting reusable components for substitution in
  existing systems
- Assists SRI teams in designing for reusability and in selecting compo-
  nents

The Library team is also the focus of standards documentation for components, interfaces, and processes. This last responsibility involving standard processes puts the Library team in charge of the development methodology
documentation. When the company decides on a standard way for performing
development and maintenance functions, the Library team houses and main-
tains the detailed descriptions of these agreed to processes and procedures.
Likewise the Library team is a suitable place to house any other agreements and
shared ideas such as values and mission statements, assumptions, process models, principles, and so forth. The Library team is not an enforcement or audit
function but it is well positioned to alert stakeholders to inconsistencies.

Fitting the teams together

Let's take a step back now and see what the system development environment
looks like as a whole.

The new model of system development consists of lots of teams—many
SAM teams, a few BPR teams, and a number of SRI teams suitable to the
amount of development going on. We can see clearly the balance of resources
between SAM teams on the *sustain* side and BPR and SRI teams on the *transform* side.

The work we think of as maintenance has been subsumed into the mission
of a number of SAM teams. SAM teams dominate the use of our system development resource and have expanded influence and responsibility. Much of the
resource represented in the SAM teams is allocated by the CIO and the technology organization, but parts of each SAM team must be allocated by the users
and other stakeholders in the system assets.

The strongest forces for change in the information ecology are the small number of BPR teams that are working to reengineer the company's basic business processes. We don't expect a lot of BPR teams, but we expect those we do have to influence significantly the way we do business. The BPR team's work extends beyond the boundaries of the information ecology, but it is in the information infrastructure and in the business application systems that their work succeeds or fails. BPR teams are allocated by corporate level authority and include appropriate representation from the information ecology.

Implementation projects come and go as SRI teams are formed, do their work, and are dissolved. SRI teams implement the new systems called for by the BPR teams and they overhaul legacy systems when the economics are right. SRI teams building new systems in support of a BPR team will have strong representation from both the business and technology sides of the linkage. SRI teams focused on overhauling an older system will be dominated by technology infrastructure and system development people.

If the company makes a commitment to reusable components, there will be Parts teams and a Library team, both of which are mostly technology people. Let's assume such a commitment to reusability and look at how the teams work together. The diagram in Exhibit 11.3 is an expanded version of the one we saw earlier in Exhibit 11.1. The teams and interactions necessary to support the commitment to reusable components are added.

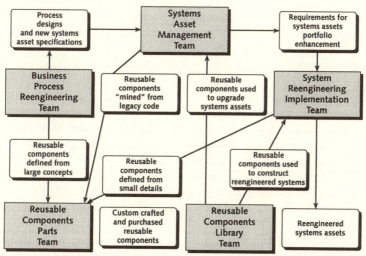

Exhibit 11.3 Process Model for System Development in a Team Oriented, Sustain and Transform Balancing Organization That Has Committed to Reusable Components.

As we've said, process designs are a major deliverable of BPR project teams. A new process design that requires a new system or set of systems calls for a new SAM team to ultimately take change of the asset. Both old SAM teams and the new SAM teams that result from BPR process redesign spin-off requirements for significant changes in the portfolio of system assets. These changes are the work of SRI teams, which ultimately produce the new system assets.

When we introduce a commitment to reusable components into the flow, we see that new components can be defined in four ways.

- *BPR teams can produce definitions of new reusable components as a result of their process redesign work.* These are definitions that derive from the broad concepts that are used in the reengineered process design.
- *SRI teams can produce definitions of new reusable components as they do the construction of new system assets.* These are likely to be definitions derived from detailed requirements of the particular implementation that will be broadened and generalized by the Parts team.
- *SAM teams can produce the definitions of new reusable components as they simplify and enhance legacy systems.* There are a lot of redundant processes in existing systems. The people who know the details of these systems best are the SAM team members. It is likely that they will "mine" from their existing systems bits of functionality that should become reusable components and be retrofitted into legacy systems.
- *Parts teams can define reusable components on their own.* Independent companies will be trying to build reusable components with broad applicability and wide market appeal.

As Parts teams develop reusable components the parts are registered with the Library team. The Library team serves as a resource to SRI teams as they build new systems and to SAM teams as they continuously improve their system assets.

Building skills

The concept presented here implies that the roles on different teams will require more differentiated skills than we typically find in the system development organizations we have today. It also implies that individuals in infrastructure operations, business operations, and other business functions will require skills different from those we typically require today.

Today, if we undertake a business process reengineering project or a systems implementation project, we expect that the same people who presently do our systems maintenance will do the work. We expect the skills to be comparable and the people to be fungible. It just isn't so. Furthermore, as the technology has matured, each of the different kinds of work has become the province of a differentiated set of automated tools. Doing this new kind of work means mastering different distinct sets of skills, concepts, and tools.

The *buyer-seller* relationship model for the business technology linkage has long been a source of constraint on the ability of technology managers to rotate staff members among different applications and roles. The buyers have often insisted on their purchases by name and have been intolerant of "staff development" at their expense. This has left the entire system development organization poorer for lack of cross-training, skills training, and role training and the buyer largely ignorant of the development process and the resulting system assets.

When these relational constraints are loosened it becomes possible to add a necessary new dimension to staff development in the system development area. The table in Exhibit 11.4 shows a framework for skills development and career planning for system developers. A similar approach would suit the business side.

	Team member	Team leader	Expert member
SAM team	1st assignment		4th assignment
SRI team	2nd assignment		5th assignment
Parts team	3rd assignment		
Library team			6th assignment
BPR team			

Exhibit 11.4 An Example of a Skills Development and Career Planning Framework for a System Developer.

The numbers in the table represent a possible career progression for a technical specialist. Each step indicates another kind of experience requiring new technical skills or role skills. A sample progression for a technical leadership career might go like the table in Exhibit 11.5.

	Team member	Team leader	Expert member
SAM team	1st assignment	3rd assignment	
SRI team	2nd assignment	5th assignment	
Parts team			
Library team			6th assignment
BPR team	4th assignment	7th assignment	

Exhibit 11.5 An Example of a Skills Development and Career Planning Framework for a Technical Manager

This conceptual framework should, in practice, be expanded to include the various skills-training steps necessary to move along a progression. The number of steps that a staff member has taken successfully becomes a value-added substitute for longevity as the basis for seniority and base compensation.

This chapter has introduced a system development resource management concept specifically designed to highlight and implement a balance between *sustain* and *transform*. We have enriched our understanding of the information ecology, as indicated in Exhibit 11.6. We started by stating that the system development resource is the highest leverage part of the organization for balancing *transform* against a preponderance of *sustain*.

We examined three team types:

- *System asset management* (SAM) teams to focus on *sustain* and fill the organization's need for stability, reliability, and continuous enhancement.
- *Business process reengineering* (BPR) teams to be the primary agents of *transform* at the corporate level, designing new processes.
- *Systems reengineering implementation* (SRI) teams, agents of *transform*, to implement significant improvements in the information ecology engendered either by the BPR teams or by the needs of the information ecology itself.

We explored how these teams work together and how allocating resources to different numbers of these teams balance the overall level of *sustain* and *transform* in the organization.

We saw how the introduction of a commitment to reusability required Parts teams and a Library team, and we examined how all five teams work together to develop and use reusable components.

We noted that these new teams call for more skill and role differentiation than our traditional approach and I asserted that freeing the system developers from the *buyer-seller* relationship would allow us to employ a more effective skills development process.

The descriptions of information infrastructure management and system development management in the last two chapters have proceeded almost completely without reference to organizational structure in the hierarchy. Chapter 12 changes that; we look explicitly at the question, *Does organization matter?*

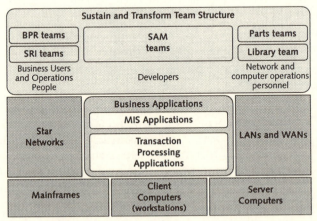

Exhibit 11.6 The Complete Information Ecology

Notes

1. I'd like to emphasize that this assertion is concerned with one's mental model of a business not with the organization of the business. Organization structure is one process variable that enables or inhibits particular kinds of group behavior but doesn't alter fundamental processes.
2. The BPR team could be long gone before the effectiveness of the new process is fully realized. This long time frame is characteristic of allocation processes and illustrates the essentially allocation rather than execution nature of a BPR team. The reward mechanism for the BPR team should take this into account.
3. Cynthia's team in Chapter 9 was an SRI team but a consultant rather than a BPR team created their design concept.
4. Each organization has a pace of change that it can accommodate. Try to change it faster and resistance becomes overwhelming or something breaks.

12

Does Organization Matter?

We have been discussing a concept of allocation and execution that uses teams as the key organizing principle. We have agreed that these teams must operate within the context of a traditional organizational hierarchy and we know that details of the organizational hierarchy are an important focus of both management and staff attention; nothing brings productive work to a halt more quickly than a good reorganization rumor. But if the linkages are supplied by partnerships and teams and all the real work is done by various process and project teams, how much do the details of the organizational hierarchy (i.e., the administrative team structure) matter to the information ecology and the effectiveness of the enterprise?

Centralize or decentralize, that is the question

Most large companies have experienced swings between "centralization" and "decentralization" in which some resource or function has been "centralized" in order to get economies of scale or "decentralized" in order to get responsiveness and effectiveness. In the information ecology the oscillation may have played out several times over the last 30 years or so. The arguments advanced to rationalize organizational changes are well known.

There's enough truth in all the cells of the table in Exhibit 12.1 so that the argument is basically "religious" and unresolvable by analysis or reason alone. The way the argument gets settled in practice depends on the power structure of the company and its present urgencies. If, for instance, IT is "centralized" and one or two highly profitable business units decide they want to own their own information technology, they probably will get what they want and the swing toward decentralization will begin. If on the other hand, IT is "decentralized" and the company comes under strong cost pressure, the pendulum may swing quickly the other way. Many large companies have experienced several full and partial swings of this pendulum. Most have settled on some compromise version.

	"Centralized" Information Technology	"Decentralized" Information Technology
Perceived Advantages	• Economies of scale • Improved technical career paths • Reduced technical and operational risk • More cross training • Flexible assignment of resources • Standards adherence	• Better control of techies by business • Improved schedule performance • Better linkage • Improved business knowledge among techies • Improved responsiveness
Perceived Disadvantages	• Lack of control by business • Poor linkage • Bureaucracy • Poor schedule performance • "Technology agenda" • Lack of business knowledge	• High cost • Poor adherence to standards • Technical skills decay • Difficulty holding quality technical staff • Increased technical and operational risk

Exhibit 12.1 Summary of the Debate over "Centralized" versus "Decentralized" Information Technology

In fact, "centralized" and "decentralized" as organizational concepts are not quite precise enough to capture the dynamics of the situation. To draw attention to more precise concepts, I'll call technology units "dispersed" when they have a solid line reporting relationship to a business unit, centralized when they have a solid line reporting relationship to a technology organization, and decentralized to describe the situation when the solid reporting line is to the technology organization but physically the unit is located with the business unit. Exhibit 12.2 shows four prototypical organizations of the information technology and the ways it is combined with business units (BU). These are highly simplified, of course, and omit details like staff structures, corporate functions, and matrix management. They ignore the reality that neither system development (DEV) nor information infrastructure (INF) can usually be divided among the business units without leaving some shared elements left to be managed by the CIO.

The top two organization concepts show the extremes. In a strictly dispersed information ecology (on the left), each business unit has its own development resource and infrastructure. In a strictly centralized information ecology (on the right), all the resources are managed directly by the CIO.

The lower two organization concepts show a couple of the possible compromises. Dispersed development (on the left) consolidates the information infrastructure under the CIO and disperses the development resource to the business units. The lower right decentralized development concept is the same except the individual development units report directly to the CIO instead of to the business units.

While you've been reading the last few paragraphs you may have already identified your favorite. I have. Every time this topic comes up we have the potential for a top-notch turf battle. People usually fight turf battles for personal power and glory, but the terms of the argument are always phrased in terms of what is best for the company. Does anybody know what's best for the company? Well, there are some people who know more about this than most of us.

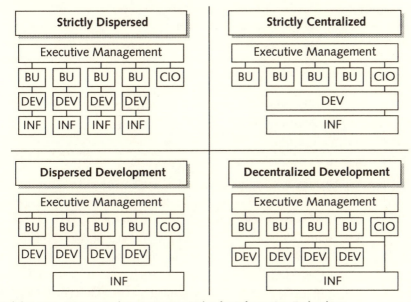

Exhibit 12.2 Prototypical Organization Styles for Information Technology

Adding some facts to the debate

In 1990 Kay Redditt and Tom Lodahl of CogniTech Services Corporation[1] working with the Canadian consultant DMR Group, Inc.[2] began a very interesting analysis that proposed to establish new measures of information technology effectiveness. They developed a carefully defined measure that they named *I/S effectiveness* (i.e. information systems effectiveness).

In late 1991 Redditt and Lodahl extended this work to determine if there was a correlation between I/S effectiveness and bottom line company financial performance measures. Based on in-depth analysis of 47 companies, Redditt and Lodahl have established statistically significant correlations between I/S effectiveness and return on equity (ROE), earnings per share (EPS), and profitability. The Redditt and Lodahl work is very interesting and quite extensive, much too extensive to review thoroughly here. I will present a number of their conclusions, however, as we go along and interpret them in terms of the models we have been discussing.

From Redditt and Lodahl's work we infer one answer to this chapter's question. They found a correlation between I/S effectiveness and corporate ROE, EPS, and profitability results and they also discovered significant organizational predictors of I/S effectiveness. Their result is that organization does matter. Their conclusions include

- I/S effectiveness increases if control over information technology deliverables is vested with a business function rather than with a pure I/S function.
- I/S effectiveness improves if some but not all of the I/S function is dispersed.
- I/S effectiveness improves if influence, not necessarily control, has moved outward and downward to business units.

I/S Function	Reports to
Cross functional development	Business unit at a high level
Cross functional maintenance	Business unit at a low level
Single function development	Business unit at a low level
Single function maintenance	Business unit at a low level
Computer operations	Business unit at a low level
Mainframe network management	Technology
LAN network management	Business unit at a low level
Technical support	Technology
I/S architecture	Technology
I/S planning	Business unit at a low level
New technology assessment	Technology
Mainframe end user services	Technology
Microcomputer end user services	Technology

Exhibit 12.3 Redditt and Lodahl Observed IT Organizational Alignment Typical of Corporate High Performers

The table in Exhibit 12.3 is a summary of the organization alignment of various information technology functions that Redditt and Lodahl found typical of corporate high performers.

High performers look like the dispersed development structure from the exhibit we looked at earlier. The low performers look quite different. Redditt and Lodahl found that corporate low performers had centralized all these I/S functions in a technology organization that reports above the level of the business units they support similar to the strictly centralized version in the exhibit.

Redditt and Lodahl give us a little more detail about high performers that helps us get a feel for what division of responsibility is highly correlated with business success.

The table in Exhibit 12.4 suggests that high-performing companies have a preference for organizing the *doing* of information ecology activities within the business and a preference for *deciding* how things should be done within the technology function. Reasonable exceptions to this generalization are that high performers want the choice of what new systems to build and the functional design of their systems to be done within the business unit and the choice of what technical projects to be done within the technology organization. I'd like to suggest that this result can be understood in the language of this book as follows:

- In high performers the relationship between business and technology people features a higher level of perceived common interest because they report within the same business unit, therefore, the corrosive results of the *buyer-seller* model are significantly reduced. Depending on the details of the relationship and the specific internal policies and procedures, the relationship within the business units might be moving toward partnership.
- In low performers, the organizational isolation of all technology people in a highly centralized unit creates exaggerated versions of the *buyer-seller* relationship slipping toward *master-slave*.
- Standards setting and pure technology projects are infrastructure considerations to which business units are indifferent.

Function	Business Responsibility	Technology Responsibility
Development and maintenance	• Project selection • Business project proposals • Business requirements • User interface design • Documentation • Programming	• Design methodology • Technical project proposals • Development standards • Development methodology • Documentation standards • Methodology
Network management	• Operations • Troubleshooting	• Standards • Architecture
Computer operations	• Scheduling • Output control	• Standards • Hardware selection • Architecture
End user support	• Troubleshooting • Small package selection • Package training • Ad hoc reports	• Standards • Large package selection • Cross functional package selection

Exhibit 12.4   Additional Detail of Division of Responsibility between Business and Technology for Redditt and Lodahl's Corporate High Performers

The Redditt and Lodahl analysis has demonstrated a correlation between I/S organization structure and corporate performance. In my opinion, the quality of business technology linkage is the hidden variable in this situation. Organization structure was significant in the Redditt and Lodahl results; companies that have dispersed the functions business units care about got better results. This is an important result. On the other hand, it is possible that organization is just one of several possible mechanisms for controlling business technology linkage. In my opinion, these significant results show us a difference in the quality of the business technology linkage based on a difference in the relationships between business and technology people.

Many Redditt and Lodahl results are consistent with this view. For instance,

- Small business units have more effective I/S than large ones.
- Business units whose employees have been on the job for a longer time are more effective.
- Organizations that cross train in business and technology are more effective than those that don't.
- Organizations in which the culture of the information ecology is the same as the culture of the rest of the business are more effective than organizations where the cultures are different.

One of their most intriguing results is that formal information ecology planning is *negatively* correlated with I/S effectiveness but planning interaction, without a formal document, is *positively* correlated with I/S effectiveness. I explain this interesting result by suggesting that a formal planning process between business and technology that results in a well-edited bound volume is likely to be a sign of a strong *buyer-seller* relationship and a poor linkage. A planning process that emphasizes interaction without a formal result is more likely to be a sign of a partnership and a good linkage.

I am inclined to believe that nearly all the Redditt and Lodahl results can be best understood in terms of factors that tend to improve or discourage linkage—this is, of course, conjecture that requires further investigation to gain the same level of credibility as the results they have already established. In the meantime, my answer to this chapter's question would be that organization matters only to the degree that it affects the quality of linkage. I will pursue that thought for the rest of the chapter.

Strategic coordination and organization

What effect does organization have on strategic coordination? Let's start to understand this question by reminding ourselves what we mean by strategic coordination. Exhibit 12.5 is the pertinent picture from Chapter 6.

Business strategy includes our selection of business scope (total market, niche market, upscale, price sensitive, all sporting goods, golf equipment and clothes only, and so forth) and what we will do to differentiate ourselves from our competitors (price, quality, image, delivery channels, and so forth). Business strategy also includes the extent to which we enter into value-added partnerships, business alliances, or other collaborative mechanisms.

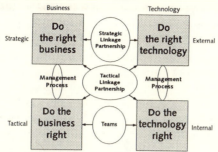

Exhibit 12.5 Business Technology Linkage Framework

Technology strategy includes questions such as will standards be open or proprietary? will electronic connectivity be general and ubiquitous or specific and tailored? to what degree will technology in the company be uniform? to what degree will we attempt to use emerging technology? will our technology infrastructure be reliable, highly reliable, or ultra reliable? which parts of the technology infrastructure do we *sustain* and which do we *transform*?

The key to linking these top-level strategic functions is including the CIO or equivalent in the CEO's inner circle, which forms a strategic linkage partnership (SLP). *For this purpose*, almost any form for the hierarchical organization will do as long as the technology view is represented in the business strategy process and an SLP exists. The CIO needs to be part of the executive management partnership in order for this business strategy to technology strategy linkage to work so, from a practical standpoint, this suggests that the CIO probably ought to report to the CEO or COO.

More interesting are the diagonal links from business strategy to technology operations and from technology strategy to business operations. I suggested a tactical linkage partnership to provide these cross linkages and described the work of this TLP as

- Review and recommend technology budgets and capital investments.
- Review and approve high-risk technology development projects.
- Develop shared procurement policies and procedures for technology.
- Endorse technology standards and processes

In Chapter 6, we said this about the membership of the TLP:

> *The membership for this tactical linkage partnership should also represent the business and technology interests but probably one step down or so in the hierarchy. On the business side the representatives are deputies, chiefs of staff, or senior executive assistants to the most senior business executives. On the technology side, the representatives are the reports to the CIO. Other representatives from functional areas, perhaps Finance, HR, or internal audit, may be necessary.*

The implicit assumption in this description was that the technology hierarchy was distinct from the business hierarchy, that is, technology was centralized. What happens to the TLP if technology is dispersed as suggested by the Redditt and Lodahl results? It seems likely to me that picking the membership for the TLP becomes more complicated.

If there is a technology manager from each business unit, do we also need a business manager to provide the linkage? This obviously depends on how well the technology manager can represent the business unit's interests. If the technology manager is a full-fledged member of the business unit leadership and part of a partnership there, no other representation from that business unit may be necessary.

If there is no partnership in the business unit or if the technology manager is not a part of it, then a business side representative will be needed. In that case, we ask, if the business representative and the technology manager are from the same business unit, can they be partners in the TLP? This is a matter of their personalities but also of their relative places in the hierarchy of the business unit. If one of the representatives is significantly different from the other in terms of authority or if there is any reason why they might not perceive common interest (different compensation plans, for instance), it will be very difficult for them to partner with each other. This dilemma must be reconciled for each business unit represented in the TLP and balance among the business units must be maintained.

Strange as it may sound after the Redditt and Lodahl results, it seems that constructing an effective cross-linkage with a strong TLP might be easier in an organization that has a centralized technology hierarchy than one where technology is dispersed. This interesting observation, however, is not an argument for centralization of technology. We know that dispersing some of technology improves performance. This is because, in my opinion, it improves business operations to technology operations and business strategy to technology operations linkage. It is quite likely that any difficulties this causes in building an effective TLP are worth the trouble.

Infrastructure doesn't divide gracefully

Since the late 1970s it has been fashionable in companies from time to time to allow or even encourage business units to procure and operate their own information infrastructure. Minicomputers and LAN server networks became the core of what was called "departmental computing." "Downsizing" was another popular thought in which mainframe computing was rearranged to run on some number of smaller computers[3] which often were considered part of the business unit's furniture. Large business units sometimes acquired their own mainframes, data centers, and networks. Having one's own infrastructure was a concomitant of the notion that accountability was only possible when a manager directly controlled all the resources necessary to perform the job. We've learned that this doesn't work very well. Imagine analogs to business unit islands of information infrastructure:

- Roads that serve a village or town but go no further than the remotest town citizen, connecting to nothing.
- Electrical generating plants that serve only their local customers with no connections to allow for purchasing more power or shedding excess.
- Railroads, all different gauges, switching conventions, stations, and loading facilities, that cannot transfer goods or people from one to another without unloading and reloading.
- Telephone companies that serve a community but can't connect to other telephone companies.

The point I'm making is that infrastructure *can* be most efficient when it is large and ubiquitous.[4] And why shouldn't it be? Infrastructure is that about which we are indifferent, remember? If it's really infrastructure we should be happy to have it managed for us by experts.

Technologies like lights-out data centers and network computing have made obsolete the idea of separate islands of infrastructure. Everything is becoming connected. Multiple networks are merging into a single multinet and all computers are becoming nodes[5] in the multinet. Breaking up the information infrastructure now because many business units use it makes no more sense than breaking up a lake because many different people own lakefront property. Recognizing the inevitable unity of information infrastructure is a strong trend in most companies that has arisen only recently. We should encourage it. This approach is consistent with the Redditt and Lodahl results, and they add the caveat that the business user of the data center, network, or other infrastructure must be able to rely on the day-to-day delivery of services, *when the business needs them, not just when IT finds it convenient.*

The Redditt and Lodahl results suggest that the user must be in control of the scheduling and deliverables. Often, however, responsibility for meeting these schedules is a two way street—in check processing, for example, the business must take responsibility for gathering checks from the branches, encoding the checks, and getting the input files to the data center, then the infrastructure operation (data center) must run the necessary application programs to post the deposits and withdrawals to the correct accounts in time for a new balance for each account to be ready on-line for the tellers, customer service rep's, and automated teller machines early the next day. If the branches don't prove their work on time, checks will be late to encoding, files will be late to the data center, and the new account balances will be late the next morning. Successful management of this complex process requires partnership-style coordination among bankers, operations personnel, application programmers, and data center and network operations.

Having endorsed unified management of infrastructure, I need to review what I mean by information infrastructure. In Chapter 10, we examined this idea: *When a system component's relationships with other system components is specified by a suitable set of standards so that one product meeting the standards can be freely substituted for another* and *the standards are acceptable to all stakeholders, then the system component should be managed as infrastructure.*

This is the formal way to say that it's infrastructure if nobody has a good reason to care about it. For instance, in today's information ecology the business is indifferent to the choice of LAN transmission protocol, but just a few years ago there was a raging battle between the advocates of Ethernet and the advocates of Token Ring technology which often spilled over into the business decision-making process because certain applications could be supported on one of these but not the other. Now no one but the infrastructure manager cares, because applications can be supported on either.

I have seen lots of turf battles between information infrastructure managers and other managers over computer and communication equipment and software. A few of these battles have been matters of personality and politics; most, however, have been about a conflict between an infrastructure manager's need to *sustain* and another manager's desire to *transform*. If the item at issue had met the criteria of the preceding principle, there would have been no reason for the argument. The infrastructure manager could have picked whatever product suited the needs of *sustain* and, because of standards, the other manager could have proceeded unencumbered with *transform*. If the item failed the criteria, it wasn't infrastructure (no matter how much it might look like it) and the question changes from product selection to allocating between *sustain* and *transform*.

Does organization matter in the management of information infrastructure? I think yes. To the extent that information infrastructure is dominated by *sustain*, I believe its purposes are best achieved by a single management hierarchy supporting it all. This hierarchy will allocate people routinely to SAM teams. Infrastructure people should be allocated to BPR teams that involve any significant infrastructure impact. SRI team leaders should decide the level of infrastructure participation needed in the team based on the degree of change the implementation requires of the infrastructure. Of course, SRI teams focused on implementing changes to the infrastructure *per se* will be staffed largely by people allocated by the information infrastructure hierarchy.

There has always been an anomaly in information infrastructure around the people who manage the infrastructure software. These people are usually called systems programmers and in many organizations represent the most expert experts in regard to the internal details and complexities of the company's computer systems. They usually disdain knowledge of the business applications themselves, but are intensely concerned with the infrastructure software on which the applications are based.

These people are anomalous because many are by inclination oriented to *transform*, but find the only work which satisfies them in the heart of the *sustain*-oriented infrastructure. These are the people who *transform* the infrastructure.

The software aspect of infrastructure is a high-potential, high-growth area. Ultimately it will be the systems programmers who will take responsibility for this aspect of the infrastructure. Unfortunately, the revolution in software infrastructure is being made by application system developers and even by users with little or no involvement from the systems programmers. This should be addressed by an increased emphasis within the information infrastructure hierarchy on systems programming.[6]

Traditionally there has been a wide gulf between the people in the information infrastructure and the people in the organization who have been asked to do new technology assessment. Infrastructure has values of nearly pure *sustain*. New technology assessment has values of nearly pure *transform*. The potential for conflict is clear. The information infrastructure hierarchy needs to specifically allocate resources to the new technology assessment team and make a clear effort to integrate their findings with the thinking of the rest of the infrastructure hierarchy. Systems programmers need to be linked to the discoveries and decisions made by new technology assessment. This same policy should be adopted with any other teams that develop with a strong focus on *transform*.

Applications are the business

System developers are the most squabbled over resource in the information ecology. Lots of people seem to think it matters who these people report to. No doubt this is because of the enormous leverage that the system developers have on our existing systems and the fact that control over this resource is essential to control over the business itself.

The Redditt and Lodahl results suggest that if system developers report to the businesses they support, I/S effectiveness, hence business outcome, improves. I said I thought this result was explained by the direct reporting relationship creating better linkage than the arms length, but internal, version of *buyer-seller*. Candidly, I think *any* relationship is likely to provide better linkage.

I think that reporting relationship of the system development resource in the hierarchy is only part of the story and becomes dominant in the absence of other strong business technology linkage mechanisms. *If we don't have good linkage, dispersing the system developers may make it better—but it can't make it good! If the linkage is good, organization in the hierarchy is much less important!*

When confronted with the symptoms of poor linkage, many managers jump to reorganization as the solution, but more often than not, the symptoms relate to a need that cannot be met by organizational change. Solid line reporting relationships in the hierarchy can provide good vertical linkages (those that involve allocation), but coordination, the kind of linkage required between and among specialties, is provided poorly if at all. Coordination is a function of horizontal linkage that can be addressed by matrix reporting lines but can best be built by partnerships and teams. Horizontal linkage is largely independent of organizational hierarchy. It is only when partnerships and teams don't exist that the weak horizontal linkages provided by having a common boss or attending common staff meetings is of any noticeable value.

Where then should the system developers report? First, I say that it doesn't matter much if we are paying attention to linkage by defining and managing the right partnerships and teams. To the degree that it does matter, I think it is best to organize along the following lines consistent with the Redditt and Lodahl results:

- *SAM process teams belong to the business, if any, that owns the asset.*[7] System developers and business people who are assigned full time to SAM teams ought to report within the business unit administrative team hierarchy if the assets being managed are clearly associated with the business unit.
- *Most SRI project team members belong to the business, if any, that will own the asset.*[8] System developers working on SRI teams where the resulting reengineered system will be an asset clearly associated with a business unit and who are likely to move to the SAM team responsible for the new asset should report in the business unit hierarchy. It may not be easy to tell at the beginning of a particular SRI project which if any of the team's system developers will end up with the new SAM team, so transfers in the hierarchy are most likely to come at the end of the project. This is also an appropriate time to transfer to their next assignments (and change the administrative team reporting relationships, in necessary) system developers who are members of SAM teams that will be disbanded.
- *Project teams building shared assets and process teams managing them report to technology.*[9] System developers working on BPR teams and SRI teams that will produce shared assets and SAM teams responsible for shared assets should report within the technology hierarchy administrative team structure.

The career mobility process described for system developers in Chapter 11 is indifferent to the hierarchical reporting relationships of the individuals as long as all managers in the various hierarchies have agreed to the process. Corporate oversight of the career mobility plan for system developers should be the responsibility of the technology hierarchy (a practice supported by the Redditt and Lodahl results).

Likewise, reporting relationship in the administrative team hierarchy doesn't matter much when all teams use the same processes for evaluation and reward.

Evaluation and reward should sort out this way:

- *The managers who allocated the teams, evaluate and reward them.* Evaluation and reward for *team performance* should be the responsibility jointly of the managers who allocated resources to the team.
- *Team members evaluate role performance and the managers who allocated the teams allocate the rewards.* Evaluation for *role performance* is a team process for which the team leader is responsible. Reward for role performance is the responsibility jointly of the team leader and the managers who allocated resources to the team.
- *Teams judge adherence and the hierarchy rewards it.* Evaluation of *individual adherence* is a team process for which the team leader is responsible. Reward for individual adherence is the responsibility of the manager within the hierarchy into which the individual reports.

Working in teams and evaluating them this way reserves the power of the administrative team hierarchy to allocate resources but takes away much of the power of the hierarchy as it pertains to execution and personal reward. In each person's selfish priority scheme, pleasing your administrative boss falls behind getting the team's work done and satisfying your teammates including the team leader. Short-term reward is based on how well the team performs and how well you perform your assigned functional role. Long-term reward and advancement is a combination of learning to do a number of roles well and adhering to the values of the organization. I suggest we summarize this thinking in another management principle.

Potential Principle: We will design and operate our formal administrative organization to facilitate the use of partnerships and teams as business technology linkage mechanisms.

So, does organization matter?

Redditt and Lodahl told us that dispersed is better than centralized for most development. I opined that this was true in the absence of good linkage but given good linkage it wouldn't matter as much.

We discussed the need for a partnership at the top to provide good strategic linkage, but we found few organizational implications. We noted that the cross-linkages between strategy and operations require a balanced partnership of techies and nontechies.

I asserted that the information infrastructure should not be "balkanized" but instead managed as a whole in the technology hierarchy. I suggested that attention needs to be paid to the boundaries of infrastructure and that careful thought should be given to how to manage the growing responsibilities of infra-structure. I emphasized the need for information infrastructure management to create links to the various forces of *transform*, especially new technology as-sessment and BPR teams.

We concluded the chapter with a discussion of how to organize the system development resource in the new world of *sustain* and *transform*. I suggested a simple plan in which members of SAM and SRI team focused on an asset be-longing to a business unit should report in that business unit's administrative team hierarchy. The rest should report through the technology administrative team hierarchy. I pointed out that adopting the teams approach for balancing *sustain* and *transform* has the effect of limiting the means by which the adminis-trative team hierarchy influences individual incentives and behavior.

Chapter 13 illustrates how all of the suggestions and ideas of this book can be put together to build effective business technology linkage in an information ecology in need of a shift from *sustain* toward *transform*.

Notes

1. CogniTech Services Corp., 320 Center Road, Easton, CT 06612. Telephone (203) 268-1401.
2. DMR Group Inc., 1200 McGill College Avenue, Suite 700, Montreal Quebec H3B4G7, Canada. Telephone (514) 866-3000.
3. IBM built one of their most successful businesses on this idea. The AS/400 family of computers was just the thing for folks who couldn't make it all the way to a LAN with their systems (or their thinking). AS/400's turned out to be mainframe com-puters in smaller boxes.
4. Careful management is required to avoid monopolistic behavior.
5. *Nodes* in a network are the lumps where the links come together. Nodes are usually computers acting as servers or workstations.
6 The Library team described in Chapter 11 is a natural analog of the systems pro-grammers and might fit into the same hierarchy.
7. Redditt and Lodahl's category called single-function maintenance.
8. Redditt and Lodahl's category called single-function development.
9. Redditt and Lodahl's categories called multi-function maintenance and develop-ment.

Implementation

The bulk of this chapter is written in the manner of a magazine article, perhaps the style of *Forbes*, *Fortune* or the *Economist*. The article describes good old NatNec six or seven years from now after a major cultural transformation has taken place and they have adopted a style of operation based on this book. NatNec has become a company that consciously balances *sustain* and *transform*. As we'll see, it has worked out very well for them.

As we read about how changes in information technology management have taken place in NatNec, we will be looking for the broad outline of how these changes can be made in a real world company. We'll summarize the major points at the end of the chapter.

Is NatNec as Good as It Looks? Maybe It's Better!

They use values and visions, partnerships and teams, pursuits and measurements, communications and computers. Should your company do the same?

I n the past five years, National Necessary Service Corporation, NatNec to most of the world, has steadily pulled away from all of its competitors, finally emerging into a class by itself. By all the usual measures of business performance— growth, market share, earnings, or return on equity—NatNec is an industry phenomenon. The market has rewarded its very strong earnings growth and outstanding ROE with the best multiple in the business. With strong stock and an uncanny skill in making acquisitions, NatNec has grown from a member of the pack to the undisputed industry leader.

If you ask Winston Burton II, Nat-Nec's CEO, why they have been so successful in the last six years, he will say, "We've been lucky and we've done a lot of things right. The most important thing I think that we've done right is to figure out how to really integrate information technology with our business. We used to be pretty much like everybody else in the way we thought about linking technology and business. After we rethought that linkage, a lot of things started working better."

Ask almost anyone at NatNec about this success and you'll hear some mention of their use of information technology. You'll also hear a lot about doing "visible" things and avoiding "invisible" things. This is NatNec shorthand for activities that support their vision for the future of NatNec. "Visible," says CEO Burton, "means we all see it; it's part of the vision. Invisible means we don't see it... and we won't do it."

What has been visible to NatNec has been a stunning series of technical achievements that have become the underpinning for their extremely strong financial performance and have established standards of excellence and performance that continue to make potential competitors hesitate to jump into this very profitable but complex industry.

NatNec has fashioned their success of equal parts leading-edge technology, aggressive financial positioning, and simple human values. A revolu-

tion started in NatNec six years ago with a different kind of leadership from a new CIO and has been focused and sharpened by a strong decisive CEO who knows a good thing when he sees it.

The NatNec story involves new mental models from top to bottom—an emphasis on balancing steadiness with change, an idea of how to separate resource allocation from execution and relate them both in a new way to hierarchy, a new view of measuring performance, a fundamental change in the way the business looks at technology, and teams, teams, and more teams.

Change from an Unexpected Direction

The emphasis on information systems and on vision at NatNec are just two of the many things that make the NatNec experience different from other companies. Many of the changes that shape NatNec's culture today stem from the arrival of Justin Jederman, NatNec's recently retired CIO. Here's how Burton remembers it. "I hired a new CIO in 1993... fellow named Justin Jederman. He was a terrific guy and had a lot of common sense ideas about how to get more value out of our resources. He called what we have an information ecology, told us that we should think about it as being kind of a jungle with the parts strongly dependent on each other. He spent a lot of time with me and with the other seniors in the firm. He showed us what we were spending and what we were getting for it. He told us that we could get back 10 to 100 times more return for our investment in technology. But, he said, we'd have to change the way we thought about a lot of things to make it happen."

"The guy came in kind of quietly and began saying all these strange things about how systems and business had to be partners, about teams, about balancing change, about values and visions. It was all new to us and, frankly, we thought he was a kook."

Justin Jederman was NatNec's CIO during the company's dramatic surge. He retired into a very active consulting practice just last spring. In a telephone interview for this article, Jederman acknowledged his contribution to the company this way, "Yes, I guess you could say that I had something to do with changing the company, but it wasn't so much that I did things differently. I think of being a catalyst that helped the company set free energy that was already there. I'm glad my ideas helped. I'm trying to spread them around now with a little consulting. I've also just finished a book."

Jederman's successor remembers it a bit differently. To Bob Roberts, NatNec's new CIO, Jederman's influence was pivotal. Says Roberts, "He was it! When he arrived I was one of his direct reports. The guy came in kind of quietly and began saying all these strange things about how systems and business had to be partners, about teams, about balancing change, about values and visions. It was all

new to us and, frankly, we thought he was a kook." Roberts remembers a particularly poor level of relations between the NatNec business people and the people who worked in technology at the time. "Until Jederman came, the technology people and the business people had as little to do with each other as possible. The relationship was very bad. Suddenly Jederman wants us to start 'sharing a vision' with them. We didn't know what that meant but we were pretty sure that the business guys weren't the ones we wanted to share anything with. They basically treated us like servants. We considered them technical illiterates. We had to do what they told us (if they ever told us anything) so we tried to keep the interaction to a minimum. Jederman changed all that. Now isolation like that is totally invisible. Cooperation and teamwork; that's visible!"

The information systems function was not alone in thinking that the relationship needed to be improved. Rose Cerrutti, Product Manager, recalls, "We used to think that people who did technology were service

---

"It's almost as if they have some special mental telepathy for deciding what to do."

---

nerds. The idea was we'd tell them what to do and they'd do it. Technology was a necessary evil. Those of us on the business side were being stupid, wasting the techie resource by not involving them in the business. On the other hand, they were kind of stupid too, copping out—either playing techie games or just shutting down and saving their energy and imagination for outside the office. After a while most of us on the business side didn't want to have anything to do with the techies. We appointed liaisons to do it for us (wow, was that a bad idea!). Later we talked a lot about outsourcing."

Like Roberts, Cerrutti sees the underlying change in attitude as very important. She says, "Now the techie is just another part of the team. We don't much think about there being a 'technology' side and a 'business' side any more. This is lots more efficient—also more fun.

"When a team gets allocated the questions are about what team roles and what functional roles we need to make the team work, not whether the people are business people or technology people. For instance, the team manager who supports my system assets is a techie, I guess, but I never think about him that way. All I know is that we have a steadily improving return on our system assets for the last four years. This team has contributed more added value than the marketing team or sales team and are second only to the acquisition team in four-year average added value increase."

Jederman seems to have arrived at NatNec with an agenda, but he was cautious about introducing it. What emerged was a top-down process in which the strategy and operations of the business began to wind together the best thinking from the traditional business leadership and the company's technology experts.

Learning New Skills

Over a period of years, Jederman seems to have encouraged NatNec to start at the top and make behavioral changes. First came values and skills training. For instance, Jason Peaks, NatNec's VP for Human Resources remembers when he first heard about it. "Jederman's people came to some of my people and asked for help in setting up skills training on communications and small group interaction. They had a list of skills they wanted to learn. About the same time Jederman and I and some of the other seniors approached [NatNec CEO] Burton with the idea of defining some common values and a shared vision. When Burton agreed, he said maybe we ought to learn some things first and handed me exactly the same list of skills!"

Jederman's list of communication and small group skills became the basis for a course that eventually nearly everyone in the company was to take. NatNec people call it "personal mastery". Peaks says personal mastery gives newcomers a sense of NatNec's style, teaches them useful communication and group work techniques that everyone else in the company also knows, and creates a bonding of common experience that encourages trust and makes working together more efficient.

Vision

Jederman didn't stop there. "Pretty soon," say CIO Roberts, "we began hearing about 'visioning.' We heard it from Jederman first, but in a couple of months it started showing up everywhere in the company. We used our new group work skills and did some sessions to see if we could generate a solid idea of what we meant by 'Shared Vision' and whether or not we wanted to spend the resources to develop one. Finally, Burton told us that executive management would develop a vision that we could build on."

In NatNec, a shared vision is a well-documented description of a desired future state for the company and a set of broad programs (called pursuits in NatNec*ese*) for moving the company toward the desired future state. It was part of NatNec's vision to dominate their industry. An important pursuit was to build market share. Subpursuits included new products and acquisitions. Both of these areas have become NatNec's strengths, clearly according to plan.

NatNec people at all levels talk about the vision. They often have different details in mind, but whether an individual works in customer service, the finance division, sales, or computer programming, they feel that their understanding of the vision (and therefore, what's visible) fits with everyone else's. This confidence grows from the significant time and dollars that NatNec spends to keep the vision alive. Nearly everyone in the company spends some time—a half day to a week—each quarter in some exercise intended to expand, refine, or coordinate the vision. NatNec executives believe that this investment pays back many times over in improved decision making.

Industry guru, Prometheus Craston, says that timely decision making has been one of NatNec's keys to success. "By the time anybody else has even gotten the facts together in a new situation, the NatNec people have already figured out what to do and are halfway there. It's amazing. It's almost as if they have some special mental telepathy for deciding what to do." Inside NatNec rapid decision making is taken for granted. CFO Colin Wright says, "One often hears, 'It's visible; let's do it!' Then people head off in all directions. It looks like magic but it's really just the power of the vision plus the effectiveness of the internal communications."

Hierarchy, Partnerships, and Strategic Allocation

An outsider often hears that NatNec pulls off this magic act without any organizational hierarchy. Human Resources VP Peaks explains, "Of course, we have a hierarchy. We use it for what it's good at and keep it out of the way of things it isn't good at. Mostly, hierarchy is useful for allocating resources and deciding in broad strokes how to use the resources. That's exactly what our hierarchy does. When it comes to doing things, that's the job of a team. Hierarchy is the coach."

Teams and partnerships are concepts that NatNec people use a lot. In NatNec partnerships are groups of people, usually small groups, usually comprised of peers in the hierarchy, which coordinate and allocate resources. Central to the company's functioning is the tactical linkage partnership (TLP) which has the key job of overseeing all of NatNec's technology based change. "We're trying for balance in several dimensions," says CIO Roberts who chairs the TLP. Emphasizing the need for constant change is an important part of the TLP. Says Roberts, "It's usually hard to make sure that we've got enough activities going on that break new ground for us. It's easy to sit back and be satisfied with a reengineered process, but if we don't stay on top of things, eventually we'll get surprised by somebody. Those surprises aren't ever pleasant.

"We've made almost a religion of knowing what returns we get."

"We're also interested in balancing risk. It's important that we don't play everything safe—nothing ventured, you know—but it's also important that the risks we take be reasonable and in the right parts of the business."

On a quarterly basis the TLP analyzes and reviews all the activity in the company that involves sustaining or transforming the company's basic business processes. They focus intently on the transforming activities and reallocate resources as they see fit. This very powerful coordinating partnership has members from all the major business and functional units. The vision and their shared sense of balance drive their decisions.

According to CIO Roberts, the overall strategic framework for the TLP comes from the work of the company's executive managers who meet twice a year as the strategic linkage partnership (SLP). The SLP makes the highest level decisions in the company about resource allocations including questions about whether or not enough investment in the aggregate is being made in new technology and how the overall resources should be balanced across businesses, markets, geography, and so forth. The SLP is chaired by CEO Burton. Roberts, who is a member of the SLP, says that it's extremely important to him as CIO to have the executive management of the company take on this specific focus from time to time. "It's the forum to deal with my partners on a vital topic for which I am steward but for which we are mutually responsible."

CEO Burton recalls how the idea of the partnerships got started, "Jederman was circulating a little presentation on relationships. He got us thinking about how the business and technology people worked together. We sort of fell into the idea of partnership as a good model and started learning how to do partnerships and be partners. I guess it was about a year after Jederman came that we set up the SLP and the TLP."

Burton responds to a query about the value of these partnerships, "It was in the TLP that we first worked out that acquisition was one of the basic business processes of this company, not just a series of ad hoc events. That's when we started to get good at it. I believe that our ability to derive value quickly from acquisitions has been and continues to be a point of major advantage over our competition."

Then Burton goes on to add, "I don't think that we ever would have gotten to understand how to balance strategically our allocation of resources to changing our basic processes if we hadn't spent so much time in the SLP working on the vision thing and understanding the fundamental way the business works. We spent hours thinking about what we wanted things to be like and what had to happen to get us there. That time investment has paid back handsomely by helping us focus on what's really important and the work that supports it."

NatNec seems to have adopted a simple principle that resources are allocated by the hierarchy, coordinated by partnerships, and used by teams. People seem to be comfortable filling positions (they call them roles) in the hierarchy, in partnerships, and in teams and doing them all concurrently. NatNec admits that this creates complication in the area of performance evaluation but they insist that the complications of their new system are much better than the confusion they left behind and that, they argue, is characteristic of most companies. Human Resources VP Peaks explains, "Partnerships evaluate themselves as teams. The success or failure of any team is evaluated by the hierarchy to determine the return the company got on the allocated resources. Other aspects of performance are evaluated within the team. Moving up in the hierarchy means that you get more involved in making allocation decisions and understanding the returns we get."

NatNec is extraordinarily concerned with the returns it gets from its invested resources. All the work that involves NatNec's information systems and operations and most of NatNec's other activities are conducted by various sorts of teams, and every team is expected to measure its return on investment. CFO Wright says, "No doubt information technology has had a lot to do with our success, but what was really important was running the company smarter. We made some changes to get more value for our investments and we've made almost a religion of knowing what returns we get.

"I guess it was two years after Jederman started messing around with these concepts that we started working on a value-added model of the company as a whole to use as the basic scorecard for investments. We built on a version of Michael Porter's value chain model and now we tie all our return on asset and investment analyses to that value chain. If we manage the added value and manage our added value increment for new investments, improved profitability is virtually unavoidable."

"Working on a SAM team is the absolute best way to learn what goes on in the business."

This thinking has led to dramatic changes in NatNec's financial management. Wright continues, "Our entire MIS process has been overhauled as a result. Our basic control reports are now translated into value added instead of contribution or pretax earnings. This was a big deal! All the score keeping changed! Here on the finance side we pay more attention to pricing consequences than we used to, but for most of our work things are simpler. A single model (even though it's fairly complex) for how the business works makes all of the MIS we used to do mostly unnecessary. It also's helped that really good automation support has been built into the new MIS. Oh yes, and I guess our shift to continuous planning has made life a bit simpler too."

CIO Roberts sees the underlying change at NatNec in yet another way, "My take is that what we figured out was not how to master the technology, I think we knew that, but how to work together. That took some learning. Especially we learned to respect each other. By 'we' I mean the techies and the business guys.

"It used to be that they were the bosses and we did what we were told. The problem was they didn't know what to tell us, especially when it came to doing anything new. After Jederman came, we started getting together and trusting each other. He set up a training program for people in I/S and the people on the business side that taught learning and team skills. It turned out to be a terrific way to build trust. After you went through that course we all felt we could trust others who had been through it too. Shared experience and so forth.

"After the senior executives did their work on vision and values, we used the skills from the personal mastery courses to extend and enrich the shared vision in the various areas where we operate. There was vision development in I/S as a whole and in a lot of I/S business areas. The personal mastery skills made vision extension a lot easier than it would have been otherwise."

Teams, Teams, Teams

NatNec believes that the function of the hierarchy is to allocate resources. Furthermore, if you allocate a resource, you are accountable for it. On the other hand, NatNec believes that if you need something done, get a team. When NatNec allocates a team, they don't just have a list of names. Teams are important concepts. CEO Burton recalls, "I guess it was also about then [shortly after the SLP and TLP partnerships were established] that [Jederman] started using the team concept in the I/S area and it began to catch on."

The members of a team are expected to fill whatever functional roles the team requires such as team leader, programmer, financial analyst, or documentation specialist. In addition, each team member is known to fill a team role based on the person's personality. NatNec believes that balancing the team's team roles makes a more effective team, so when a team is being formed a choice may be made between two financial analysts based on which one is a "completer finisher"—a person who likes to get things done—and which is a "shaper" —a person who likes to decide how problems will be solved.

Teams report to whomever allocated the resources that the team represents, usually one or a small group of managers from the hierarchy. As soon as teams are formed they establish their goals and objectives and the measurements they will use to determine success. These tie into the vision's pursuits; the work of the team must be visible to all the members.

Teams are set up for both projects and processes. Process teams tend to

---

"I know what I have to do to make the team succeed. I know what I have to do to succeed personally. And, surprise, they're the same things!"

---

be more stable; project teams disband at the end of the project. When the work is done, team members evaluate each other (including the team leader) in their functional roles and they measure each other in what NatNec calls individual adherence [to NatNec's values]. The success of the team as a whole is measured against the goals and objectives set up by the team at the beginning. Hierarchy members allocate performance bonuses to teams based on these results. The bonus is apportioned by the team leader with consultation with the HR function based on the individual team member's functional role performance. Individual adherence rarely plays a big part in bonus allocation but it does weigh heavily on team staffing and promotion decisions.

The fundamental engine for change at NatNec is a business process reengineering (BPR) team. These very powerful high-level teams tackle whole business processes or major subprocesses. Chuck Shoop, a member of the BPR team working on service distribution, enthuses, "This is the most exciting work that a person can do in this company! Our job is to tackle the entire service distribution function of the company, all products, all geography, all customer segments, and make it add more value. Anything goes in the way of ideas, all doors are open to the team. Everybody wants to get involved."

BPR teams are idea generators and high-level designers. When implementation is required, various focused implementation teams are allocated based on BPR team recommendations. When system development work is required to implement a BPR design (and it usually is), a system reengineering implementation (SRI) team is allocated. SRI teams have responsibility for building or acquiring what NatNec calls "system assets." System assets are NatNec's name for all the systems, procedures, processes, and equipment necessary to perform some business process. These are not necessarily assets in the accounting sense but are certainly assets in the

---

"This is a company that got its act together in a lot of very important ways."

---

popular sense. Each system asset is expected to earn its way in "value added" as defined in the overall NatNec MIS system.

John Smythe works on an SRI team. In his view, "Building systems in this environment is very interesting. We put enormous focus on what the system's functionality and user interface should be. We usually either build prototypes or increasingly sophisticated versions of the final system. Either way we try to get real-world experience with a design as we build and test it.

"In the old days, we spent most of the effort on a new development on things that were basically internal to the application. You know, file layouts, databases, ways of organizing functions, user interface layout —stuff like that. Now almost all of that is in the infrastructure. As application developers we mostly fit together a lot of components that already do the basic parts of the job. In a typical system, we write less than 5% new code. Sometimes we don't write code at all. In fact, 'Write no code' is one of our principles."

When Smythe and his SRI teammates complete a system, the new system asset is turned over to a permanent system asset management (SAM) team. The SAM team's mission is to make sure that NatNec gets maximum value for the system asset. Their work includes what others might call maintenance, but it also includes a great deal of oversight of how the system is used and how it evolves.

Pauline Tertius is the team leader for a well-established SAM team. She says, "Working on a SAM team is the absolute best way to learn what goes on in the business. The system assets we manage are the highest return part of the value chain for this business. Our job is to make sure we keep getting that return and it keeps getting better."

When asked for specifics, she continues, "We do the normal care and feeding of the computer applications and we pay attention to how efficiently these applications use the infrastructure. More important, though, is we pay attention to how people use the asset to add value. We are on top of the efficiency of the human interface so that the operations people can be as efficient as possible. We also have one particular system asset that has a direct customer POS interface, so we pay a lot of attention to how efficiently customers use that."

Asked why she cares about customer's efficiency, she replies, "First, it's a service thing. We compete on ease of use for the customer. It's part of our value added. Then we are interested in how much alternative service these customer-originated transactions require. Sometimes this makes us reevaluate our underlying business model."

Human Resources VP Peaks tells the impact that the emphasis on teams has had for HR, "When we first made the commitment to teams as the fundamental organizational unit, we did an exhaustive review of all of our policies and procedures to identify which ones had to be changed to fit the new management style. Most of the changes came in the compensation plans, performance appraisal system, and in career planning.

"Oh, I'm sure that most of the ideas we use are used in other companies somewhere, but I think what's different is how we've put them all together: values, principles, vision, teams, ticket punching, etc.

"[Ticket punching is] our slang (I think it came from the military) for a career plan and a progression of responsibility. Everybody knows what is expected in terms of learning different roles and different skills. When the skill is learned or satisfactory performance in the role is demonstrated, the person has gotten another punch in the ticket. Ticket punches translate into salary increases and promotions."

Respect and Trust

Many NatNec long timers credit Justin Jederman's ideas for the profound change that has taken place here in the way that business and technology people work together. When asked what working at NatNec is like, one system developer from an SRI team says, "This is a great place to work. I worked in four companies before joining NatNec and this is the only company I've ever been in where I was considered part of the business instead of part of the problem. I know what I have to do to make the team succeed. I know what I have to do to succeed personally. And, surprise, they're the same things!"

A business person from the same SRI team answers in the same vein, "There's a good sense of belonging to something. The values, principles, and the vision are all out there where we can all see them. I'm really committed to the vision. Most of us are. And that makes things so much easier. We almost never have arguments about opinions. If we find ourselves arguing about facts, we dig out the facts, we don't just keep arguing."

CEO Burton describes the change this way, "We used to think of our computer systems as tools for doing the business. We figured out that the computer systems and the people who used them *were* the business. It was a subtle shift but it really made a difference in how we treated the people with technology skills.

"When we started treating them as partners, they started acting like partners and the huge body of skills and experience they represent was finally brought to bear on making money. Before that we treated them like service providers or contractors—we told them head down and code, do what you're told. It drove the best ones away and alienated the ones who stayed. These are very smart people and we used to throw away that brainpower even though we were paying for it."

A visitor quickly feels the real respect and trust that suffuses these working teams. There's also energy, lots of energy. The complex team assignments keep things from being boring. An SRI team member says, "Teams are everything. I'm on four teams right now in addition to my administrative team. I usually am a resource person as my team role. That means I can usually find out information or get hold of the things we need on the team, so I do that on all the teams I'm on. I get different functional roles though. On one team I'm the team leader, on another I'm a product expert, I'm just a regular team member on the other two." These multiple assignments are the norm at NatNec and become more complex as you climb the hierarchy ladder. The complexity of this staffing arrangement and the measurement and evaluation processes that go with it are only a few of the features of NatNec that would be impossible without the complete dedication the company has made to automating itself.

Dedication to Technology and Change

There are no paper-based processes at NatNec. Every employee has access to a suitable workstation and all the workstations are interconnected by NatNec's sophisticated internal data communications network. NatNec's general wisdom says that "People do the thinking and the network does the work." NatNec was an early adopter of full multimedia documents in their operations and led in the conversion to desk-to-desk teleconferencing. They have been at the forefront of the groupware revolution and today are testing the possible applications of bio-computing, intelligent agents, and nano-machines. They believe in learning how to use new technology first and they trust that their investment in understanding will let them know when to jump in with big money. NatNec considers their ease with adopting new technology as just one aspect of an overall commitment to mastering change. CEO Burton says, "If there is one thing that we want to do better than anyone else, it's change. As an organization we want to know

all we can about the process of change and as individuals we want to have the skills that allow us to change efficiently. We can't know too much or be too good at change. It's a constant challenge to balance doing what we do to add value today with what we have to do so that we can continue to add value tomorrow."

Industry consultant Craston comments, "You hear a lot about how NatNec has gotten on top of things by using technology better. That's certainly true, but it doesn't begin to tell the whole story.

"This is a company that got its act together in a lot of very important ways. Technology was a part, but I think that the principles that Just Jederman and Win Burton brought to managing the company—mutual respect, trust, partnerships, teamwork, visioning, measurement, return on investment, and so forth—all of this was fundamental change in the way these people thought about working together. That's what's worked for NatNec."

National Necessary Service Corporation is a lively place full of lively people who believe in NatNec's vision. So far it's worked better than anyone (except the NatNec people) would have believed possible. At NatNec the vision is still polished every day and every day NatNec people reshape their world to look like their vision. Will it continue? Well, at NatNec they say, "It's visible; let's do it!"

Summary

NatNec certainly prospered by adopting the ideas in this book. The application of the ideas in a real company will take a course that is unique to the character and circumstances of the company, but experience in large-scale change suggests a broad outline of what works.

A champion of change. Successful major change requires a leader who serves as the central figure and the driving force for the change. This champion articulates the main ideas and continually exhorts the benefits of the change. The champion must be in the innermost leadership of the company, preferably at the very center. If the CEO is not the champion then the champion must be seen to have the CEO's strong support and backing. In the article CIO Justin Jederman was the original champion but then the role gradually shifted to CEO Win Burton.

A vision for change. An indispensable component of this kind of broad change is a shared vision. A process is necessary for developing the vision (complete with desired future state, pursuits, and measures), syndicating the vision to all the stakeholders, and keeping the vision fresh as time passes and the environment changes. In the article, CIO Jederman fostered the idea of a vision, but CEO Win Burton pushed it through and ensured that resources would be available to keep it alive.

A rational basis for change. A significant portion of the key players in a company will find it difficult to support change unless they believe that they understand the logical basis for the change—they need more than just the vision, they need a sense that there is an underlying rationale that guides the change. Frameworks like the common interest-relative authority grid, the Henderson work on partnerships, the Henderson and Venkatraman model, and the Redditt and Lodahl work on I/S effectiveness and organization can satisfy these people.

Business technology linkage. In the article, NatNec adopted strategic linkage and tactical linkage partnerships exactly like the ones described in this book as the coordinating and linkage mechanisms for strategy and high-level allocation. NatNec also uses the partnership model as the coordinating mechanism for middle-level managers who share common resources. For execution work, NatNec has bought into the concept of dynamic teams. Business and technology people are carefully mixed on teams focused on particular processes and projects.

Sustain and *transform* **balance.** A program for change needs to take into account the permanent and necessary tension between *sustain* and *transform*. NatNec used the mix of teams described in this book as the balancing mechanism. A company troubled by a disproportionate amount of *transform* might need to introduce stability and the associated values with a more traditional organizational style.

Measurement and reward. Every plan for change must embody careful alignment of the measurement and reward mechanisms with the goals of the organization. NatNec developed a value-added model for each of the important processes of the business and used it across the board to measure and reward performance. Individual performance was evaluated against a set of well-defined team roles and a separate set of desired personal behaviors. Rewards are linked to individual, team, and overall business performance.

Use of technology. NatNec looked hard at using technology as a facilitator of all company processes. They invested in infrastructure and began to pride themselves on being exploiters of technology (not experimenters).

Focus on the process of change. Change is not a blip in an otherwise placid continuity; change is a process that is continuous and unavoidable. We can manage the change or not, but we can't avoid it. NatNec decided to view change as another process of its business and learned to be good at it. The practical consequences of this view included specific skills training in communications and change management.

Each company will have its own story. The stories with the happy endings will have most of the features of this broad outline.

Appendix A

A Management View of the New Technology

Most companies have become masters of information technology over the course of the last 30 years. Large computers systems and networks of terminals have become commonplace and the skills to build and operate these large systems have become part of the repertoire of corporate management.

The comfort that comes from information technology mastery has been challenged forcefully by an entire revolution in the underlying technology of computing and communications, which started with microcomputers and the first PCs and has spread to every part of the information ecology. Most important to the general manager are those elements of the new technology that have changed computing hardware and software economics.

I suggest that understanding this new technology has important benefits for us as senior executives. We are not going to be writing programs or plugging in wires, but we will be involved in important decisions that arise as the tension between *sustain* and *transform* grows. Insight into the technology will help us

- Appreciate the real obstacles to *transform* that exist and help us distinguish them from the obstacles that only exist in the minds of the forces of *sustain.*
- Appreciate how different preferences for specific standards, vendors, and products arise between the supporters of *sustain* and *transform* and understand where we need to be on these questions conceptually and practically.
- Identify expressions of cultural difference between *sustain* and *transform* masquerading as technical or organizational problems.

The politics of the information ecology are inextricably tangled with its technical complexities. Most of us have absorbed an appreciation for the present technology in the 15 years or so we have been using it. Now, in order to effectively manage the struggle between *sustain* and *transform* and to deal with the growing complexity of the information ecology, an appreciation of the new wave of technology is indispensable.

This appendix explores the new technology in just enough detail to foster such an appreciation. We examine network computing, which is revolutionizing the infrastructure of the information ecology, and reusable software, which is revolutionizing the way application systems are built and maintained. In each section, we describe the path most companies have traveled to get to their present *sustain*-dominated information ecologies then we describe the new technology and how it's different. In the final section of the appendix, we examine the benefits that are driving us toward these new technologies and the problems we are likely to encounter trying to implement them.

Network computing

Most large companies have followed a familiar path over the last 30 years as they have implemented information technology. This path has left them with a very expensive technology infrastructure, an inherently fragile suite of legacy application systems that are difficult and expensive to maintain, and an information systems organization that is well suited to sustaining this obsolescent environment but is ill equipped to *transform* it. In the last few years, the microcomputer and associated technical advances in electronic communication have enabled a new, much cheaper and more flexible infrastructure for computing called network computing. The next sections describe the familiar path most have followed and introduce network computing, the new microcomputer-based infrastructure.

Most Companies Have Followed a Familiar Path to Their Present Automation

Sometime in the 1950s or early 1960s most companies bought or leased a computer, probably from IBM. It had to have air conditioning, extra power, and a raised floor. The computer probably was justified on savings in the payroll department, accounting department, or maybe, inventory control.

At first slowly and then in a rush, people from all over these companies wanted to put their work "on the computer." Every year or so more computer equipment was needed. Every three to five years a major upgrade required "conversion" of the applications.

In the late '60s and early '70s the computers companies were using integrated circuits that were manufactured on boards (literally, boards) that, in order to share a common power supply, slipped into a wired up metal cage called a "frame." The most important components of the computer were on the "main" frame.

Most large companies gradually grew into a situation where they had many computer rooms, now called "data centers"—large, secure, environmentally controlled spaces with a raised floor on which sit a large number of featureless boxes that look a good deal like refrigerators.[1] In a good modern data center, most of the actual work of telling the computers what to do and when is managed by one of the computers. Like airline pilots, an operator is required only when something goes wrong.

The computer operator doesn't have to sit in the cold room with the computers any more and rarely does. Consequently we can turn the lights out in the machine room. Most modern data center managers have made a goal of the lights out data center, a code phrase for maximum automation of the data center functions. When it is achieved, it means that, not only does the computer operator not have to be in the same room, he may not even have to be in the same state! If this kind of remote operation can be made to work, then a single site with people in it could run computers in lots of "lights out" sites, which may be geographically remote.

In addition to computer operators to operate three shifts, 365 days a year, a data center operations group has experts who:

- Tune the computers for maximum practical use of the equipment.
- Install and maintain the hundreds of programs that comprise operating systems, data base management systems, terminal control systems, printing control systems, and so forth.
- Control which application systems[2] are in production and when they should run and what internal computer resources and priorities they should have.
- Provide data security to make sure only authorized terminal users can look at or update important computer files.
- Plan and manage a backup and recovery process to handle emergency situations in which the data center is unavailable for some reason.[3]

Most companies have a data communication network that connects terminals all over the company to its mainframe computers. Mostly these networks are connected to IBM computers and use IBM's proprietary data communications technology.

Conceptually you can imagine that each terminal is at the end of a wire—one wire for each terminal. The other end of each wire is attached to the mainframe computer, forming the "star network" illustrated in Exhibit A.1. The terminals never talk to each other, only to the mainframe computer. The terminals aren't expected to be good for anything by themselves; they've got to be connected to the mainframe to be useful.

The star network that supports mainframe computers is usually very sophisticated and requires a lot of experts to keep it going at the very high reliability that we demand of these networks. There may be as many operators and experts to support a mainframe's network as there are experts and operators to support the mainframe computers themselves. The mainframe computers and the network that serves them are really one complicated device assembled to do a company's information processing.

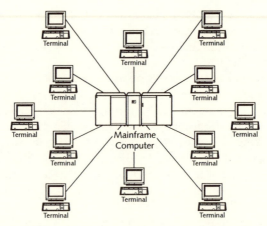

Exhibit A.1   In a Star Network Each Terminal has a Logical Connection to the Mainframe

There is another kind of data communication networking going on in many companies that uses local area networks (LANs). For most of us, the first LAN arrived six or seven years ago. It started out when a department with ten or so PCs decided they would like to share a printer or a device to share files. Like rabbits, the longer a company's had LANs, the more they've probably got.

When we make the mental picture of a LAN, we imagine a loop of wire with each PC connected to its own place on the loop (see Exhibit A.2). There's no middle and no top to the flow of data on the loop.[4] Like a broadcast, when one of the computers sends a message out on the loop, every other computer on the loop hears it. Even though all the computers hear the message, only the computer to which the message is directed pays any attention. Some kinds of LANs have rules about how the computers have to take turns broadcasting on the loop (like token rings). Other LANs (like Ethernets) let the computers broadcast any time they want to and have rules for dealing with the situations when they bump into each other. In the early '80s, there was a fierce "religious" debate about which kind of LAN was better. It was never resolved and now nobody cares. They both work fine.

LANs grew in most companies as communication islands. The computers attached to a LAN could talk to each other but that was it. As the information ecology evolved, existing LANs grew larger and more and more LANs were started. Gradually a demand emerged for the PCs and workstations attached to LANs to communicate with computers on other LANs. Also, computers on the LAN increasingly wanted to communicate with the mainframes. To meet these requirements techies started installing connections between and among LANs and other connections between LANs and mainframes. These weren't local anymore; they covered a wide area, so the connections and the LANs together came to be called the wide area network or WAN.

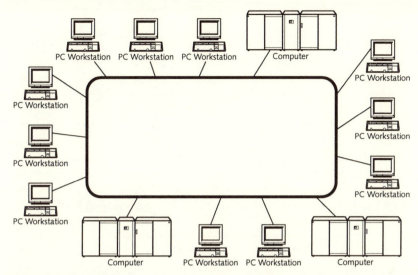

Exhibit A.2   Each Computer on a Local Area Network (LAN) Can Talk to Each of the Others

In most companies there's a star network that connects a large number of terminals to mainframe computers. Some, perhaps many, of the terminals in the star network are PCs or other workstations pretending to be terminals. There are islands, big and small, of computers that communicate with each other over LANs. And, there is probably a pressure to begin or continue to interconnect the LANs with each other and with the mainframes. Most companies either have a WAN or soon will.

There are also isolated computers. Perhaps, a department computer that isn't attached to anything. More likely, personal computers that just sit on somebody's desk and do word processing or spreadsheets. No matter how useful these computers may be standing alone, they will be worth a great deal more when they join a communication network—electronic mail, at least! As long as people think of that PC as a computing device, the best it will do is make one person more productive. As soon as we begin to treat it as a communications device, it has the potential to make whole work groups more productive.

Network Computing Offers a Compelling Alternative to Traditional Mainframe Computing

Network computing is basically a substitution of many microcomputer-based computers for a few mainframe computers and the computer-to-computer communications necessary to get them to work together. The next section describes how the work of an application is divided among various computers. The section after that describes how the communication between computers works.

Client Server

The story of the tower of Babel illustrates the key role communications plays in combining individual efforts. Life without communication and cooperation would be simple, sterile, and primitive beyond imagining. Network computing is all about arranging things so that our computers can communicate and co-operate.

"Client server" is the popular buzzword in network computing. Techies will tell you that this phrase may refer to several different kinds of computer cooperation. They're right, of course, but we have no need to examine the subtleties. We can be quite content with a very homey understanding of clients and serv-ers. Take the dialog in Exhibit A.3, for instance. If Dad and Sally were comput-ers, we would examine this transaction and say that Sally is the "client" and Dad is the "server." It's that simple.

> "Dad, please pass the potatoes."
>
> "Here they are, Sally."
>
> "Thanks."
>
> "You're welcome."

Exhibit A.3   Simple Analog of Client Server Dialog

Computers can be either clients or servers. They can change roles to suit different circumstances. Typically the desktop computer (workstation) is the client and the computers in the back room(s) are the servers. Computers that most often act as servers can, if need arises, request services from other servers and therefore temporarily become clients. As a matter of fact, however, in most present day network computing designs computers mostly stick to one role or the other.

Even clever computers aren't as flexible as people are. In order to make a re-quest and response work between computers, the question must be asked and the response sent in a carefully constructed way. Between computers, the dialog would be more like Exhibit A.4.

"Dad	this is Sally	please pass the potatoes."
"Sally	this is Dad	here are the potatoes."
"Dad	this is Sally	I have successfully received the potatoes."
"Sally	this is Dad	I understand that you have successfully received the potatoes."

Exhibit A.4   Simple Analog Dialog Restructured to Look More Like a Computer Conversation

The rules for these conversations are called remote procedure calls. In order for computers to interact this way techies have to agree on a specific remote procedure call standard and all the computers in the network have to have programs that implement the standard.

Cooperation among computers means nothing more than the ability to exchange messages and to act on those messages. This is very simple and it's very powerful. To illustrate, let's begin by elaborating our dinner conversation a little, as shown in Exhibit A.5.

"Dad	this is Sally	please pass the potatoes."
"Sally	this is Dad	we don't have potatoes."
"Dad	this is Sally	what do we have that's like potatoes."
"Sally	this is Dad	rice."
"Dad	this is Sally	please pass the rice."
"Sally	this is Dad	here's the rice."
"Dad	this is Sally	I have successfully received the rice."
"Sally	this is Dad	I understand that you have successfully received the rice."

Exhibit A.5   More Complex Analog Dialog

In this more elaborate scenario, Dad and Sally both did some processing in order to complete the transaction. first the "Dad server" had to signal the "Sally client" that the request couldn't be honored. "Sally client" had to determine whether to quit or to continue in some way. When the "Dad server" got the query, he had to determine what was like potatoes. And then "Sally client" had to decide whether or not rice was sufficiently like potatoes to be worth asking for. This is pretty simple stuff around the dinner table, but it's a big deal for computers. Exhibit A.6 shows how a similar logical problem might arise in a computer application.

"Database	this is Workstation	please pass the Robert Smith file."
"Workstation	this is Database	we don't have the Robert Smith file."
"Database	this is Workstation	what do we have that's like the Robert Smith file."
"Workstation	this is Database	R. Smith file."
"Database	this is Workstation	please pass the R. Smith file."
"Workstation	this is Database	here's the R. Smith file."
"Database	this is Workstation	I have successfully received the R. Smith file."
"Workstation	this is Database	I understand that you have successfully received the R. Smith file."

Exhibit A.6   Sample Client Server Dialog

In this case, the workstation client needed to decide what to do when the requested file didn't exist. It might have been programmed to ask for similar files or it might have been programmed to create a file if none existed or it might have been programmed to display the situation on the screen and ask the user to decide what to do. The data base server needed to know how to decide what it meant for a file to be "like" another file. So in this case there had to be decision-making logic in both the client and the server. They cooperated by sharing the work of coming up with a file that's "like" the Robert Smith file.

Networks and Protocols

In the preceding example we saw the messages the computers exchanged and inferred the processing that was required to act on those messages. You can easily imagine that most of the logic of implementing a business process in network computing is involved with designing the messages that are passed back and forth and on designing the details of how clients and servers act on the various messages. These details of the business process are what really matter to us as business managers because they represent the work we really want to get done. For the techie, however, these details, although important, are only a small part of the overall challenge of making computers work together. To the techie, the problem of what to communicate is dwarfed by the problem of how to establish reliable and flexible communications.

"I think what we have here is a failure to communicate"… this cliché is usually good for a laugh in a tense moment. It's a cliché because it's so often true. And it's true even though human beings are especially designed for communication. Communicating computers are like the singing dog. It's not a surprise the dog doesn't sing well; it's a surprise it sings at all. Communication between piles of silicon and copper seems even more unlikely. But before we dig into all the things we have to do to get computers to communicate, let's look at all the things that have to go right to get people to communicate.

- *Signaling.* first of all, we have to agree that we will communicate by modulating sound waves in frequencies between 2000 and 12000 cycles per second. We didn't get a lot of choice about that, after all we come with a certain set of lungs, larynx, mouth, teeth, lips, and ears, which pretty well lock us into those frequencies. Of course, we could have agreed to communicate by modulating the position of our arms and hands as people do in sign languages. A person who speaks and a person who signs may both be eloquent, but without an agreement or a translator they will not be able to communicate. So we have to agree on a signaling scheme.
- *Flow control.* Given a signaling scheme, we have to agree on some flow control. Most people have trouble communicating if everyone is talking at once so we adopt some form of agreement that lets one of us talk and then another and so on. You know, people clear their throats when they are about to speak or they lean forward or they raise a hand. These flow control mechanisms change from situation to situation and can be very different in different cultures, but they always exist in one form or another or communication is disrupted. People from different cultures who are

used to different flow control find it difficult to communicate without someone to moderate (translate) in their dialog.

- *Language.* Given signaling and flow control, we have to agree on a language. In spoken communications, this involves the choices of symbols (vocabulary), pronunciation of the symbols and the grammatical rules for combining the symbols into messages. Any confusion about what a word means, about how a particular word is pronounced, or about how words are combined to make ideas puts the communication at risk.

Given signaling, flow control, vocabulary, pronunciation rules, and grammar we can expect basic communication. In our subtlety as human beings we have evolved other languages of posture, emphasis, gesture, and facial expression that we use to embellish and amplify our spoken communications. Often the purpose of these additional languages is to improve the chances that we accurately communicate what we wish to communicate by introducing some nonsyntactical redundancy.

Most people share more or less the same signaling scheme, although there are wide variations among individuals and cultures. flow control varies within language groups and in different situations. Choice of language and the fine details of employing it are varied to an enormous degree. And the choice of nonsyntactical redundancy languages is often idiosyncratic to some obscure group. When you think about it, human communications is a bit of a singing dog too.[5]

In order for us to communicate reliably we need a lot of agreements as shown in Exhibit A.7.

Agreements about what can be talked about
Agreements on redundancy processing
Agreements on language and usage
Agreements on flow control
Agreements on signaling

Exhibit A.7   Agreements Required for Communication

It's important to note that what is needed is "agreement," not any particular agreement. For instance, one set of agreements might look like Exhibit A.8.

Agreements about what can be talked about	level 5	Talk about business topics
Agreements on redundancy processing	level 4	Pounded fist means important
Agreements on language and usage	level 3	American English
Agreements on flow control	level 2	When chair acknowledges raised hand
Agreements on signaling	level 1	Speak

Exhibit A.8   Example Communication Protocols for a Business Meeting

This set of agreements (let's call them protocols) would work for a business meeting. A different set of protocols could work too. For instance, level 5 could be "Talk about religion" while the rest of the protocol stack stays the same. The meeting would be different, but it would work. Or, perhaps, we might change level 3 to be "Mandarin Chinese"—different, but it still works. Level 2 could become "When no one more important than you is trying to talk" or level 1 could be "Cluck tongue and hiss in Morse code." The point is that there are choices of the protocols at each level in the stack and, if we are careful in defining the levels, each level can change more or less independently.

Standards for Network Computing

The purpose of the network is to support communication among application programs running on separate computers. In order to fulfill this purpose, network computing needs to agree on a set of protocols similar to the example we discussed. Over the years, there have been a number of proprietary protocol sets (the most famous is IBM's System Network Architecture, SNA) and there are now some developing international standards (most notably, OSI from ISO). The details of these data communication protocols are a lot more complicated than most people care about—real techie territory—but the agreements deal with more or less familiar topics as can be seen in Exhibit A.9.

Agreements about what can be talked about	Agreements on the kinds of messages which can be exchanged between computers Agreements on displaying and accepting information from people
Agreements on redundancy processing	Agreements on error handling
Agreements on language and usage	Agreements on codes and characters, message formats, and error correction
Agreements on flow control	Agreements on setting up and completing communication sessions
Agreements on signaling	Wire standards, electrical pulse standards, and connector standards

Exhibit A.9   Protocols for Computer Communication

Because of the history of this technology, different people in a large organization are likely to be involved with different levels in this protocol stack.

- People in the facilities area or telecom department are concerned with wires, connectors, and being able to get electrical conductivity from one place to another.
- Communications people in the data center are involved with some of the kinds of codes and session connections (especially between computers and terminals).
- People who install LANs are interested in all of these things too, but they probably have different preferences.

- Application programmers will be the ones interested in how application programs talk to each other.

Each of these groups of people is thinking about a different thing when they use the term "network." "Network management" is something that they all believe is important, but they probably don't agree on what it means or how to do it. We noted earlier that, if the protocol levels are carefully selected, they can be considered separate from each other and one protocol level could change, affecting only the adjacent layers. Many organizations have not yet settled on a set of protocols that provides this independence. Furthermore, there is probably a lot of uncertainty around who is responsible for what in the area of LANs, the interconnection of LANs, and the connection of LANs to mainframe data centers. Consequently, it's likely that there is a lot of confusion about making the network part of network computing work in most companies.

In addition to this confusion, one of the biggest challenges we face in transforming our information ecologies to network computing is making sure we can support the transformed environment when we get there. Network computing is very different from what we are used to. The people we have to manage our present computing environment have learned painfully over years how to keep our systems working every day and, if they break, to fix them fast. This same need for high reliability and quick response to problems will be a requirement of the new environment too, but the nature of the problems and the skills needed to cope with them will be different.

Confusion about who should be in charge of what in network computing is compounded also by a set of turf issues and personal agendas. In many companies, ventures into network computing were taken first by an end user. Typically, some business area had a need and decided to solve their problem without reference to the company's technology area. This has led in different companies to a variety of outcomes, but few of them have been particularly good. It is not unusual for there to be a significant struggle in the organization over control of network computing decisions and resources. The struggle can be obvious or it can be underground but its symptoms will be fierce arguments over obscure technical issues. When a senior executive is called on to settle such a struggle, he should forget the technical details and try instead to see the situation as an opportunity to balance the company's needs for *sustain* and *transform*.

Reusable software

This section describes how most companies developed their computer applications by "computerizing" existing business departments, a process that led ultimately to a huge tangle of legacy software. Following that, we describe the changes in the technology that are making possible a whole new set of application systems at a fraction of the cost of the systems already in place.

Most Companies Are Struggling with a Set of Computer Applications, Built Over a Period of Many Years, That Are Very Expensive and Complex to Operate and Maintain

The first computers were justified on cost savings in payroll, accounting, or inventory control—very basic parts of businesses. These first applications were quickly joined by others as understanding grew of the potential that existed for saving money by replacing human labor with computers.

Typically, a company would "computerize" some department. If things worked out well, the cost of the new computer system and the reduced cost of the department would be less than what the department cost before being "computerized." Sometimes there would be other benefits, perhaps improved timeliness or quality, but these were rarely important parts of the motivation or justification.

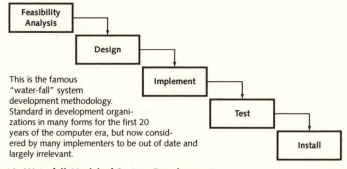

Exhibit A.10 Waterfall Model of System Development

This process of incremental automation has dominated the history of computer use in almost every big company and it's worth a brief examination of how each step was taken to help us understand the consequences that we are living with today.

In order to "computerize" a department, systems people always did some version of the steps in Exhibit A.10.

- *Feasibility analysis* involved examining an existing department's processes and costs to determine whether or not the potential benefits of "computerizing" were sufficient to warrant the development and on-going computer operating and support costs. Obviously, departments with big payback were likely to be done first. Payback usually meant displacing lots of people by having the computer do some relatively simply work. Departments that were smaller or where the work had a lot of nonroutine activity were likely to be "computerized" later or not at all.

- *Design* involved figuring out in a lot of detail the answers to straightforward questions. What information flows into the department and how can it be captured in "machinable" form? What information needs to be retained in the department, how long, who might need to see it, and in what form? What information in what form needs to be produced by the department and where does it go?

When answers to these question were worked out, the designers built computer programs to meet these requirements. Once the design was set, implementation, test, and installation—fairly mechanical processes—followed.

The archetype for most early computer applications was: take in data, process the data, write the data out. This linear process was appropriate to most of the simple work that was being computerized. Exhibit A.11 shows this flow from bottom to top. Information enters these applications at the bottom, is processed and stored in the middle, and output emerges from the top. This image of the applications leads to the techie jargon "stovepipe systems."

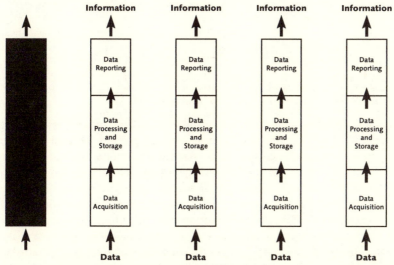

Exhibit A.11 Stovepipe Systems Were Built to Computerize Functions a Department at a Time

So, department by department, these applications were developed; the biggest, most labor intensive departments first. As department after department was "computerized," the company's suite of applications came to reflect the organization chart of the company. For a long time, nobody really noticed that we were organizing computer applications the same way we had organized manual operations and nobody asked if that was a smart thing to do.

As time passed, technology and business needs combined with a growing understanding of how to use computer systems and the original suite of applications was revised, replaced, upgraded, and generally improved. Often this meant substituting on-line data capture for card punching, on-line inquiry for paper reports, and fixing it so when data had to flow from one department to another, it was translated and transferred automatically by the machines instead of by people,[6] as shown in Exhibit A.12. But even with the new improved versions of these systems, they most often retained their identity, identifiable by name and function with the department that was originally "computerized."

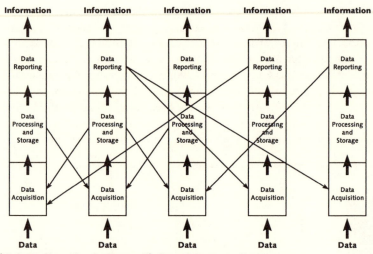

Exhibit A.12 Stovepipe Systems with Some Interconnection

As companies have automated more and more of their internal information flows, the stovepipe systems have become increasingly interconnected and the flow of information between and among systems has become at least as complicated and expensive as the applications themselves. The result, which techies call "spaghetti systems," is like a hanging mobile where moving one part starts up unpredictable motions in every other part. Such highly interconnected systems, illustrated in Exhibit A.13, are extremely difficult to maintain or change, and consequently routine maintenance absorbs an ever-increasing proportion of most companies' development staffs. In companies where this syndrome has reached an advance state, 80% to 90% of "development" effort is used up just dealing with wiggles in the mobile—forget about hanging on any new pieces.

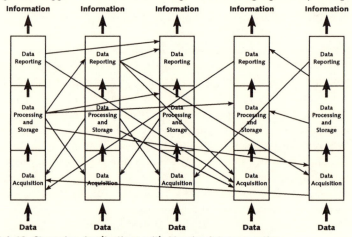

Exhibit A.13 Stovepipe Applications with Massive Interconnection

This typical history has produced a legacy of hard to maintain stovepipe systems with a spaghetti tangle of internal connections. This result was as inevitable for most companies' systems, given the typical history, as it was inevitable that a thousand-year-old city would have a tangle of too narrow streets at its center, buildings built on the rubble of preceding buildings, and modern amenities like power, water, and sewers available only at an enormous cost and complexity.[7] We don't need to beat ourselves up because we have what we have, but we do need to understand and begin to deal with the reality of this costly legacy.

Two Important Changes in the Technology Make It Possible to Build a Very Large Percentage of New Applications by Using and Reusing Standard Parts

Even though the business application is the most important part in the information ecology, it is an increasingly small part. The amount of code in new systems that is specific to the business the system supports is becoming smaller and smaller, in some cases vanishing altogether. Let's find out where the vanishing application is vanishing to.

Here's an illustration using two business applications. I am going to make them very simple intentionally so we can focus on the concepts instead of the details. The two applications are:

- *Inventory control:* keeps track of the number of items in stock of each item type.
- *Personnel:* keeps track of the employees name and addresses, dependents, work location, and benefit choices

The major functions in these simple applications are shown in Exhibit A.14.

Inventory Application	Agreements on error handling
Add, delete, or modify an item record	Add, delete, or modify a personnel record
Find all the items of a certain type (all the bolts, all the fuses, all the wheelbarrows, etc.)	Find all the employees with a certain characteristic (all the supervisors, all the married people, all the people living out of state, etc.)

Exhibit A.14 Basic Functions of Two Applications

The program functions that have to be written by the development people look something like the expanded list in exhibit A.15. You needn't study this exhibit but you might want to note that the entries are similar to the point of being boring.[8]

Different type styles are used in the table to emphasize the few portions that are different between the inventory control application and the personnel application. Spend a little more time to note the pattern—the actions that have to be done (display, accept, retrieve, update, and so forth) are the same in both applications, but the objects of the actions are different.

Inventory Application	Agreements on error handling
display a menu of choices (add, modify delete an **inventory item** record)	display a menu of choices (add, modify delete a **person** record)
display an Add screen and accept **inventory item** description data from the keyboard	display an Add screen and accept **person** data from the keyboard
add the new **inventory item (inventory item id, description, type, initial amount, etc.)** to the data base	add the new **person (person id, name, address, dependents, etc.)** to the data base
display a Modify screen and accept **inventory item** identification data from the keyboard	display a Modify screen and accept **person** identification data from the keyboard
retrieve the existing **inventory item** record from the data base	retrieve the existing **person** record from the data base
display the existing **inventory item** data and accept changes from the keyboard	display the existing **person** data and accept changes from the keyboard
update the **inventory item** data in the data base and write a transaction history record	update the **person** data in the data base and write a transaction history record
display a message saying update complete	display a message saying update complete
display a Delete screen and accept **inventory item** identification data from the keyboard	display a Delete screen and accept **person** identification data from the keyboard
retrieve the existing **inventory item** record from the data base	retrieve the existing **person** record from the data base
display the existing **inventory item** data and verify that this is the record to delete	display the existing **person** data and verify that this is the record to delete
delete the data base **inventory item** record and write a transaction history record	delete the data base **person** record and write a transaction history record
display a message saying update complete	display a message saying update complete
display an Inquiry screen and accept **inventory item** description data from the keyboard	display an Inquiry screen and accept **person** description data from the keyboard
search the data base and identify all the records that match the **inventory item** description request	search the data base and identify all the records that match the **person** description request
display the first matched **inventory item** record and accept a command from the keyboard to display the next record, start another search, or quit.	display the first matched **person** record and accept a command from the keyboard to display the next record, start another search, or quit.

Exhibit A.15 Two Business Applications Written to Highlight Similarity of Structure and Differences in Subject

There are 392 words in the table in Exhibit A.15. Only 36 are in large font bold, indicating that they are different from one application to another. This provides an unscientific, but quite reasonable, analog of the amount of custom code compared to general purpose code that would be required if we used the best new technology to actually build these two applications. Using today's best tools, the two application might be more than 90% the same! With this thought in mind we begin to wonder why we have a team of programmers doing inventory systems and another team of programmers doing personnel systems.

No one doubts that there are profound differences between items in the inventory and people in our organizations. It doesn't follow, however, that there are profound differences between the processes needed to keep track of what we want to know about items and people (counts, descriptions, records of changes, and so forth). The fact is that there is much more similarity than difference in these processes.

Those of us who have spent the last 30 years or so building the information ecology didn't figure that out right away. In fact, we built very similar systems over and over before we figured out what we were doing. Naturally, we got pretty good at doing the same thing again and again. We called that experience. If we continue to do it, we will have to call it stupidity.

Very early in the development of the information ecology we figured out that the computer itself, while certainly necessary, wasn't part of the business application. That is, if we designed it correctly, the same computer could be used for inventory control as for payroll and so on. Over a wide range, we could have a "general purpose" computer.[9] During the late '60s and '70s, we began to understand that the same "general purpose" concept could be designed into data communication networks and on-line computer applications. The spread of this "general purpose" thinking was slowed, but not stopped, by the PC revolution of the late '80s. Today, the general wisdom is that the hardware part of the information ecology either is or should be considered "infrastructure," components that can be common to any business application we wish to deploy.

The same shift from special purpose to general purpose has been happening with the software part of the information ecology. Exhibit A.16 illustrates the shift. The lower part of each column is an estimate of the amount of custom and general purpose code used in a "typical" business application that uses best practices of the period.

- *Before 1960,* a computer application was likely to be entirely custom.
- *During the 1970s,* operating systems were introduced and began to perform functions like loading and starting applications, sharing peripherals like printers and tape drives, and keeping track of the use of the computer.
- *By 1980,* common code was in use to control terminals and mass storage devices.
- *By 1990,* most applications used common code to control databases.

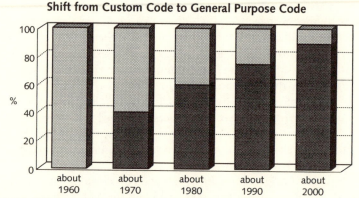

Exhibit A.16 Shift from Custom Code to General Purpose Code

The trend will continue. By the end of this decade we will have moved to general purpose software for almost everything including the user interface on the PC. Network computing will be well established and the application will "float" on a ocean of networking support services. One consequence of this is that the business application, as we presently understand it, begins to vanish. Already a business application constructed with the best new technology is 80% general purpose pieces. Soon, the 80% will grow to 90%.

Look back for a moment to the side-by-side chart in Exhibit A.15 that shows the process steps in the inventory and personnel applications. We noted that about 90% of the process description was the same. The 10% that was different deals with **inventory items** and **persons**.

In the real world, **inventory items** are toasters, bolts, electrical subassemblies, or some other things that we store and keep track of and **persons** are two-legged creatures we say hello to, go to lunch with, and get orders from. I'd like to call this real world the business domain. We will distinguish the business domain from the information domain in which **inventory items** are collections of information about id's, types, descriptions, and amounts and **persons** are collections of information about names, addresses, salary, and work location. The business domain consists of the real-world items that we deal with every day. The information domain consists of the abstract items that we keep track of and manipulate in our application systems. Exhibit A.17 illustrates how items in the business domain have corresponding items in the information domain.

We have to take the business domain pretty much as we find it—things are things, people are people, events are events. On the other hand, we get to construct the information domain any way we want. Historically, techies have constructed the information domain to suit themselves and the convenience of the machines in the data center—12 holes and 80 columns to fit on a card, 132 characters to fit on a printed line, 35 lines and 60 characters to fit on a screen, and many more and subtler accommodations. It seemed easier to do it that way, but bad stuff happened.

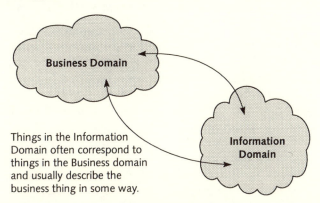

Exhibit A.17   Our Information Ecology is Built on Mapping the Business Domain of Real World Things and Ideas to the Information Domain Represented in Our Systems

Every time we built a new business application, we designed a new piece of the information domain. Each stovepipe had its corresponding version of part of the information domain. Mostly the stovepipe applications ignored each other when they did the information domain designs and definitions. One result was that a thing in the "real world" might be represented in part or whole by many different things in the aggregate information domain. The truth is we just didn't think this out very well at the beginning. By the time we became aware of the confusion that could result from very sloppy correspondence between the information domain and the business domain, it was too late. We were in the soup… and here, in the soup, we remain.[10]

"Snap-Together" Systems Offer a Cost-Effective Approach to the Common Elements of Applications

The best new tools allow us to concentrate on the things that are different from one application to the next. The tools provide common, general purpose pieces of the systems. The two applications that we have been looking at from Exhibit A.15 are simple transaction processing systems. Some of the tools that provide common, general purpose parts of transaction processing systems are

- *Screen builders:* tools that allow us to present data on the screen and accept data from the keyboard.
- *Database management interfaces:* tools that allow us to send requests for data to a database, receive data records back, send new data to the database, order the data base to delete or modify records, and deal with situations when the add, delete, or modify fails for some reason.

- *Transaction loggers:* tools that allow us to keep a history of all the transactions that change a data base to support finding out who did what, rebuild data if it fails, or roll back some updates if they are done in error.

There are literally hundreds of tools like these that provide generic pieces of systems. Entire systems can often be built by connecting these generic pieces. The jargon talks about snap-together systems.[11]

The growth of snap together systems has been largely in the new world of network computing.[12] Consequently, snap-together tools tend to be divided into those that build parts of a client function and those that build parts of a server function. Client pieces tend to focus on the user interface: screen building, data input editing, logic controlling the interaction with the human user, and communication that sends and receives data from a server. Server pieces tend to deal with data processing: storing, retrieving, and updating data; processing transactions; and communicating with client systems.

Objects Are the Reusable Building Blocks for Business-Specific Parts of Modern Applications

Some of the best thinking today about how to represent the business domain inside a computer involves conceiving of the information domain as a collection of objects that correspond in a more or less natural way to identifiable things in the business domain. This has proven to be a very powerful techniques in some special purpose information domains. There is good reason to believe that these benefits will generalize to our familiar problems. What I'd like you to know about objects is this.

- Objects exist in the information domain and most often correspond to familiar things in the business domain.
- The familiar things in the business domain may be "real" (an inventory item, a person) or conceptual (a project, an agreement, prospect).
- When an object is properly defined in the information domain, it is very easy to define similar objects. For instance, if we have bed as an object it is very easy to have twin bed, double bed, queen bed, king bed, child bed, rollaway bed, Murphy bed, and so forth.
- Objects are defined with certain useful processes attached. For instance, the object loan has associated processes like approve, draw down, payment, pay off, and so forth.
- Although objects can be very complex things in the information domain, they are very easy to use.
- Objects can result in an very great potential increase in productivity for developers who work with them.

The Superior Cost-Effectiveness of Network Computing and Reusable Software Is Undeniable but Not Easy to Get

This appendix concludes with sections that explain why this new technology is strategically important, describe the nature of the benefits the new technology brings, and discuss some of the reasons why these benefits require serious management attention to achieve.

Timing and Economics Make the Technology Important

The wave of change being produced by this new technology is not superficial; it's profound. When the wave has passed our businesses will be very different—some of them unrecognizable, some of them gone. The power of this wave comes from its timing and from the economics of the new technology. The timing is important because in the last few years most large companies' information ecologies have reached a maturity level where

- *The company's business processes are absolutely dependent on the legacy technology.* Most information ecologies have spent the last ten years or so completing the automation of the old business processes and fine-tuning them. No one can go back to manual processes and no one is very satisfied with what they have.
- *Most companies are reluctant even to try to change legacy technology because it's so complex and expensive.* Most companies feel that they are spending too much money already just to maintain what they have. Many have experienced large expensive failures of "great new systems" built from existing technology.
- *Reengineering of basic business processes is becoming the most obvious route to competitive advantage.* Many technology forecasters have been pointing out for ten years or more that new powerful new business processes can be built from new technologies. This idea has now become part of mainstream thinking.

The economics of the best new technology are important because

- The cost to build reengineered business processes with the new technology is a tenth or less what it cost to build the legacy systems that will be displaced. The new techniques require the presence of a suitable infrastructure of PCs, LANs, and data communications, which has taken time to put in place. The new technologies, however, can lay new applications on this infrastructure at a breathtaking pace and at a very attractive price.
- The cost to operate the reengineered business processes will be half or less the cost of operating the old processes. The new technology is conceptually simpler than the legacy systems. This translates directly into reductions in the cost of complexity which pervades legacy systems.

The timing and the economics together make it possible to totally replace old business processes with new reengineered business processes and to do so at a fraction of the time and money it took to establish the business processes supported by the legacy systems.

The Quantitative and Qualitative Benefits of the New Technology Are Substantial

The power of network computing yields benefits in two ways. first, communicating and cooperating computers can divide up and share work in ways that make the network of computers much more productive than the sum of the computers if they are isolated. They can be used for larger and more complex applications and are much more cost efficient. As an illustration, if NatNec converted to pure client server computing, Exhibit A.18 shows they could expect data center expenses to drop drastically with only a minor offsetting increase in network costs.

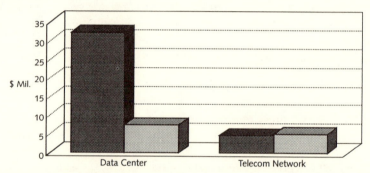

Exhibit A.18 Impact of Network Computing on Representative Company's Infrastructure Expense

Second, networked computers can provide services that are not practical for traditional technology. These enhanced services yield benefits that include

- Much better information availability for users
- Much better presentation quality to enhance understanding and reduce training time and cost
- More efficient work flow organization for human processes
- Better group member communication
- Ability to separate work group members geographically
- Ability for group members to cooperate even when they work at different times

What these benefits add up to is the possibility of new applications that make work groups and processes that involve many people enormously more efficient. For the most part, it is these cooperative processes that are the most important in our companies. The processes where we add the value for which we are paid.

Personal computers and personal computing amplified the ability of individuals, but they were still individuals. Communication and cooperation among networked computers is the key to amplifying the communications and cooperation among our people and, consequently, amplifying the value they add.

Let's imagine that we have a strong set of open standards in our company and a full complement of snap-together tools that adhere to the standards. What have we accomplished?

Snap-together subsystems for system implementers are analogous to power tools for construction workers. We still have to do all the work but we don't have to do it by hand. The pieces of systems that are common can be created with a fraction of the effort of hand crafted development. Like using power tools on a construction site, there are tremendous productivity advantages; snap-together systems give a 10 to 1000 times improvement in developer productivity.

On the other hand, there is (like in construction) only part of the job in which the power tools are helpful. There is another part of the development job where we figure out what must be done to provide the business function and translate that understanding into system components that fit with the snap together subsystems. Although 80% to 90% of the code can come from snap-together systems, only about half the work of building a new system can be done that way (see Exhibit A.19).

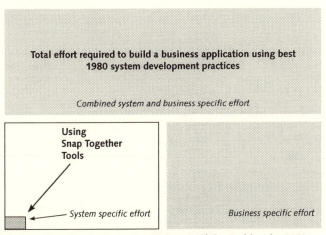

Exhibit A.19 Snap Together Systems Can Reduce Half the Problem by 90%

So the huge productivity gain applies only to a portion of the overall development effort. What do we do about the other half?

Someday, very soon, object technology will become routine for our developers. A well-chosen combination of open standards, snap-together tools, and objects will produce a profound affect on the cost of building applications systems—something like Exhibit A.20.

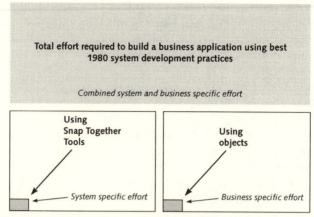

Exhibit A.20 Combining Reusable Technology and Snap Together Systems Cuts Software Development to a Tiny Fraction of Traditional Best Practice

The picture intends to show that the best new tools and techniques for systems development are 10 to 100 times as productive as the best practices of 1980. Productivity in the systems development activity is not as well documented as we would like for many reasons, but a growing body of formal measurement and anecdotal evidence is emerging that supports this range of productivity improvement.

- The benefits of network computing and reusable software are very substantial.
- Network computing yields a factor of two to ten reduction in infrastructure cost over a comparable traditional mainframe computing environment.
- Once a network computing environment has been established, incremental investments are small and relatively easy to make.
- Reusable software yields a factor of 5 to 100 reduction in software development and maintenance costs compared to traditional custom program development.
- A large number of application systems developed from reusable software components is intrinsically more reliable than an equivalent amount of business function developed by traditional methods because there are fewer unique code modules to contain defects

The benefits of the new technology offer an overwhelming motivation for change, but getting there isn't easy.

Difficulties in Introducing New Technology

It is relatively easy to build the network computing infrastructure. We can write a check for the workstations and servers, hire electricians to do the wiring, buy circuits from the phone company, and mix in a little data communications expertise. Fairly soon we have a network where all the computers can talk to each other. Once it's in place, however, troubles begin.

The complexity of the network computing environment is at least 10 times the complexity of the corresponding sized traditional mainframe environment. Complexity is expressed by the different ways things can fail. Because there are many more failure modes there are correspondingly more failures that must be identified and resolved without interrupting user service. We have become accustomed to a very high level of availability in our computer systems. It is a challenge to manage a network computing environment to the same levels. The tools, techniques, and skills appropriate to the traditional environment don't transfer directly to the network computing environment, so the infrastructure management itself needs to undergo a transformation.

Thus, it's relatively easy to get into a network computing infrastructure, but difficult to manage it. The application side of the situation is quite different.

Like infrastructure organizations, system development organizations also suffer from a lack of tools, techniques, and skills suitable to the new technology. With applications, however, the difficulty is much more involved with getting to the new environment than maintaining it. Actually, maintenance in a world of reusable components will be significantly less complex and easier to manage because much more of each application system will be standard, pretested components.

It's likely that your company has a few people who have been experimenting with snap-together systems, but they are probably not in the mainstream of your system development organization. They may even be exclusively found in some business unit that has decided to do its own thing. Wherever these experimenters are found, it's likely that they are not accepted as "real systems people" by either the system developers or the information infrastructure people. Many of your technology professionals will have an attitude that systems built this way are "too easy," "not really serious," or "just toys." Turf struggles over control of this technology are just beginning.

Notes

1. The spinning tape drives so popular in movies are gradually losing their importance and are disappearing. Instead there are more refrigerators that accept data cartridges instead of tapes.
2. An application system is a set of programs that does the actual work of your business (payroll, order entry, inventory control, and so forth).
3. Fire, flood, power outage, and bomb threats are the most popular emergencies with earthquake and insurrection making the list in some places.
4. *Egalité, fraternité, communiqué*!
5. And we haven't even mentioned the kind of rules that produce statements like, "We don't talk about that sort of thing at dinner."
6. I once saw an application in which a set of numbers was taken from a computer report, typed into a word processor, printed, and faxed across an ocean. For every number on the fax, a person looked up a corresponding number on a terminal and wrote it on the fax. Since a fax of a fax is hard to read, the marked up fax was typed

on a word processor and the result was faxed across another ocean where the look-up process was repeated on another terminal. The completed version was once again typed on a word processor and faxed back to the originating point, where the completed document was typed into a terminal!

7. I remember hearing once that since modern cities were too expensive to operate and too valuable to discard, we ought to turn them all into museums!

8. A good rule of thumb is "If it's boring to do, describe, review, or check, a computer ought to be doing it."

9. This wasn't always so clear. In the late '50s and early '60s IBM marketed completely different lines of computers for "business" and "scientific" applications. There were even a few computers that were specifically designed for particular industries like insurance.

10. Any comprehensive, unified view of the information domain would lead to solving most of the problems of the spaghetti stovepipe systems. *Corporate-wide data architectures* used to be a popular approach to this problem. These corporate-wide efforts all failed. Often, however, significant benefits resulted even from the failures. Even a little clean-up of the information domain can help a lot.

11. "Snap-together systems" isn't very well established jargon. Other jargon that tends to refer to the same general purpose pieces of systems includes *component systems, middleware, development environments, productivity tools,* and other phrases in that vein.

12. Mainframe computing has been involved, for the most part, only when developers have found it necessary to connect a mainframe's data or processing power into a network application.

Appendix B

Summary of Suggested Information Ecology Management Principles

Simplification We will invest to simplify our information technology infrastructure, applications, and management processes.

Scarce Resource We recognize that skilled personnel is the scare resource in the information ecology and we will manage our investments in hardware and software to make maximum use of the scarce resource.

Aggregate Economics We will analyze and manage information technology expense and capital investment in the aggregate.

Vision We will invest in the creation and maintenance of a shared vision to support resource allocation and other key decision-making activities.

Linkage We will invest in describing, designing, measuring, and improving our business technology linkage.

Partnership We will adopt the partnership relationship model as the primary organizational mechanism for planning and allocating resources and we will invest time, energy, and money to understand, establish, and improve partnership skills.

Team We will use teams as the primary organizational mechanism for carrying out processes and projects and we will invest in understanding, establishing, executing, and evaluating team activities.

Reward We will arrange our evaluation and reward systems so that members of a given partnership or members of a given team are subject to compatible compensation schemes.

Tracking	We will track and report our use of resources at the team level.
Groupware	We will invest in understanding, implementing, and using technology to support group work.
Infrastructure Investment	We will determine the level of capital that we wish to devote to the information infrastructure and maximize the useful value of the infrastructure within that level of capital over time.
Standards	When a system component's relationships with other system components is specified by a suitable set of standards so that one product meeting the standards can be freely substituted for another and the standards are acceptable to all stakeholders, then we will manage the system component as infrastructure.
Balance	We will invest time and resources in balancing our efforts to sustain our business with our efforts to transform it. The primary means for striking the balance will be an adjustment of resources among cross-functional teams that manage our systems as assets and other cross-functional teams that reengineer our processes and implement discontinuous change.
Organization	We will design and operate our formal administrative organization to facilitate the use of partnerships and teams as business technology linkage mechanisms.

Selected References

Arnold, William W., and Jeanne M. Plas, *The Human Touch*, John Wiley & Sons, Inc., New York, 1993.

Badaracco, Joseph L., and Richard R. Ellsworth, *Leadership and the Quest for Integrity*, Harvard Business School Press, Boston, 1988.

Benjamin, Robert I., and Jon Blunt, Critical IT Issues: The Next Ten Years, *Sloan Management Review*, Summer 1992, 7-19.

Benson, Robert J., Greg Goluska, and Karl Stolze, Case Study: On Competitive Response Utilizing Information Technology, *POSPP Report P-89-1 PII 1236*, November 1991.

Bergman, Pat, Transforming a Utility into a Productive Business Partner: An Approach To Information Systems Personnel Reskilling and Retraining For Achieving Successful Internal Partnershipping Within The Enterprise, *POSPP Report P-86-0 PII 0130*, October 1990.

Bernardin, H. John, and Richard W. Beatty, Can Subordinate Appraisals Enhance Managerial Productivity? *Sloan Management Review*, Summer 1987, 63-73.

Booz, Allen & Hamilton and CIO Magazine, A Prescription for I/S Effectiveness In The '90's, *The '92 CEO/CIO Survey*, April 1992.

Brynjolfsson, Erik , Thomas W. Malone, Vijay Gurbaxani, and Ajit Kambil, Does Information Technology Lead To Smaller Firms?, *CISR WP No. 211*, November 1989.

Buchholz, Steve , Aftershock: Helping People Through Corporate Change, *POSPP Report P-76-1 PII 1103*, October 1991.

Buchholz, Steve and Thomas Roth, Wilson Learning Corporation, edited by Karen Hess, *Creating the High Performance Team*, John Wiley & Sons, Inc., New York, 1987.

Carson, Neill, Making Sure Your Bank's Work Teams Are Accountable, *American Banker*, August 19, 1992, 2,9.

_____, Information Politics, *Sloan Management Review*, Fall 1992, 53-65.

Davenport, Thomas H., Michael Hammer, and Tauno J. Metsisto, How
     Executives Can Shape Their Company's Information Systems, *Harvard
     Business Review*, March-April 1989.

Davenport, Thomas, and James V. McGee, Toward an Ecology of Information,
     Ernst & Young Mastering the Information Environment Research Note, 1994.

Davenport, Thomas H., and Nitin Nohria, Case Management and the Integra-
     tion of Labor, *Sloan Management Review,* Winter 1994, 11-23.

Davenport, Thomas H., and James E. Short, The New Industrial Engineering:
     Information Technology and Business Process Redesign, *Sloan Manage-
     ment Review,* Summer 1990, 11-25.

Davis, Stan, and Bill Davidson, *2020 Vision,* Simon & Schuster, New York,
     1991.

Dejarnett, Larry, The Transformation of I/T: The New Rules of the Game,
     POSPP Report P-8-2 PII 0142, February 1992.

DeMarco, Tom, *Controlling Software Projects: Management, Measurement, and
     Estimation,* Yourdon Press, Englewood Cliffs, New Jersey, 1982.

Eccles, Robert G., The Performance Measurement Manifesto, *Harvard
     Business Review,* January-February 1991, 131-139.

_____, *The Transfer Pricing Problem: A Theory for Practice,* Lexington Books,
     Lexington, Massachusetts, 1985.

Eccles, Robert G., and Nitin Nohria, *Beyond the Hype: Rediscovering the
     Essence of Management,* Harvard Business School Press, Boston, 1992.

English, Tom, Self-managed Teams - The Pros and Cons, *POSPP Report P-52-2
     PII 1115,* June 1992.

Fairley, Richard E., *Software Engineering Concepts,* McGraw-Hill Book
     Company, New York, 1989.

Flynn, S., 1991/1992 Information Technology Budgets and Practices Survey,
     Gartner Group IS Strategic Analysis Report IS: R-962-114, June 30, 1992.

Fritz, Robert, *The Path of Least Resistance: Learning to Become the Creative
     Force in Your Own Life,* Fawcett Columbine, New York, 1989.

General Electric Company Corporate Information Systems, *Software Engineer-
     ing Handbook,* McGraw-Hill Book Company, New York, 1986.

Gold, Charles L., IS Measures - A Balancing Act, *CITAS Research Note CITA27,*
     May 1992.

_____, Measuring Information Processing, *POSPP Report PII #0148.06 P-5-9.*

Hammer, Michael, Reengineer Work: Don't Automate, Obliterate, *Harvard
     Business Review,* July-August 1990, 104-111.

Hammer, Michael, and James Champy, *Reengineering the Corporation,* Harper
     Business, New York, 1993.

Handy, Charles, Balancing Corporate Power: A New Federalist Paper, *Harvard
     Business Review,* November-December 1992, 59-72.

Hemingway, John, *Building the Perfect Team,* Briefcase Booklet, Video Arts
     Ltd., Printed by B&H Printing Services Ltd, Watford, England, May 1991.

Henderson, John C., and N. Venkatraman, Strategic Alignment: A Framework for Strategic Information Technology Management, *CISR WP No. 190,* August 1989.

_____ ,Strategic Alignment: A Process Model for Integrating Information Technology and Business Strategies, *CISR WP No. 196,* October 1989.

Hensley, Sue , Reaching Their Potential, *POSPP Report P-56-2 PII 1115,* June 1992.

Hoerr, John, The Payoff From Teamwork, *Business Week,* July 10, 1989, 56-62.

Jaques, Elliott, In Praise of Hierarchy, *Harvard Business Review,* January-February 1990, 127-133.

_____ , Managerial Leadership: The Key To Good Organization, *The World & I,* October 1991, 535-542.

Johnson, H. Thomas, and Robert S. Kaplan, *Relevance Lost: The Rise and Fall of Management Accounting,* Harvard Business School Press, Boston, 1987.

Jones, Capers, *Programming Productivity,* McGraw-Hill Book Company, New York, 1986.

Kanter, Rosabeth Moss, *The Change Masters: Innovation for Productivity in the American Corporation,* Simon and Schuster, New York, 1983.

Kaplan, Robert S., and David P. Norton, The Balanced Scorecard - Measures That Drive Performance, *Harvard Business Review,* January-February 1992, 71-79.

Katzenbach, Jon R., and Douglas K. Smith, The Discipline of Teams, *Harvard Business Review,* March-April 1993, 111-120.

Keen, Peter G. W., *Competing in Time: Using Telecommunications for Competitive Advantage,* Ballanger Publishing Company, Cambridge, Massachusetts, 1988.

Lane, Ray, and Ray Hall, Yes, There Is A Way To Measure MIS Investments, *Business Month,* August 1989.

LaPlante, Alice, TeleConfronting, *Forbes ASAP,* May 1993, 110-126.

Lee, Chris, Talking Back To The Boss, *TRAINING, The Magazine of Human Resources Development,* April 1990.

Luginbuhl, Daryl, Application Development for the 90s, *POSPP Report P-85-1 PII 1501,* November 1991.

Maglitta, Joseph, Information . . . Please, *Computerworld,* January 10, 1994.

McGovern, Patrick, Plug In for Productivity, *New York Times,* June 27, 1993, editorial page.

McMenamin, Stephen M., and John F. Palmer, *Essential Systems Analysis,* Yourdon Press, Englewood Cliffs, New Jersey, 1984.

Musser, Cherri M., Implementing the I/T Vision: Business Process Reengineering, *POSPP Report P-12-2 PII 0142,* February 1992.

New Science Staff, Charting the New Information Landscape, *New Science Associates Intelligent Document Management Strategic Directive,* September 1, 1992.

Peters, Tom, *Thriving On Chaos,* Alfred A. Knopf, New York, 1988.

Pressman, Roger S., *Making Software Engineering Happen: A Guide for Instituting the Technology,* Prentice-Hall, Englewood Cliffs, New Jersey, 1988.

Rockart, John F., and James E. Short, IT and the Networked Organization: Towards More Effective Management of Interdependence, *CISR WP No. 200,* December 1989.

Ross, Alexander, The Long View Of Leadership, *Canadian Business,* May 1992.

Rosser, B., and R. Small, Conventional methods for justifying IT expenditures are obsolete, *Gartner Group Continuous Services Research Note IS: K-980-911,* July 28, 1992.

Rubin, Howard, CASE Success and Software Metrics: The "Odd Couple," *CASE Trends,* April 1992, 38-41.

_____, Inside the Information "Black Hole," *The Rubin Review,* Fourth Quarter 1992, 1-2.

Schindler, Max, *Computer-Aided Software Design: Build Quality Software with CASE,* John Wiley & Sons, New York, 1990.

Senge, Peter M., The Leader's New Work: Building Learning Organizations, *Sloan Management Review,* Fall 1990, 7-23.

_____, *The Fifth Discipline: The Art and Practice of the Learning Organization,* Doubleday Currency, New York, 1990.

_____, Transforming the Practice of Management, *Presented at the Systems Thinking in Action Conference,* November 14, 1991.

Tapscott, Don, and Art Caston, *Paradigm Shift: The New Promise of Information Technology,* McGraw-Hill, New York, 1993.

Weinberg, Gerald M., *Quality Software Management: Volume 1 Systems Thinking,* Dorset House Publishing, New York, 1991.

Wilzbach, Peter M., Moving Towards Empowerment Quickly, *POSPP Report P-18-2 PII 0142,* March 1992.

Wurman, Richard Saul, *Information Anxiety,* Doubleday, New York, 1989.

Yukl, Gary, and Manus Associates, Involving Others In Decisions, *Manus Associates internal document,* 1987.

Zuboff, Shoshanna, *In the Age of the Smart Machine: The Future of Work and Power,* Basic Books, Inc., New York, 1988.

Index

About the Author

BRUCE W. HASENYAGER is a senior executive with 30 years of experience managing technology for demanding businesses. He has held executive management positions with Citibank, Kidder Peabody, Merrill Lynch, and Chemical Bank, where his application of technology to system-development management was the subject of a Harvard Business School case study. He served most recently as Chief Technology Officer for the Houston-based investment management firm AIM Management Group.